# THE GROLIER CLUB

## 1884 – 1984

## ITS LIBRARY, EXHIBITIONS, & PUBLICATIONS

### NEW YORK · 1984

LIBRARY OF CONGRESS CATALOGUE CARD NUMBER 83–82710

ISBN 0–910672–01–6

# Contents

| | | |
|---|---|---|
| Subscribers | | 9 |
| Preface | *Robert D. Graff* | 11 |
| Plates | | 15 |
| The Grolier Club Library | *Robert Nikirk* | 35 |
| Incunabula | *William H. Scheide and Mina R. Bryan* | 48 |
| Post-1500 Printed Books | *Ruth Mortimer* | 53 |
| Booksellers' and Auction Catalogues | *William S. Reese* | 59 |
| Private Library Catalogues | *William P. Barlow, Jr.* | 68 |
| Autograph Manuscripts | *Herbert T. F. Cahoon* | 74 |
| The Print Collection | *Phillip D. Cate and Herbert D. Schimmel* | 80 |
| Archives | *P. William Filby* | 84 |
| The Library as a Resource for the Collector and Scholar | *Douglas F. Bauer* | 90 |
| Educational Uses of the Library | *Terry Belanger* | 102 |
| The Clubhouse | *Wendell Garrett* | 106 |
| Publications | *C. Waller Barrett* | 112 |
| Publications of the Grolier Club, 1884–1983 | *Allen Asaf* | 117 |
| Exhibitions | *G. Thomas Tanselle* | 165 |
| Exhibitions and Meetings, 1884–1983 | *Allen Asaf* | 175 |
| Index | | 225 |

# Subscribers

Dr. Abram J. Abeloff
George Abrams
Frederick B. Adams
Thomas R. Adams
Reginald Allen
Elmer L. Andersen
T. R. Anderson
Rodney Armstrong
Lee Ash
Joseph Auerbach
Gabriel Austin
Clifford J. Awald
Donald K. Bain
James F. Barnett
C. Waller Barrett
William P. Barlow, Jr.
Wayne E. Batcheler
Douglas F. Bauer
William B. Bean
Theodore S. Beardsley, Jr.
Alexander Gordon Bearn
Irving A. Beck
David P. Becker
Frederic C. Beil, III
Terry Belanger
David E. Belch
Richard Dyke Benjamin
Abel E. Berland
John Bidwell
Lyman G. Bloomingdale
Emmet J. Blot
Joseph Blumenthal
Fred. J. Board
W. H. Bond
Dr. Hans Rudolf Bosch-Gwalter
Ann Bowden
George M. Bowles
T. Kimball Brooker
Alan Willard Brown

Thomas S. Brush
Herbert T. F. Cahoon
David Giles Carter
Phillip Dennis Cate
Daniel D. Chabris
Carlo A. Chiesa
Herbert L. Cohen
Herman Cohen
Morris L. Cohen
George B. Cooper
John M. Crawford, Jr.
Timothy J. Crist
Clifford Currie
William J. Dane
William Henry Porter Davisson
Donald C. Dickinson
James R. Donnelley
Robert O. Dougan
Donald D. Eddy
J. M. Edelstein
Augustín E. Edwards
Alfred Eisenpreis
Parmenia Migel Ekstrom
M. Wieder Elkind
Henry N. Ess, III
Robert N. Essick
Charles Peaslee Farnsley
Donald Farren
Charles E. Feinberg
Alan M. Fern
Charles D. Field
P. William Filby
Walter Fillin
John F. Fleming
H. George Fletcher
Roland Folter
Edward Jenkins Foote
Charles Alvin Foster
David A. Fraser

Bert Freidus
Helmut N. Friedlaender
Joan M. Friedman
Jenkins Garrett
Morris A. Gelfand
David R. Godine
Jack Golden
Lucien Goldschmidt
Mrs. John D. Gordan
Ronald M. Gordon
George Talbot Goodspeed
Paul Gourary
Marjorie S. Graff
Robert D. Graff
Neal F. Grenley
Charles F. Grosnell
Philip Grushkin
Rollin Van N. Hadley
Jack W. C. Hagstrom, M.D.
Robert Halsband
Richard A. Harris
Horace Hart
James D. Hart
Dorothy L. Hatch
Iola S. Haverstick
Mrs. Allen T. Hazen
August Heckscher
Charles L. Heiskell
William H. Helfand
John B. Hench
Wolfgang A. Herz
Peter N. Heydon
Jonathan A. Hill
Kenneth E. Hill
Arthur Cort Holden
David J. Holmes
Harrison D. Horblit
Arthur A. Houghton, Jr.
Alfred H. Howell

Andrew Hoyem
Clarence Hugo
Harold Hugo
Mrs. Donald F. Hyde
Nico Israel
Robert J. H. Janson-La Palme
Grady E. Jensen
Gordon W. Jones, M.D.
William L. Joyce
Jamie Kamph
Herman W. Kapp
Alan H. Kempner
Chester Kerr
John E. Kilgore, Jr.
Douglas Maitland Knight
Marie Elena Korey
Hans P. Kraus
Mrs. Valerian Lada-Mocarski
Benjamin J. Lake
John Lancaster
Dr. Lawrence Montague Lande
Daniel J. Leab
Rensselaer W. Lee
Abe Lerner
Richard A. Linenthal
Edward S. Litchfield
Charles R. Long
Richard M. Ludwig
Beverly P. Lynch
Richard Maass
Mrs. Stephen F. Mandel
Stanley Marcus
Francis A. Martin, Jr.
H. Bradley Martin
Alexandra Mason
Mrs. Linton R. Massey
Stephen C. Massey
William Matheson
David Hunter McAlpin
Marcus A. McCorison
David Jackson McWilliams
Paul Mellon
Jerrold I. W. Mitchell
Rev. William J. Monihan, S.J.
Davis W. Moore

Peter M. Mortimer
Ruth Mortimer
Andrew Breen Myers
Andrew T. Nadell, M.D.
Weston J. Naef
Edward Naumburg, Jr.
Kenneth Nebenzahl
Elizabeth S. Niemyer
Robert Nikirk
Haskell F. Norman, M.D.
Alfonso A. Ossorio
Katharine F. Pantzer
Wyman W. Parker
Eugene P. Pattberg
Frederick Woodworth Pattison
John F. Peckham
Hon. Carl H. Pforzheimer, Jr.
Robert S. Pirie
Lawrence Clark Powell
Richard E. Priest
Ronald R. Randall
Joseph T. Rankin
Gordon N. Ray
William S. Reese
Mrs. E. W. Reilley
Mary T. Reynolds
Mary L. Richmond
Elizabeth M. Riley
Arthur G. Rippey
Arnold A. Rogow
S. Wyman Rolph, III
Albi Rosenthal
Samuel R. Rosenthal
Anthony Rota
Frederick G. Ruffner
Rudy Lamont Ruggles
Herbert J. A. Runsdorf
Charles Ryskamp
Dr. Morris H. Saffron
William Salloch
Otto Schäfer
Otto Schäfer, Jr.
Robert D. Schapiro
William H. Scheide
Herbert D. Schimmel
Stuart B. Schimmel

Leonard B. Schlosser
Henry Schniewind
Alice D. Schreyer
John Mackay Shaw
Milton R. Slater
John J. Slocum
George Staack
George E. Staehle, M.D.
Lewis M. Stark
Geoffrey Steele
Roderick Stinehour
Stephen Roderick Stinehour
Frank S. Streeter
Norman H. Strouse
Larry E. Sullivan
Charles J. Tanenbaum
G. Thomas Tanselle
W. Thomas Taylor
Eugene Victor Thaw
Michael M. Thomas
Lawrence S. Thompson
William B. Todd
Daniel Traister
Jacques Vellekoop
Arthur E. Vershbow
Richard Vogler
Alexander D. Wainwright
William Bond Walker
James E. Walsh
Harry L. Wechsler
Sidney Wechter
Edward R. Weidlein, III
James L. Weil
James M. Wells
Michael Winship
Edwin Wolf, 2nd
Denis B. Woodfield
Daniel Woodward
William P. Wreden
Stuart Wright
Marjorie G. Wynne
Ralph Webster Yarborough
Herbert C. Zafren
Ben D. Zevin
Charles Zitner

# Preface

## ROBERT D. GRAFF

A CENTURY of effort in the public interest has brought "The Grolier Club of the City of New York," as its constitution describes it, worldwide membership and considerable renown. From a modest beginning in 1884 in a private house on East 36th Street, where our nine founders met, until today, that general craving for cultural fellowship that animated much of late nineteenth-century American society has been harnessed to public purpose within the Club's field of interest. Today there are 653 Grolier members, men and women, many of them still residents of New York City, many others living in thirty-four states and in nine countries abroad—an enlarged sphere of influence.

New York's exuberant growth, its contemporary quality, and its world-girdling influence were and are created from myriad economic, cultural, and interpersonal transactions. These have produced a seductive quality of life that brings everyone here from everywhere in the hope of partaking of it. The shared sense of exhilaration arises from a torrent of knowledge and cultural performance, vast amounts of both, daily created and daily countermanded, duly recalled and more frequently discarded. Amidst this flux and welter, certain persons and certain institutions become the public's *cicerones*. They illuminate the meaning of some aspect of the moment; they link today with yesterday and with what tomorrow may be. Their connoisseurship, called by many names, points the way. They set standards. They endure. Among such path-finding institutions, large and small, the Grolier Club has earned its modest place.

What is the Grolier Club? It is basically a network of persons sharing a belief in the importance of knowledge and artistic creativity as contained in books, prints, and the graphic arts. Named for Jean Grolier (1479–1565), a powerful royal treasurer under four French kings but remembered by us as a humanist, patron, and bibliophile, the Club is a somewhat starchy group with an educational mission self-imposed. It is a band of women and men who believe in the virtues attending excellence in the conduct of human affairs; and, as behooves a freely inquiring institution in a free society, sharing our views with the public in a variety of ways has been the chief Grolier activity since its first day.

Thus the Club has organized and encouraged attendance by the public at over six hundred scholarly exhibitions devoted to manuscripts, books, prints, photographs, and related examples of communication of knowledge ranging from Mayan vases and codices with their cargoes of pictograms to laser printing. Gutenberg is only one of the Club's patron saints. We have published 145 volumes devoted to bibliographic and aesthetic matters; the quality of their contents or of their design has made many of these books collectors' items. We have organized lectures, short courses, symposia; we have provided critical and creative insights for the body politic over the years. At age one hundred, our doors remain open to the public just as, we hope, the Grolier remains open to new ideas.

Beyond these activities, the Grolier has made two other social contributions in its first hundred years. One is an appreciable addition to knowledge in the Club's chosen fields. Our contributions have been threefold: the concepts and contents of our exhibitions; the creation of a valuable, open bibliographic resource in the form of the Club's library; and our publications, large and small, often scholarly, frequently beautiful, issued year after year. As a second form of social contribution, Grolier members can lay claim to inventing, or at least proving the usefulness of, two methods for extending the range of support for cultural institutions. The

first, historically, was organizing groups of Friends, as they came to be known, to provide an enlarged constituency for institutions beyond the Boards of Trustees—a richer source of collection and operating support. The second was, along with the Archives of American Art, putting cultural tourism on the map of institutional support. The Grolier's 1959 tour to libraries, museums, and private collections in England and France inaugurated the current era of museum-sponsored tours.

Our centennial year will encompass an accelerated publication program of which this volume is the centerpiece; large and small exhibitions gracing the clubhouse for all to see; special exhibitions honoring the Club in various institutions throughout the city; and an international colloquium to be held in April 1984. During our centenary we will be engaged in scholarly conversation about the future of books, the evolving role of libraries, the place of aesthetics in education and of education in life, and the functions of twenty-first-century book and print collectors.

This particular volume, *The Grolier Club, 1884–1984: Its Library, Exhibitions, and Publications*, therefore, is our promise of a second century of continuous Grolier outreach into the world. The essays within these covers are also a look backward at our history and inward at our Pierian spring. They touch on various facets of what, to date, we have done, and, by inference, who we are. A few of our members, *mirabile dictu*, have never set foot inside the clubhouse. For them this book serves as an introduction to 47 East 60th Street. For our other members, and for the many members of the public who are familiar with the place, the book suggests sources of serendipity and scholarship available to all whose interest in the materials qualifies them to do research within our walls.

As for the authors of the essays, they are all members of the Club. The breadth of their interests is illuminated by the subjects of the chapters. They reflect the intellectual span of the membership and the range of our members' capabilities, be they amateurs or professionals in their field.

This book also introduces the Grolier Club to its second century. What will the next hundred years hold for those persons who share our interests and concerns? No one knows. But we might consider, on the basis of present evidence, a few currents and directions. A further burgeoning of new knowledge and new kinds of knowledge seems probable. Some of this knowledge will be presented and preserved in new forms; much of it will still take the form of books. It appears probable that intellectual and aesthetic dialogue will continue to use books for purpose and for pleasure. Despite contradictory trends, one can assume more persons will learn to read than ever before in history. Books in demand will be available on demand in urban centers and elsewhere. We may witness the emergence of universities not only as generators of knowledge but as major economic generators as well. They may support themselves in greater part beyond philanthropy. It is quite conceivable that different human beings could emerge from achievements in biology, psychology, and computer science, from gene splicing, and from a greatly changed learning environment. Forthcoming generations may be literate, computer literate, and visually literate—all three. Life in the United States probably will be based on many forms of lifelong learning. Institutional change will accompany and fulfill this need.

Such trends in the years ahead, if they materialize, bode well for persons devoted to "literary study and the arts of the book." Their interests will become increasingly central to society. It appears probable that, amidst the social processes of the twenty-first century, the Grolier Club will have an important role to play. This is the agreeable challenge that faces us today as, with this book, we celebrate our centennial year.

# Plates

The Grolier Club library in 1983. It was designed by the architect of the building, Bertram Grosvenor Goodhue, in late seventeenth-century English style, with walnut woodwork and paving of marble and slate.

The second home of the Grolier Club at 29 East 32nd Street, New York, photographed in 1895. It was designed in the Romanesque style by Charles W. Romeyn and Company, built of pressed brick and terra cotta, and completed in 1889; it survives as a designated landmark. By 1913 the Club was already seeking a building site farther uptown.

The present clubhouse, 47 East 60th Street, New York, designed by Bertram Grosvenor Goodhue in the Georgian style, is built of red brick and marble and was completed in 1917.

The exhibition hall as it appeared in 1929; it was altered to its present state in 1954. Some 600 public exhibitions have been held by the Grolier Club since May 1884.

My dear sir:

I accept, with pleasure, your invitation to meet some book lovers at Mr. Robert Hoe jr's, on January 23ᵈ at half-past eight, evening.

Yours very truly,

Theo. L. De Vinne,

Jan. 14, 1884.

To Mr. Arthur Turnure.

Theodore Low De Vinne accepts Arthur B. Turnure's invitation to the gathering which led to the founding of the Grolier Club on January 23, 1884. This letter represents a starting point for the Club's century-old archive, which contains much of cultural and social interest beyond Grolier Club activities.

The Grolier Club silver punch bowl. Late nineteenth century, date and maker unknown, diameter 15½ inches. Gift of Robert Hoe, January 1898.

Samuel Putnam Avery was the most generous benefactor of the Grolier Club among its early members, presenting printed books, reference sets, fine bindings, prints, and *objets d'art*. This etched portrait by François Flameng, from the 1876 oil by Raimundo de Madrazo, is in the Club's extensive collection of portraits. Gift of Edward A. Bierstadt.

One of two fragments on paper from the 36-line Bible, Bamberg, Gutenberg or Pfister, ca. 1458–1460, 12⅞ x 7⅞ inches, recovered from a bookbinding. There is no copy of the 36-line Bible in the United States and even fragments are rare. Gift of David Wolfe Bruce, 1894.

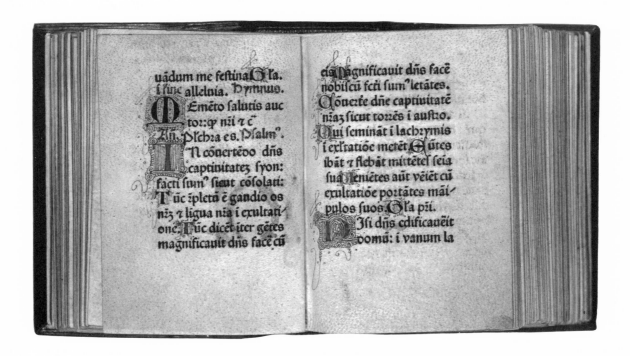

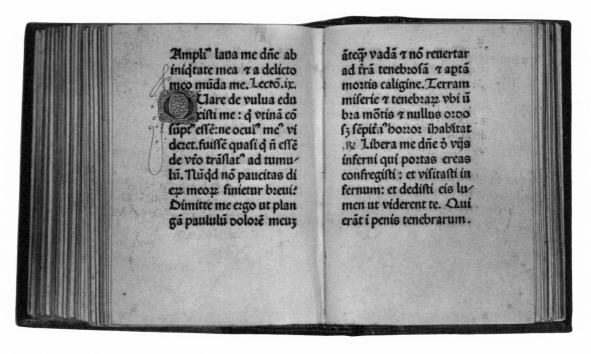

Office of the Blessed Virgin printed on vellum in black and red with illuminated capitals, Venice, Nicolaus Jenson, 1475. This is one of two known copies of this miniature book; the type page measures 1 15/16 x 1 3/8 inches. Its sixteenth–century–style binding is by Louis Hagué. Bequest of Mrs. William Loring Andrews, 1931.

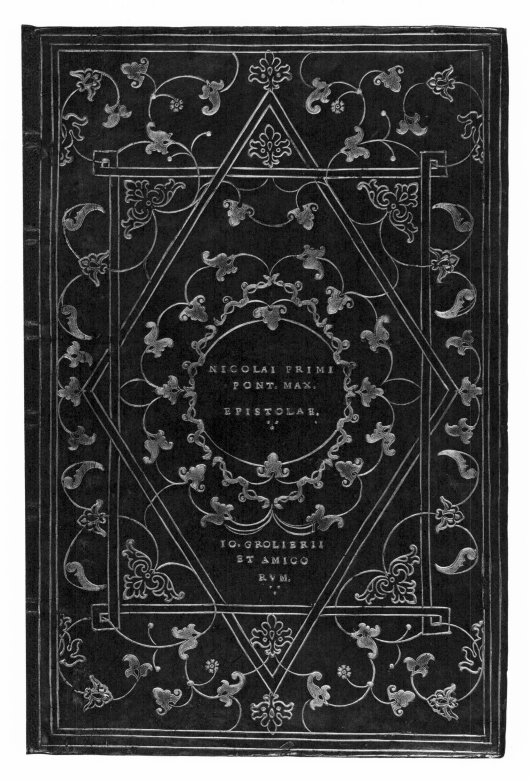

Binding of gold-tooled brown calf made for Jean Grolier by the Cupid's Bow Binder, Paris, late 1540's, on the *Epistolae* of Pope Nicholas II, Rome, 1542. This is one of four books from Grolier's library in the Club's collection. Purchased from the estate of Lucius Wilmerding, 1951.

# A DECREE
## OF
## Starre-Chamber,
## CONCERNING
### PRINTING,

*Made the eleuenth day of July
last past.* 1 6 3 7.

❡ Imprinted at London by *Robert Barker*,
Printer to the Kings moſt Excellent
Maieſtie: And by the Aſſignes
of *Iohn Bill.* 1 6 3 7.

First edition of the infamous decree regulating printing in England; its text was chosen for the first publication of the Grolier Club, issued in December 1884. Freedom of the press is one of the notable subject collections in the Club library.

# CATALOGUS

Variorum & Insignium

# LIBRORUM

Instructissimæ Bibliothecæ

Clarissimi Doctissimiq; Viri

# LAZARI SEAMAN, S.T.D.

Quorum Auctio habebitur *L O N D I N I*
in ædibus Defuncti in Area & Viculo
*Warwicensi, Octobris* ultimo.

---

Cura *GULIELMI COOPER* Bibliopolæ.

---

*L O N D I N I*,

Apud { *Ed. Brewster* & *Guil. Cooper* } ad Insigne { *Gruis* in Cæmiterio *Paulino*, *Pelicani* in Vico vulgariter dicto *Little-Britain*. } 1676.

Title page of the catalogue of the first English book auction, conducted by the London bookseller William Cooper on October 31, 1676, and eight following days. The library belonged to the eminent Nonconformist divine, Dr. Lazarus Seaman. It is a cornerstone in the Grolier Club collection of book auction catalogues. Gift of the children of Waters S. Davis, 1941.

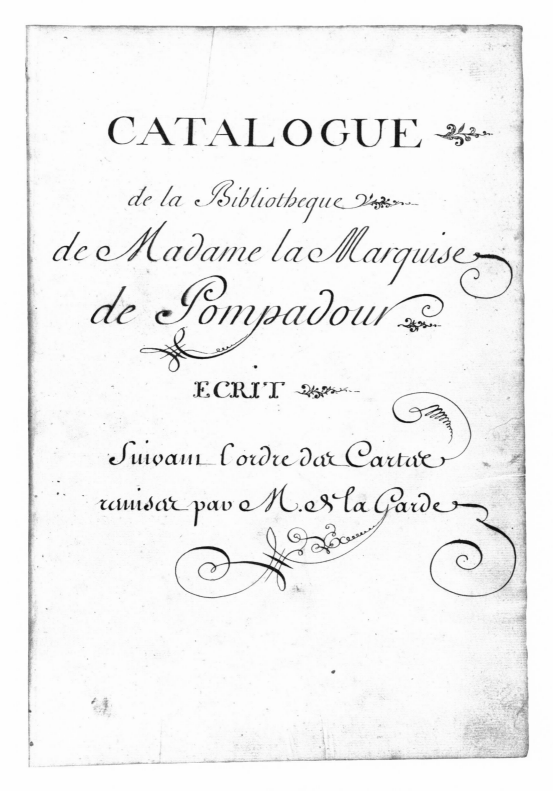

CATALOGUE

*de la Bibliotheque*

*de Madame la Marquise*

*de Pompadour*

ECRIT

*Suivant l'ordre des Cartes*

*remisar par M. de la Garde*

Among the Grolier Club's large collection of private library catalogues and inventories is this folio listing some of the books belonging to Madame de Pompadour. As it contains valuations, it was probably prepared after her death. It was once owned by the French bibliophile Baron Pichon and in May 1945 was recovered from among the personal possessions of Adolf Hitler at Berchtesgaden. Purchase, 1978.

*Dibdin*

8192 Clericus et Hammondus—Vetus Testamentum ex transl.
I. Clerici, cum ejusdem Paraphrasi, Comment. Dissert. &c.
—Novum Testamentum ex Transl. vulgatâ cum Paraph. et
Annot. Hammondi, ex Anglica illustravit, &c. Clericum
—et Clerici Harmonia Evangelica, 7 vols. *very neat, calf full
gilt, 5l 15s 6d*            Paris. 1735

*Cochrane*

8193 Cotelerii Patres Apostolici, Gr. et Lat. 2 vols. *neat, 2l 2s*
                             *Antverpiæ*, 1700

*Bp of London*

8194 Critici Sacri sive Doctiss. Virorum in S.S. Biblia Annota-
tiones et Tractatus, 9 vols.—Thesaurus Theologico-Philo-
logicus, 2 vols. et Novus Thesaurus Theologico-Philologi-
cus, 2 vols. together 13 vols. *fine copy, bound by Montague, 16l*
           *16. 16. 0*                Amst. 1698-1732

8195 Cypriani Opera, recognita stud. et operâ Steph. Baluzii, *very
neat, 2l 5s*                          Paris. 1726

*Rev. J. Law*

8196 Cyrilli Opera Omnia, Gr. et Lat. ex recens. Mills, *neat,*
*10s 6d*                             Oxon. 1703

8197 I. Damasceni Opera Omnia, Gr. et Lat. studio Le Quien,
2 vols. *best edition, vellum, 3l. 10s*        Paris. 1712

8198 Aliud exemplar, 2 vols. *vellum, 3l 3s*        ib. 1712

8199 Dissertatio et Animadversiones ad nuper inventum Severæ
Martyris Epitaphium, *18s*         Panormi, 1734

8200 Epiphanii Opera Omnia Valesii, 2 vols. *vellum, 3l 3s*
                              Coloniæ, 1682

8201 Aliud exemplar, 2 vols. *very neat in russia, gilt leaves, 4l 4s*

*Bp of London*

8202 Episcopii Opera Omnia Theologica, 2 vols. *vellum, 1l 11s 6d*
                              Rotterod. 1665

8203 Eusebii et Aliorum Historia Ecclesiastica Gr. *very neat, 15s*
                         Lutet. Stephani, 1544

8204 Eusebii et aliorum Historia Ecclesiastica Gr. et Lat. ex vers.
et cum notis Valesii, observationibus Gul. Reading illustrata,
3 vols. *neat, 5l 5s*      —           Cantab. 1722

8205 Eusebii Præparatio et Demonstratio Evangelica, *15s*
                          Lutet. Steph. 1544

8206 Alia editio, 2 vols. *very neat in russia, gilt leaves, 3l 10s*
                            Coloniæ, 1688

8207 Gibsoni Codex Juris Ecclesiastici Anglicani, 2 vols. *neat in
russia, gilt leaves, 4l 4s*            Oxon. 1761

*Cochrane*
*Do*

8208 Gregorii Nazianzeni Opera Gr. Lat. ex interpret. Billii
Prunæi, curâ Morell, 2 vols. *very neat, 2l 2s* Paris, 1630

8209 Gregorii Nysseni Opera Omnia, 2 vols. *vellum, 2l 2s* Paris. 1615

*Drury*

8210 Gregorii Nysseni Opera Gr. et Lat. 3 vols. *best
edition, 3l 3s*      —          Paris. Morell, 1638

*Dibdin*

8211 Grotii Opera Omnia, 4 vols. *neat in russia, 3l 10s* Amst. 1679

8212 Heinsii Exercitationes Sacræ ad Novum Testamentum,
*10s 6d*                         Elzevir, 1639

8213 Hieronymi Opera Omnia ex recensione Benedictinorum,
5 vols. *best edition, vellum, 9l 9s*       Paris. 1693

8214 Hildeberti Opera Marbodi, curâ Beaugendre, *half-bound,
uncut, 1l 11s 6d*                  Paris. 1708

*Thorpe of Cam:*

8215 Irenæi Opera Gr. et Lat. ex recensione Grabe, *very neat, 15s*
                            Oxon. 1702

A representative page from an 1822 Payne and Foss catalogue showing the names of buyers. The Grolier Club owns the annotated master catalogue set from 1815 to 1850 of this major English bookselling firm. It is part of the Club's collection of book trade materials dating from the seventeenth century. Gift of Robert Hoe, 1889.

I beg you to distinguish the Greek edition of Pilpay's fables published
at Berlin, the Geoponica, and the sequel of Aeschylus published at Hale & to spare
no trouble in getting them. Mr. Monroe our minister plenipotentiary
at Paris will receive the books & pay you for them. I shall be happy
always to hear from you, to learn that you preserve your health,
and that you have not suffered by the civil storms which have been
blowing over your head, being with great & sincere esteem and
attachment Dear Sir

your friend & servt.

Th: Jefferson

Books which mr. Froullé is desired to send me.

XLIVe livraison. Encyclopedie. Planches de la botanique. premiere livraison. this vo-
    -lume contained 200. pages of Discours and from the 1st. to the 100th. plate.

the next volume of Planches de la Botanique (the label being rotted off, cannot be copied) it
    contained Discours page 201. to 352. & Plate 101. to 200.

another volume of which the label was rotted. the title page Ornithologie printed
    in 1790. it contained the Introduction lxxx. pages. plate 178. to 230. of
    birds, and plate 1. to 18. of Quadrupeds.

LIe livraison. Encyclopedie. Planche d'hist. natur. XIIe partie. Insectes. it contained
    Discours page. 193. to 320. and plate 66. to 165. of Insects.

the above is a description of the 4. volumes wanting to be replaced in the former
    part of the work.

Encyclopedie methodique. whatever has come out since the 52d. livraison, to
    wit the 53d. & subsequent livraisons.  52
Copede? whatsoever has come out since his four first volumes. 12mo. of Oviperes.
Schutz Aeschylus. Halae. I have the Prometheus vinctus. Agamemnon. Septem adversus
    Thebas. & Persae which came out in 1782.3.4. and I want what has come out since.

Thomas Jefferson writes to M. Froullé, bookseller in Paris, from Monticello on May 26, 1795, ordering twenty-
four other books and replacements for parts of the *Encyclopédie* damaged in transit. Page three of a three-page
autograph letter. Gift of William Bradford Osgood Field, 1932.

Probably the best-known work of art in the Grolier Club collection is the portrait of Nathaniel Hawthorne by Cephas Giovanni Thompson. Oil on canvas, 30 x 24 inches. It appeared on a twenty-cent postage stamp in 1983. Gift of Stephen A. Wakeman, 1912.

Invitation to a Ladies' Day lecture by a well-known collector of Japanese prints at the Grolier Club in 1896. The Club has a complete file of such ephemera printed for members since 1884.

FRA·LUCA
DE·PACIOLI
OᶠBORGO·S
SEPOLCRO
BʸSTANLEY
MORISON
THE·GRO-
LIER·CLUB
NEW·YORK
MCMXXXIᴵᴵ

The title page of the Grolier Club's edition of Pacioli's Renaissance treatise on letter forms. The book, designed by Bruce Rogers using his Centaur type, is among the best known of the 145 books produced by the Club since 1884.

# The Grolier Club Library

## ROBERT NIKIRK

THE Grolier Club was launched with all the optimism and enthusiasm typical of nineteenth-century Americans organizing a new enterprise. The mixture of men and their motives was right and 1884 was a propitious time. The ingredients were an eager, and rather touching, pursuit of culture; a general inclination, prevalent in the 1880's, for joining anything that promoted uplift; and a spirit of reform, a serious strand in American life and politics of the decade. In the fledgling Grolier Club, this spirit hoped to reform the arts pertaining to the production of books, which, in the eyes of the founders, had fallen to a very low ebb indeed. Not to be discounted, of course, was the enjoyment evident in all this. The tangible results from their banding together created a personality and position for the Grolier in New York and the larger world in a remarkably short time. The most visible of these was, of course, the program of free exhibitions intended to show the public artifacts of a kind never seen by them before: medieval manuscripts, bookbindings ancient and up-to-the-minute, prints old and modern, Japanese prints, and French posters, to name only a few. Another near-immediate result was the issuing of finely made books to exemplify the high ideals of the founders. True, these works came out in severely limited numbers for subscriber-members only but soon enough became sought-after collectors' items. The third undertaking, and the least visible, was the establishment of a library. For this, only a few members were necessary as godfathers, 35 and those most familiar with the mysteries of book collecting and its attendant muse, bibliography, took the lead. Creating a library of standard reference works on bibliography and printing was certainly a fresh idea, especially for a men's club of the period, and the library was, quite properly, treated as a favored child. "It is the aim of the Council to gather together for the use of the members all the standard bibliographical works, as well as books relating to the art of printing." This was the first statement of purpose in print and appeared in the *Yearbook* for 1887. Gifts from members and appropriations brought in thirty-two volumes valued at $595 by 1888. Today, of course, anyone with a demonstrable need for our library is welcome in it. Containing around 70,000 items, the Grolier library may be outdistanced in some of its specialty areas by larger institutions, but no other significant library containing similar materials is so easy to use.

Two events in the history of the library may be regarded as of particular importance: the devising of the classification system in 1901 by Henry Watson Kent and Richard Hoe Lawrence and the Harper Bequest of 1957. After a period of fourteen years during which the library was supervised by three members, Alexander W. Drake, Beverly Chew, and Richard Hoe Lawrence, a professional librarian was hired in September 1900. Henry Watson Kent came from the Norwich Free Academy in Connecticut, a highly qualified thirty-four-year-old who had been in Melvil Dewey's first class (1887) in the newly founded library school at Columbia University. He immediately perceived the need for a classification system to control the rapidly growing but nevertheless narrowly focused collections of specialized materials, then already numbered at around 6,000. With a singular grasp of the situation, diligence, some advice from Dewey, and the experience and guidance of Lawrence, the system was ready for use in 1901. It still serves its purpose well, though it distances the Grolier from the Library of Congress system now widely used in this country. In short, the Kent-Lawrence system *defined* the library, made order out of a miscellany, and enabled it to continue to grow according to a plan. After a short four years full of achievement (including the bibliographical work on our *One Hundred Books Famous in English* *Literature*), Kent departed for a position at the Metropolitan Museum of Art which led to a distinguished and pioneering career in the new profession of museum work. He kept up a close and affectionate connection with the Grolier, even serving as president from 1920 to 1924.

The Harper Bequest of 1957 provided, at long last, an independent income for the acquisition of books, for certainly in recent years the library could not have been kept current through gifts and Council appropriations. A library endowment fund was first proposed by treasurer Robert Jaffray in 1920 "to avoid appropriations from current revenue." He urged, of course, gifts of money and bequests. Thus was born the concept of a Library Fund—to buy books. But it gradually evolved into that very useful mechanism for receiving tax-deductible gifts to fund Club activities benefiting the public such as exhibitions, a large share of building maintenance and staff salaries, and other worthwhile activities *except* the purchase of books. Thus, the Harper Bequest arrived at a most opportune time in our history.

Its origin lies in the affection formed by Lathrop Colgate Harper for nine institutions close to him during a long career as a New York rare book dealer. His plan was to bequeath to each of them trust funds providing income for the purchase of books. He predeceased his wife, but with an uncommon sympathy she carried out his plan handsomely by adding to his her own fortune accumulated as a popular syndicated columnist. The Grolier was left three trusts: for incunabula, for books about books, and for books more than one hundred years old. The incunabula fund is rarely touched and the latter two generally suffice for annual acquisitions. They are supplemented by the Book Fund, which is replenished by gifts and sales such as those of 1968, 1969, and 1972. The Harper Bequest, at around $250,000, remains the largest gift ever received by the Grolier Club.

In order to avoid here a long account of regular purchases over a hundred years, it may be assumed that the Grolier library keeps up with current publications in its special fields though some key works were missed, especially in the 1940's and 1950's. Growth, then, has been on a reasonably regulated course since 1901.

We should now look back to those donors who have made significant gifts to the library in the past century. A Golden Book would be headed by Samuel Putnam Avery, our Maecenas of the early days and (the Harper Bequest apart) the Grolier's most generous benefactor. An art dealer and collector and a much-loved figure in cultural and club life in New York, Avery made frequent trips to Europe and after 1884 arranged for frequent gifts to the Club library and building. Until his death in 1903, a steady stream of the newest reference books, key older works in the history of bibliography, bindings of four centuries, fine printing of all periods, and prints of interest to bibliophiles provided the broad foundation on which the collection grew. After his death, the Avery family gave the collection of miniature books which are attracting more attention in the 1980's than ever before. Too much cannot be said about Avery's foresight and generosity in promoting the growth and position of the Grolier Club and its library.

In July 1894 the Bruce family, New York typefounders since the early part of the century, donated a library of ninety-four incunabula and several hundred sixteenth- and seventeenth-century books, collected with a typographical slant and with many containing references to the invention of printing. Assembled by at least two generations, it may well have been the first collection of its kind formed in the United States. For that reason alone the incunabula perhaps should have remained intact as a collection; but after due process, thirty were sold by order of the Council in 1967.

We find that the most active members of the Club were also the most frequent donors of books and prints, especially Avery, Robert Hoe, William Loring Andrews, R. H. Lawrence, Beverly Chew, Edwin B. Holden, and E. G. Kennedy. Generosity often continued even after death. Beverly Chew left us his large collection of silver and embroidered bindings, English portrait prints, and several oil portraits—all received in 1924. Mrs. W. L. Andrews left us several of her husband's most prized books, including the miniature Nicolaus Jensen *Officium B. V. M.* of 1475 in a

Louis Hagué binding, as well as the library's imposing late eighteenth-century Dutch tall clock.

Daniel B. Fearing of Newport, Rhode Island, and angling fame, began in 1908 to give a collection, finally totaling 525 books ranging from the sixteenth through the nineteenth century, with the stipulation that those not wanted could be sold or exchanged. Leonard L. Mackall, a writer and journalist, in 1927 began making gifts soon numbering in the hundreds, most of them with his characteristic sprawling ink inscription filling the free endpapers. He expressed the wish that his books join "the most important bibliographical collection in America." Though some of the Mackall books are no longer in the collection, many of those remaining are of prime historical importance for the study of printing and bibliography. In 1932 a fund was established by the children of George Livingston Nichols through the sale of part of his library given for the purpose. In 1936 John A. Penton of Cleveland gave fifty editions of Frederick Locker-Lampson's verse along with the poet's delightful and important scrapbook filled with watercolors or drawings by his friends Richard Doyle, Kate Greenaway, Walter Crane, and Ernest Griset, and a series of autograph letters.

Other special collections came from Charles Williston McAlpin during his lifetime and after his death in 1942; of particular note are most of the early books designed by Bruce Rogers and representative runs of the turn-of-the-century English presses, especially the Doves. That aficionado of the Daniel Press of Oxford, Joseph M. Andreini, presented our collection in 1910. In 1942 we received the Melbert B. Cary, Jr., bequest of "one of the finest existing collections of Goudyana," much of it in splendid fitted cases made by Gerhard Gerlach.

Of medieval manuscripts, few of our dozen or so examples are outstanding but in their range of date and quality they form an ideal collection for teaching purposes and are often thus used. All are recorded in de Ricci's 1935 census. The most important is an eleventh-century Italian large folio example, a text of Gregory the Great's *Moralia in Job* with echoes of Irish decoration. We value it all the more because of its provenance: Mateo Canonici, Walter Sneyd, and our donor, Archer M. Huntington. A fine and delicate two-volume French Bible of the thirteenth century was bound by our early member William Matthews and his invoice is preserved in it. Several examples of *Horae* in various sizes and of varying quality were given by the Bruce family, Beverly Chew, D. B. Fearing, and Edward Bement.

It should be mentioned in passing that in addition to printed books and European manuscripts, we could put on a small exhibition of examples of writing from all over the world—all donated by members. Asia is especially well represented; besides Chinese and Southeast Asian examples, we have fifty Japanese woodcut books of the nineteenth century.

The Grolier Club is forever in the debt of members who took a special interest in building up its famous collection of booksellers' and auction catalogues. Today this section of the library is perhaps the best known and is certainly the most heavily used. Many recent scholarly editions of writers and composers have drawn on it. S. P. Avery gave many French sale catalogues of three centuries. William M. Ivins, Jr., in 1925 presented 250 French sale catalogues, duplicates from the vast collections formed by Seymour de Ricci, himself a loyal member and donor. In 1931 a major purchase of 975 catalogues from E. P. Goldschmidt was effected, probably through the intercession of Lucius Wilmerding, who took a great interest in this aspect of collecting history and who gave large numbers of catalogues. But our greatest benefactor in the catalogue field was Waters S. Davis, who, after his election to membership in 1932, found here an outlet for his catalogue mania. His innumerable gifts included the first English book auction of 1676. After his death, his children saw to it that the remainder of his collection came to the Grolier, along with his still useful handwritten notebook indexes. Finally, during the financial campaign of 1961, the Robinson brothers, booksellers of London, presented sixty-two rare English auction catalogues of the period 1674–1695 that all at once made the Grolier collection the largest in this country.

Thanks to the particular affinity of our librarian, Gabriel Austin, for catalogues, the collection grew remarkably during his six-year tenure

beginning in 1963. In 1967 alone, an unusually complete run of 300
French sales from 1840 to 1870 were purchased from "a castle library."
Major purchases were made in the Major J. R. Abbey sales in 1966 (and
in the A. N. L. Munby sale a decade later). Gabriel Austin, together with
our member Richard E. Priest, labored mightily over many months
recording catalogues on a card system of their own devising and physi-
cally moving the collection so related materials would be shelved together.
Their index continues to serve every day as a virtual catalogue of our
collections of booksellers' and auction catalogues. All of this just mentioned only supplements the material gathered in annually by subscription
and from the booksellers of Europe and America. Related to this was one
of our most welcome acquisitions: in 1979 new enameled metal shelving
was installed using every available inch on the fourth floor, a project
conceived, designed, and carried out by member Douglas F. Bauer. But
very soon we will have to find yet more space for the catalogue collections which grow by purchase and accumulation at a remarkable rate.

Of the periodical collection, often regarded as an unglamorous country
cousin in research libraries, we can be proud. It has been formed over a
hundred years not only by subscription but also by the purchase of society publications and bibliographical, typographical, and bibliophilic periodicals.

Another section of the library, still largely unknown to members and
specialists alike, is the collection of bookbindings. It has several examples
of outstanding artistic and historical importance and overall amply demonstrates the history and progress of binding. Examples are always on
display in the second floor room. As it happens, the Grolier Club's founding coincided exactly with the birth of modern interest in the study of
historical bookbindings, in common with many other of the applied arts.
Some Grolier members eagerly collected old and new bindings. Contemporary work from the ateliers of Paris and London demonstrates skill of
astonishing virtuosity to today's eyes. Robert Hoe, first president of the
Grolier, owned the finest collection of bindings old and new ever formed
by an American; fellow Club members followed him as best they could. 41

But it was once again the inimitable S. P. Avery, collector of historical examples and patron of contemporary binders, especially French, who first saw the usefulness of putting together a wide-ranging collection for the enjoyment and instruction of Grolier members and students. His donations covering four centuries eventually made up one of the first institutional collections in this country. In 1894 the Bruce gift of incunabula added several original fifteenth-century examples, and the Chew bequest of 1924 brought us fifty-one seventeenth- through nineteenth-century bindings, mostly miniature, of silver repoussé and filigree, needlework, enamel, tortoise shell, and other unusual materials. Two modern bindings are of exceptional interest. One is Roger Powell's imaginative design on green morocco incorporating scientific symbols in gilt and inlay on a copy of our *One Hundred Books Famous in Science* presented as a thank-you gift following a 1964 visit sponsored by the Club. The other is a large quarto of red morocco shimmering with radial tooling, one of the *irradiante* series designed by Paul Bonet in the late 1940's and presented to us by Mrs. Valerian Lada-Mocarski.

The broad scope of our bindings collection includes quite a number of other out-of-the-way treasures such as the dedication copy to King Edward VI of John Bale's 1548 *Illustrium Maioris Britanniae scriptorum* in its contemporary German calf and heavily gold-tooled binding, Roger Payne's diminutive binding containing his last known invoice, Octave Uzanne's personal nine-volume set of his periodical *Le livre moderne* (1890–1891) in extraordinary emblematic bindings with endpapers of cut-up Japanese wood-block prints, several of the Sienese wooden bindings painted in the fourteenth-century style, fine fore-edge paintings, a sizeable group of armorial and other association bindings, representative examples *à la fanfare* and *à la cathédrale*, bindings by May Morris, Katherine Adams, and Sarah Prideaux, and so on.

One of the high points of late nineteenth-century French binding was executed by S. P. Avery's favorite artist, Charles Meunier of Paris. On this large folio *tour de force*, Meunier reproduced with incredible skill the painting by Flameng called *Grolier in the House of Aldus* by means of leathers which are inlaid, onlaid, painted, gilded, marbled, tooled, and incised. The lower covers and doublures, rarely seen, are also elaborately worked. It houses J. F. Jacquemart's 1861 album of historic binding reproductions. This association item, almost a talisman to us, was retained by the Avery family until presented to the Club in 1919.

But what of books from the library of Jean Grolier? Strange to tell, of the four we now own, the first did not come to the library until 1930, though dozens of examples had passed through the collections of members since 1884. In the 1919 *Yearbook* the librarian wrote: "Members of the Club and visitors are constantly disappointed not to find a book here from the library of Grolier, and it is earnestly hoped that, at a not too distant day, this greatest need of the library may be supplied." The great day was a full eleven years distant when, in 1930, Mrs. Meredith Hare, daughter of former member Dean Sage, presented his copy of the 1537 Marinus Barletius, a fine folio example bound by Claude de Picques. In 1935 the folio Paulus Jovius of 1549, perfectly genuine but clumsily repainted in the nineteenth century, was presented by the Seth Sprague Terry family. A particularly suitable association copy, Grolier's copy of the octavo two-volume 1504 Aldine Homer containing his painted arms and emblems and handsomely decorated initial letters, was bought privately from the collector Edward C. Streeter in 1940. It is in an English binding of around 1820. Our prize Grolier binding, a splendid folio example in brown calf tooled by the Cupid's Bow Binder on the 1542 *Epistolae* of Pope Nicholas I, was removed from Lucius Wilmerding's fabled library before the auction by order of the family so it could be sold privately to the Club as a memorial to that devoted and beloved member.

Books and manuscripts, bindings and prints, archives and paintings, clocks and bronzes—and members—have all had a professional caretaker since 1900 called The Librarian. It is perhaps not too much to say that the Grolier Club at any given time is in some degree a reflection of the incumbent, a combination of librarian, curator, and manager. As the librarian of the Sorbonne, the Abbé des Housayes, wrote in 1780: "Your librarian, gentlemen, is in some sort your official representative. To him is remitted the deposit of your glory. To him is entrusted, as a duty, the important mission of maintaining, and even of increasing, your brilliant reputation whenever a stranger comes to examine the precious treasures of your library." Following the short but effective tenure of Henry Watson Kent from late 1900 to 1904, Miss Ruth Shepard Granniss, a graduate of the library school at Pratt Institute, presided over the Club's library and daily affairs (for such is also the charge of the Grolier librarian) until 1944. Nothing describes her distinguished career of forty years better than the text of the beautifully printed citation presented to her upon retirement. "With complete understanding of the purposes of the Club and sympathy with all its efforts to make its objects known and understood, with fine scholarship in the literature of the subjects pertaining to the arts of the book and other subjects, with intimate acquaintance with the books of the library in her charge and an exact knowledge of their bibliography . . . with enthusiasm and courtesy she has welcomed every opportunity to serve the Club." Her retiring modesty while in the forty-year employ of male bibliophiles was marked, but so was her quiet strength of personality. A few members today can recall businessmen who left their offices early to take tea with Miss Granniss at the Club. The period after her retirement, in her native town of Guilford, Connecticut, was marred by a growing infirmity, and she died in March 1954. An intensely private person, she always successfully warded off any attempt to photograph her. Miss Granniss still ranks high in that small group of American women of achievement in the world of books during the first half of the twentieth century. Her publications of various lengths number some eighteen. Anyone at all familiar with the Grolier library is guided daily by her careful work over forty years and, indeed, one often encounters her handwriting in helpful notes.

Adjutant from 1923 in the library with the title of curator was George Leslie McKay, appointed to the post of librarian upon the retirement of Miss Granniss. A prolific bibliographer, he published standard works on

44

John Masefield, H. Rider Haggard, and Robert Bridges, as well as com-
piling the vast Edwin J. Beinecke collection catalogue on Robert Louis
Stevenson. His most universally useful work is perhaps the complete
record of American book auctions from 1713 until 1934, with its still-
standard introduction, in daily use in libraries and bookshops all over the
country. He continued bibliographical work after retirement in New
Haven, where he died in 1976. His successor, appointed in 1957, was
Alexander W. Davidson, a graduate of Williams College, a member since
1936, and a well-known and popular figure in the New York rare book
trade, having been a longtime associate with the firm of L. C. Harper
as an Americanist. He had a personality suited to the position and helped
set in motion several significant changes in the building and Club programs, among them the renovation and furnishing of the second floor
room and its consequent series of exhibitions from members' collections.
He also organized the long-term restoration program for library books,
their first overhaul since the founding in 1884. Having been an intimate
of the Harpers for many years, he was of great help to all the institutions
sharing in the will in straightening out the complications inherent in such
a large estate (which included rental property in the Bronx). In 1960
Davidson was incapacitated by a stroke and never resumed his duties
full-time though he continued as "consultant librarian" through the end
of 1961. He died in May 1967.

Davidson's successor, another graduate of Williams, J. Terry Bender,
also had a degree from the library school at Columbia. After working in the Columbia library, he went to Stanford, eventually becoming
chief of special collections there until appointed our librarian in mid-
1961. He brought to Grolier's house notable social gifts, energy, and
perseverance, all of which were needed in ample measure, for during his
tenure the library book rehabilitation was completed and the building
itself utterly disrupted during the renovation when new wiring and air
conditioning were installed. Holding the Club together in that period of
siege was no small feat, and when he left to become curator of rare books
at Syracuse University in July 1964, he left behind many grateful and     45

pleasant memories. He remained at Syracuse until 1969, when he was called to Hofstra University to take over their rapidly growing collections, especially of modern writers, thus once again joining the New York book scene. At Hofstra he carried out his duties with characteristic élan until resigning to become an independent rare book and manuscript appraiser. Stricken with lung cancer, he died after a short illness in March 1977.

Gabriel Austin was first hired in March 1963 as curator, a title in abeyance since the days of George L. McKay but revived for his use. He was appointed librarian in July 1964. A member since 1959, Austin emerged as a most useful linguist and *cicerone* on the fabulous Iter Italicum of 1962. While moving easily in the social milieu of the Grolier, he also restored the roles of scholar and acquisitor to the position of librarian. He was also in large measure responsible for the success of the outstanding exhibitions of the late 1960's. His tenure here culminated in a first-rate work of investigative scholarship, a census of all the known books from Grolier's library built upon our Carolyn Shipman book of 1907. *The Library of Jean Grolier* (1971) called for all his accumulated knowledge of catalogue sources for tracing provenance and will remain the standard work. Upon resigning in July 1969 to become head of Sotheby Parke-Bernet's book department, he was succeeded in September 1969 by Harvey A. Simmonds, still another graduate of Williams, then employed at the Berg Collection of the New York Public Library. Also a graduate of the library school at Columbia and with excellent background for the position of librarian, he seemed to take hold well at the Grolier, but resigned the position in early January 1970. In his address to the membership at the 1970 annual meeting, President Howell said: "We must respect this decision as a part of the basically beneficial process of finding one's best role in life, and accept this resignation with sincere regret." Simmonds's successor, a candidate for the position back in the summer of 1969, was the present writer, then a cataloguer at Sotheby Parke-Bernet by way of the book trade in New York. A graduate of New York University and a former staff member at the Corning Museum of Glass, he has been a member of the Grolier since 1966.

This brief sweep over the hundred-year history of the Grolier Club library has omitted facts and persons eminently worthy of mention in a centennial volume. The entire story can be had only by reading all the *Yearbook* reports of the Library Committee in sequence; perhaps they should be reprinted with a thorough index. What cannot be conveyed here is the flavor of our library: not only its scope, but also its various settings in the clubhouse, especially the jewel of a library room, and its numerous quirks and byways. Most of all, what we cannot recapture in this sketch is the flavor of the personalities and temperaments of those devoted Grolier members who established our great library and of their successors who nurtured it and passed it on to our care.

# Incunabula

## WILLIAM H. SCHEIDE
## AND MINA R. BRYAN

THE second article in the Grolier Club Constitution reads in part, "Its object shall be the literary study and promotion of the arts pertaining to the production of books." Such an object inevitably involves what in the last five centuries has been, in Western civilization, the principal art "pertaining to the production of books," namely, the art of printing. And this in turn directs attention to the importance of the origin and early history of alphabetic printing with movable type. It seems appropriate to emphasize that the significance of this question was recognized by the Club in its earliest years. The Club's collection of incunabula, now comprising fifty-two books, had an auspicious and distinguished beginning.

The story begins with George Bruce (1781–1866), typefounder, printer, and publisher, in connection with his printing and publishing establishment, which introduced stereotyping in America. Later he abandoned his printing and publishing and, with his brother, established the first type foundry in New York. They developed a typecasting machine in 1838 which was taken up in many countries and was successful enough to threaten the traditional trade of typefounding. His son, David Wolfe Bruce (d. 1895), joined him in the firm. In 1876 Theodore Low De Vinne, one of the nine founders of the Club, dedicated his *The Invention of Printing* "To David Wolfe Bruce in acknowledgement of his instruction about types not to be had by reading, of assistance in studies not to be found in public libraries, of companionship more pleasant than books." It is not, therefore, surprising that both father and son were interested in the invention and spread of printing in Europe. Father and son collected books on the subject for over fifty years. In 1894, a year before his death, David Wolfe Bruce, who became a member of the Grolier Club in 1885, gave the Club his incunabula along with many other early books, as well as his own highly interesting six-volume catalogue. These still form the nucleus of the collection.

The Club incunabula begin with two conjugate leaves on vellum of the 42-line Gutenberg Bible, largely complete though damaged from once being folded and cut for use as bulk in a binding, and another large fragment (a complete leaf on paper was given in 1922 by J. C. McCoy). Of equal interest are the two large Bruce fragments on paper of the 36-line Bible printed at Bamberg in an earlier state of the Gutenberg type, although printed after the 42-line Bible. As there is no copy of this Bible in America, the fact that one of these fragments is the largest example in the United States is significant.

Books printed in Cologne, Strasbourg, Augsburg, Nuremberg, Basel, Rome, Venice, Lyon, and Westminster not only illustrate the spread of printing, the development of Gothic, Roman, and Italic types, and their refinement during the last half of the fifteenth century, but also present a selection of the most popular and influential books printed—theology, law, and Greek and Latin classical literature. It is possible to mention only the most outstanding books in the gift, and space does not permit discussion of the original and other early bindings present in the collection.

The Mentelin German Bible printed in Strasbourg in 1466 is the first Bible, and probably the first large book, to be printed in a vernacular language. It is also important because it preserves the text in purer form than found in other manuscripts from which later editions were printed.

Pomponius Mela's *Cosmographia*, a popular and often reprinted geography, was printed by Erhard Ratdolt in Venice in 1482. Ratdolt was one of the first printers to use woodcuts to illustrate his books.

Saint Jerome's *Vitae Sanctorum Patrum* was printed in Latin over and over again. It was also printed in Dutch, German, French, and Italian in a number of editions. The only English edition in the fifteenth century, *The Lyff of the Faders*, was printed by Wynkyn de Worde at Westminster in 1495, and a copy is in our library. The book is profusely illustrated with crude cuts; the largest woodcut is repeated six times, and the forty smaller cuts account for 155 illustrations. Wynkyn de Worde, the successor to William Caxton, England's first printer, records that it was "translated out of French by William Caxton of Westminster, late dead, finished on the last day of his life."

There is a copy of the *Horae ad Usum Parisiensem* printed in Paris by Phillippe Pigouchet for Simon Vostre on April 25, 1500. This is a fine Book of Hours on vellum. Pigouchet specialized in printing these small devotional books. They were produced not only for the local market but for other French cities and also for England.

Many of the first owners of the Bruce books were monasteries which probably bought them from the printers, as we know from early manuscript ownership inscriptions. Bruce copies derived chiefly from two German collectors, Dr. Georg Kloss and a Berlin lawyer named Barnheim. Many Barnheim books found their way into David Wolfe Bruce's library by way of a Stargardt auction of Barnheim's library in May 1873. One of the Bruce books, a Petrucius *Disputationes Questiones et Concilia*, has an interesting provenance because it can be traced from the late fifteenth century. It traveled from Rome, where it was printed by Adam Rot in 1472, to Ulrich Fugger, who in 1509 presented it, according to an inscription, to a German Augustinian convent. Around the year 1800, during the period of secularization of religious houses, it went to the Bavarian Royal Library, which later sold it as a duplicate. At some point it was acquired by the Berlin lawyer Barnheim and from his sale passed (perhaps directly) to Bruce. The Grolier Club's is one of two copies in this country; the other is in the Library of Congress in the John Boyd Thatcher collection.

Among the many benefactions of Samuel Putnam Avery and one of the most prized books in the Grolier Club library is the noble first edition of St. Augustine's *De Civitate Dei*, printed at the Benedictine abbey of

Subiaco by Conrad Swynheym and Arnold Pannartz in 1467. Only three titles printed by this, the first press in Italy, are known today. This fine large copy has an illuminated first page of text and decorated initials throughout.

The rarest book in the collection was once owned by William Loring Andrews, a founder of the Club. This superb miniature book, an *Officium Beatae Virginis Mariae*, was printed in 1475 on vellum in black and red by Nicolaus Jensen in Venice and has added illumination of borders and initials in gold and colors. It is the only copy in this country and one of two copies known; the other is in Naples. In a Louis Hagué binding, it was in the sale of the library of Ambroise Firmin-Didot in 1879, another member of a famous family of typefounders and printers. It came to the Grolier Club in the bequest of Mrs. Andrews in 1930.

Two other nineteenth-century members of the Club donated incunabula. Edwin B. Holden gave a popular and widely printed Biblical commentary printed in Venice in 1478 by Franciscus Renner de Heilbronn. This book has a presentation inscription from Walter Savage Landor to Robert Southey in 1824. Marshall C. Lefferts presented a fine copy of Boccaccio's *Genealogie Deorum*, printed in Venice by Wendelin de Spire in 1472, the first printing of this popular work. Boccaccio's books printed in the fifteenth century illustrate the importance of the invention of printing in recovering and widely reproducing the treasures of classical history and literature.

The twentieth-century additions to the library have all been accomplished by purchase from the Harper Fund, with the exception of a Solinus, *Polyhistor*, printed in Venice by Nicolaus Jensen in 1475, which was the gift of Philip Hofer. It is bound in blue morocco gilt by Lefebure and comes from the libraries of A. A. Renouard and the Russian imperial summer palace at Tsarkoe Selo. This work, a description of the ancient world with remarks on natural history, religion, and social questions, was compiled in the third century A.D. and revised in the sixth century. It was also among the popular and influential books which transmitted the knowledge of the ancient world to the beginning of the Renaissance.

The Lathrop Colgate Harper Fund for the purchase of incunabula was one of the provisions in the bequest of Mrs. Harper in 1957. Mr. Harper's will provided a number of bequests operative upon the death of his wife if he predeceased her, which was the case. Mrs. Harper carried out the original bequests, but, in turn, supplemented his intentions with her own considerable estate. One of the books bought with the Harper Fund, Johann Tritheim, *Catalogus illustrium virorum* (Mainz, Peter Von Friedburg, after August 14, 1495), has the following note: "Sold to the Grolier Club by authorization of the Board of Trustees of the Pierpont Morgan Library on January 19, 1961. Frederick B. Adams, Jr., Director." This is a book of considerable bibliographical interest, the *viri illustres* being all German men of letters, many of them Tritheim's contemporaries. He gives in each case the names of their works, and at the end of his treatise "confesses" to a long list of his own publications. The book has the bookplate of James P. R. Lyell.

Thus, the first incunabula in the Club's library were the gift of inventors and other collectors, with post-1957 additions purchased from funds provided by one of the great scholar-dealers in incunabula. As a result of these gifts and purchases, the collection now contains representative examples demonstrating the beginning and spread of printing from 1455 throughout the fifteenth century.

# Post-1500 Printed Books

## RUTH MORTIMER

GROLIER CLUB publication no. 21, printed at The De Vinne Press in 1895, has the title *A Description of the Early Printed Books Owned by the Grolier Club with a Brief Account of Their Printers and the History of Typography in the Fifteenth Century*. The books described were not all incunabula. Included were sixteenth-century books that contained references to the invention of printing. Each book so catalogued had two reasons for being in the library. Its text was a literary contribution to printing history; its physical form was evidence of the state of the art to date. There is some merit in applying to the post-1500 books in the library the principle that shaped the notable hourglass colophon in Johann Tritheim's *Compendium* printed in Mainz by Peter Schoeffer in 1515. The colophon is reproduced and translated in the 1895 Grolier Club volume as one of the documents of printing. Schoeffer chose to make a claim for Johann Fust as the inventor of printing, within a decorative arrangement of type that drew attention to the text. Collectors, printers, artists, and printing historians are alert to the implications of form as well as information, and they are well served by the juxtaposition of original editions with modern critical works.

There is a natural inclination toward major figures and landmark volumes of the sixteenth century. The Grolier Club copy of Geoffroy Tory's *Champ fleury* (Paris, 1529) was purchased by council order in 1889 and rebound in 1975 using the die from the binding of the 1909 Houghton Mifflin edition. Another Tory volume is the 1509 Paris edition of Baptista Mantuanus, with Tory's preface and marginalia. This has the earliest block of the device of Jodocus Badius Ascensius showing the printing press in operation.

Within the library, it is possible to study letter forms by reading sixteenth-century theorists such as Tory and Albrecht Dürer or comparing a writing book such as Ugo da Carpi's *Thesauro de scrittori* of 1530 with Charles Snell's *Art of Writing* (London, 1712; bound with *The Standard Rules of the Round and Round Text-hands*, 1728) or the *Arte de escribir* of Torío de la Riva y Herrero (Madrid, 1798). The Grolier Club copy of a Vatican type specimen book of 1628, *Indice de caratteri, con l'inuentori, & nomi di essi, esistenti nella stampa Vaticana, & camerale*, is one of only two copies known, as is also *Épreuves des caracteres de la fonderie du Sr. Marquet*, printed at Lyons (undated, eighteenth century). *A Catalogue and Specimen of the Large and Extensive Printing-type-foundery of the Late Ingenious Mr. John James, Letter-founder, Formerly of Bartholomew-Close, London, Deceased . . .* , an auction catalogue for June 1782, is equally scarce.

Personalities are reflected in such unusual works as the 1569 obituary of the Basel printer Joannes Oporinus, *Oratio de ortv, vita, et obitv Ioannis Oporinus Basiliensis . . .* by Andrea Jociscus Silesius, or George Stanhope's funeral sermon for a bookseller (London, 1724), or two editions of Johann Conrad Zeltner's lives of celebrated press readers, *C. D. Correctorvm in typographiis ervditorvm centvria, speciminis loco collecta* (Nuremberg, 1716 and 1720, the latter being T. L. De Vinne's copy). While there are standard works—Joseph Moxon's *Mechanick Exercises* (1677–1678), Samuel Palmer's *General History of Printing*, the 1733 issue—there is also a copy of Samuel Palmer's *Proposals for Publishing a General History of Printing* (London, 1729), and a curiosity such as *Le bureau typographique; livre elementaire, a l'usage des enfans* (London, "Au Magasin des Enfans," 1808). Much of printing history is directed at a small readership: there were only eighty copies printed of Edward Rowe Mores's *A Dissertation upon English Typographical Founders and Foundries* ([London], 1778), and Delandine's *Histoire abrégée de l'imprimerie* was printed in 1814 in Lyons in an edition of one hundred copies.

Freedom of the press is a subject significantly treated in the library. There is the text of Henry VIII's "Acte concernyng printers and bynders of bokes" as part of the *Actis Made in This Session* printed in folio by Thomas Berthelet in 1534. There are two issues of the Star Chamber decree of 1637, and other English ordinances in seventeenth-century editions. The 1692 *Orders, Rules & Ordinances* of the Stationers' Company is an interleaved copy with manuscript additions. A tract volume includes two pamphlets printed in 1774, Catharine Macauley's *A Modest Plea for the Property of Copyright* and William Enfield's *Observations on Literary Property*. The material here, while strong in London-printed texts, is not limited to them. There are successive editions of the *Index librorum prohibitorum* beginning in 1559—and the record of controversies surrounding single works such as *Ad censuras theologorum parisiensium, quibus Biblia a R. Stephano . . . responsio* (Geneva, 1552). There is the 1687 *Édit du roy pour la réglement des imprimeurs* (bound with the *Réglement des relieurs*).

Such works dealt with restrictions on printing; a more pleasurable consideration is the extension of the text by means of illustration. The techniques of book illustration, although all are represented by example and theory, might best be examined by looking at the technique that was developing and challenging the traditional methods during the century in which the Grolier Club was founded. The wood block and the copperplate were both available to the fifteenth-century printer, although it was not until the sixteenth century that the engraving seriously displaced the woodcut on the printed page. The chemical method of printing, whereby an image was transferred from the plane surface of the lithographic stone, was invented by Alois Senefelder at the very end of the eighteenth century, and the library has the first edition of the English translation of his account of the method, *A Complete Course of Lithography* (London, 1819). The library also has the first lithograph produced in America in the *Analectic Magazine* for 1819 (Philadelphia) and the first book published in America on the process, F. C. Lawsher's *Die lithographische Hochätzkunst*

(Baltimore, 1835). The early manuals by Engelmann and Raucourt (both the original and the English translation by Charles Hullmandel) are here as one would expect, but less expected are the instructional and promotional books of the 1820's and such doomed experiments as *The Parthenon* (1825–1826), where a typeset text was laboriously applied to the stone. The procedure can be followed in the library through the monuments of chromolithography late in the nineteenth century. Artistic lithography was quite rightly surveyed in a Grolier Club exhibition in 1896.

The library is fortunate in the range of examples by which it can demonstrate the enhancement of the printed book by color, in illustration, in ornamentation, and in the ink and paper used for the text itself. There are works on color theory, such as Le Blon's *Coloritto or the Harmony of Colouring in Painting* (London, 1756), a dual-language edition, with its color plate of a palette. Contemporary with the *Coloritto* is *Le livre de quatre couleurs* by Caraccioli, printed in 1760 in gold, blue, brown, and orange, the Grolier Club copy in a four-color binding. The Grolier Club copy of an anthology of *Pieces of Ancient Poetry from Unpublished Manuscripts and Scarce Books* (Bristol, 1814) is one of six copies printed on blue paper, of an edition limited to 102 copies. Printing on blue paper was a characteristic method of producing special copies in the sixteenth century, but the paper experiments in the nineteenth century went to such lengths as the *Aristarchus; or Principles of Composition* (London, 1822), in which each signature is on a different colored paper, or *The Modern Thinker* (New York, 1870), printed section by section in colored inks on colored papers.

The library has Charles Gillot's *El plus ultra*, issue no. 1 of a periodical color-printed on colored paper in Paris in 1893. The Gillot piece, however, is overshadowed in the library by a proof copy of *Le livre moderne; Revue du monde littéraire et des bibliophiles contemporains* (1890–1891). This is Art Nouveau artist Octave Uzanne's own set, bound in eight volumes together with an index volume produced in February 1892. Bound in are proofs, original drawings, and working layout. Notices of the *bibliophiles contemporains* include references to the Grolier Club. The library catalogue contains twenty-six entries for Uzanne, including other special copies of his works.

A recitation of the name labels in the press alcove of the library would result in an outline of the history of the private press movement with the addition of the better commercial presses involved in good printing. Here are many productive interconnections among Grolier Club members. A strong collection of the Gilliss Press—one press responsible for early Grolier Club publications—gives that press its rightful place in American printing history. Robert Hoe's *A Short History of the Printing Press* was printed by the Gilliss Press in 1902. A full section is given over to the Melbert B. Cary, Jr., collection of Goudyana—a solid working collection with proofs and layouts by Frederic and Bertha Goudy. The major Frederic Warde archive at the Grolier Club, Warde's own designs for his books at every stage of preparation—drawings, layouts, proofs, clippings —extends to other areas where books from Warde's library have been integrated in the Club library as a whole. The Grolier Club copy of Strozzi's *Poetae*, for instance, printed by Simon de Colines in Paris in 1530 in a type influenced by the original Arrighi italic, is Warde's copy, dated March 1925.

While the library is rich in press books, a press collection is also judged by its preservation of ephemera. Perhaps the most intriguing example of ephemera is an extraordinary scrapbook for the Lee Priory Press. Formerly belonging to Archdeacon Francis Wrangham, it contains autograph letters, press announcements, and broadsides. There are eight books from this press, dating from 1814 to 1820. The Daniel Press, the private press of the Rev. C. H. O. Daniel, Provost of Worcester College, Oxford, was active at the time the Grolier Club was founded, and it exemplifies the ideal community of literary interests. The box marked for the Daniel Press on the library shelves is full of the characteristic blue-paper–covered volumes.

There are excellent association copies throughout the library. The 1554 Paris edition of Quintilian belonged to the historian Jacques Auguste de

Thou. A 1555 Paris edition of Aristotle's *De arte poetica* belonged to W. W. Greg. The 1636 *Alphabetum chaldaicum* was once in John Evelyn's library. A 1543 Paris Cicero representing the first use by Robert Estienne of an Aldine-derived italic letter has the bookplate of Anna Damer, friend of Horace Walpole, which was designed by another friend of Walpole, Agnes Berry, in 1793. The 1795 Worcester edition of Charlotte Smith's *Elegiac Sonnets*, the book in which Isaiah Thomas used the first wove paper made in America, is a presentation copy from Thomas to Harriet Lee in 1797. There is good provenance for the Grolier Club copy of Jean de La Caille's *Histoire de l'imprimerie et de la librairie* (Paris, 1689). This belonged to Georges Lepreux, historian of French printing, and has his manuscript annotations; it was given to the library by Daniel Berkeley Updike.

One of the headings in the Grolier Club library's classification scheme is "Celebrations of the Invention of Printing." The library itself offers cause for continual celebration, in the quality and diversity of its examples of the art of printing.

# Booksellers' and Auction Catalogues

## WILLIAM S. REESE

THE library of the Grolier Club contains one of the largest and most accessible collections of booksellers' and book auction catalogues in the United States. The collection has grown over the years through generous gifts by members, purchases, and the preserved accretion of generations of catalogues. Now properly shelved and arranged on the entire fourth floor of the clubhouse, the collection is perhaps the most readily available and useful collection the researcher may call upon in America.

Auction and booksellers' catalogues are by their very nature ephemeral. Some are published with an eye to posterity, either to record some great collection or to mark an anniversary; most catalogues, however, are issued as articles of commerce and are disposed of once their currency is passed. Even today, when readers have become increasingly aware of their value as reference tools, most booksellers' catalogues go straight to the wastebasket once they have been read. Such was even more true fifty and a hundred years ago. Virtually any catalogue issued before 1900 is scarce, and many exist in only a few copies. A collection such as the Grolier possesses could not be reproduced. Its strength is not only in the high points mentioned here, but in the mass of obscure and often unrecorded material, as irreplaceable as the more famous rarities and perhaps of the greatest value to the bibliographical or literary student. In addition, many of the catalogues have distinguished provenance and manuscript notes which add to their usefulness and interest.

The most impressive section of the Club's holdings is the group of English catalogues. This is not surprising, since a large percentage of the Club membership has been interested in English books, and as the English trade was the preeminent book market for American collectors in the nineteenth and early twentieth centuries. The interest of members in English bibliography also led to the acquisition of many older English catalogues. These include the first three English book auction catalogues: the 1676 sale of the Rev. Lazarus Seaman's library, and the 1677 sales of Thomas Kidner's and Humphrey Henchman's libraries. Also included in the collection is the Richard Smith sale of 1682, notable for its many Caxtons and books from the library of the great English bibliophile Humphrey Dyson. A. N. L. Munby applauded the Smith library as the most important sold in England in the seventeenth century. It is appropriate that at the Munby sale the Club secured the personal copy of that great bibliographer of catalogues.

The crown jewels of the Club's catalogue collections are the sixty-odd English auction lists of 1678–1695 presented to the Club in 1962 by the noted booksellers Lionel and Philip Robinson. This extraordinary run, largely from the Bibliotheca Lindesiana, comprises about a quarter of the items noted in Munby and Coral's *English Book Sale Catalogues* for the period up to 1700. Most English book auctions of this period were run by bookdealers as an alternative method of disposing of stock, and such prominent bookseller-auctioneers as Edward Millington, William Cooper, and Robert Scott are well represented in the Robinson gift. With the Club's other holdings in this early period it is the equal of any collection in the field, after the British Library.

Representative of the great age of English bibliomania, which began with the sale of the Duke of Roxburghe's library in 1812, are the Club's copies of virtually all the important sale catalogues of the period. Many of these, notably that of the Roxburghe sale itself and the catalogue of the fifth Duke of Marlborough's 1819 dispersal of his White Knights library, are annotated with buyers and prices realized. At the Lord Northwick sale in 1965 the Club obtained a set of twenty-six bound volumes with over two hundred Sotheby catalogues for the period from 1825 to 1832, especially prepared for Samuel Leigh Sotheby. Printed on paper both heavy and large, the catalogues are usually annotated by Sotheby, and provide a nearly complete record of his firm's activities at the time. The Club can boast duplicate copies of some of these catalogues, annotated by observers rather than the house. One, at least, is quite rare: the sale catalogue of the artist Thomas Rowlandson's prints, drawings, and paintings at Sotheby's in 1828. It is one of only two copies in America. A number of the earlier English catalogues are partially or wholly devoted to prints and pictures, making them valuable references for the art historian as well as the bibliographer.

One of the most attractive items in the collection, both for research value and for bibliographical association, is the Britwell Court set of the *Bibliotheca Heberiana*. The library of Richard Heber, one of the greatest of English bibliomaniacs, was dispersed from 1834 to 1836 in thirteen sales in England after his death. (There were more sales on the Continent. The Club has these catalogues, but they are not part of the set.) The parts were uniformly bound in blue gilt-tooled morocco by the English binder Hayday, in ten volumes, with interleaved sheets bound in containing annotations of all the prices and buyers. All this data was taken from the notes of William Tindall, the clerk of the sale. The set was made up for Joseph W. K. Eyton in 1842, and passed through several hands before coming into the possession of the Christie-Millers. It was sold in the Britwell Court sale of 1927 and later presented to the Club by W. B. Osgood Field. From the time of the Heber sale on, the Club possesses excellent runs of the major English house catalogues.

The first private English booksellers' catalogue in the Club collection was issued by the Newcastle-on-Tyne dealer William London, *A Catalogue of the Most Vendible Books in England* . . . (London, 1658), with its rare *Supplement* (London, 1660). This early effort is a most impressive one, listing thousands of books by category, as was then customary, and providing a good idea of what books were generally available at the time, although not necessarily from London. A similar catalogue was issued in 1674 by Robert Scott, listing over 7,000 items available from him. Scott was widely lauded as the leading European bookseller of his day. The Club is fortunate to have the Sir William Twysden–Sir Thomas Phillipps copy with annotations by the former. Scott catalogues of private libraries for sale en bloc in 1677 and 1686 are also present, as well as his auction catalogues in the Robinson gift. There are several other massive catalogues combining books in print and antiquarian material in the Club's collection. The largest of these was issued by the London bookseller Lackington in 1793, listing some 20,000 lots. This bookseller was evidently used to the problems of collecting payment from peers and other recalcitrant customers, because he notes, "Not an Hours Credit will be Given to any Person, nor any Books Exported, or sent into the Country, before they are paid for."

The Club's holdings in nineteenth-century material include entire sets of dealers' catalogues, with long runs of such important booksellers as Thorpe, William and Richard Baynes (the Phillipps-Munby set of their catalogues), and Willis, later Willis and Sotheran, finally Henry Sotheran. Certainly the most interesting of this period is the long, nearly complete run of catalogues from the great firm of Payne and Foss, issued from 1815 to 1850, here present in the shop's master copy, with all the purchasers marked. Robert Hoe presented this to the Club in 1889; in the accession book it was valued at fifteen dollars. It is hard to imagine a more glorious piece of bibliographical history than the detailed record of this firm's activities. In the latter half of the century begin the sets of such prolific cataloguers as Francis Edwards, Maggs, and Quaritch, all of them present in virtually complete runs. In addition to these larger sets, there are numerous odd groups or single catalogues in the nineteenth and early twentieth centuries. During the last twenty years, the Club has been much

more systematic about filing currently issued catalogues, especially of

English and American dealers. The result is that a comprehensive modern archive is building up.

American auction catalogues have always been a strong point in the Club holdings, although the Club has always deferred to the American Antiquarian Society as the preeminent repository in this area. It is probably the most used section of the collection. The longtime librarian of the Club, George L. McKay, published *American Book Auction Catalogues, 1713–1934* in 1937. He leaned heavily on the Club's holdings in its preparation. Catalogues in the Club's collection are noted in the published text; those acquired after 1936 are in the Club's master copy. This adds greatly to the ready reference value of the material, especially since McKay also indicated whether Grolier copies are annotated or priced. There were few notable book sales in America before 1850; after that time the Club has copies of almost every major sale, including the dispersals of the libraries of many Grolier members. Such sales as those of Grolier founders Brayton Ives in 1891 and Robert Hoe in 1911–1912 were landmarks in American book collecting. At $1,932,000, the Hoe sale realized the largest total of any book auction to that time and was eagerly watched by the world at large as well as by bibliophiles. The Club possesses six volumes of scrapbooks kept day to day by Ruth Granniss, the librarian, as well as a priced set of the catalogue. After the period covered by McKay, the holdings of book auction catalogues from the major American houses are virtually complete.

The first catalogue of an American bookseller in the collection is Henry Knox's thin trade list, issued at Boston in 1772, one of two known copies. More extensive, and rarer, since the Club has the only perfect copy, is *Samuel Campbell's Sale Catalogue of Books for 1789*, issued in New York that year. This lists 1,500 titles and reflects Campbell's position as a leading New York importer of books. Bound with it is Campbell's catalogue for 1794. Almost all of the early American catalogues are lists of European imports with new and antiquarian books mixed. The flamboyant New York dealer William Gowans was among the first to issue strictly antiquarian catalogues. The Club has an excellent run of his catalogues from the 1840's and 1850's spiced with highly original discourses. He was also the first American dealer to issue specialized catalogues by subject area.

For the period after the Civil War, there is a nearly complete set of 120 catalogues issued by David G. Francis between 1867 and 1896. In 1884 the firm of Francis P. Harper published its first catalogue. By catalogue 119, Lathrop Harper had joined the firm, later continued under his name. Happily the Club has a complete run of Harper catalogues, as few have done more for the library of the Grolier Club than Lathrop C. Harper. While Harper was beginning, the rare book department of Dodd, Mead also issued its first catalogue, in 1882, and this firm remained one of the dominant New York dealers until the turn of the century. The Club has a nearly complete run of its catalogues through 1909. All the catalogues of Goodspeed's, except the first, are present, as well as all 248 catalogues issued by James F. Drake from 1905 to 1939. Most of the well-known American dealers of the post–World War I era, from Rosenbach on down, are well represented. As with the English catalogues, the last twenty years have seen much more order and completeness in the Club's archive of American dealers' catalogues. Almost all the major dealers' catalogues are now saved, and incomplete runs are filled in when possible.

Perhaps the least-known segment of the Club's catalogue collection is the excellent assemblage of French material, primarily auction catalogues. Two Grolier members deserve much of the credit for building the holdings of the Club: Lucius Wilmerding and Waters S. Davis. Wilmerding was one of the best-known bookmen of his time, a president of the Grolier, and for many years chairman of the Library Committee. Davis is less known, but he was one of the library's greatest benefactors until his death in 1941. Feeling that the Club was weak in French bibliography, they took it upon themselves to remedy the deficiency. The two assembled much of the present collection for the Club in the 1930's.

The earliest French catalogues the Club owns are difficult to categorize, as they occupy a position midway between sales catalogues and inventory lists. The catalogue of Jean des Cordes, canon of Limoges, was compiled primarily as an inventory. There is no question, however, that the *Bibliothecae Cordesianse catalogus*, issued at Paris in 1643, was intended to aid in selling the collection. Cardinal Mazarin purchased the library intact only to see it dispersed when he was driven from Paris in 1649. The arrangement and scope of the polymathic Cordes catalogue made the work useful as a subject bibliography long after the dispersal of the books. The catalogue of the de Thou library occupies the same ambivalent position. The *Catalogus Bibliothecae Thuanae*, issued at Paris in 1679, was compiled as an inventory list but not used at the dispersal of the library when the books were sold in large lots. Most of the de Thou holdings, although not all, passed into the Ménars library. However it is classified, the Club has a fine copy, redolent of provenance: it belonged to the French bookseller Prosper Marchand and then the English collector William Dampier, and came to the Club from Samuel P. Avery.

The holdings of French catalogues are somewhat scattered until 1800, but after that they are very strong. Certainly one of the most interesting pieces is the *Catalogue de livres de la bibliotheque de feu M. Le Duc de La Vallière* (Paris, 1788). This sale was one of the most important of the eighteenth century, drawing collectors from all over Europe. The Club is fortunate to have recently acquired a copy of the first part of the sale, in three volumes, annotated by the famous English bibliophile Michael Wodhull, who attended the sale. The Club also has a set of the second part of the La Vallière library, but as this was sold as a unit the catalogue is not annotated. Another catalogue of bibliographical distinction is the Firmin-Didot sale, held in Paris in 1810. The dispersal of this great printer's collection provides many clues to his taste and to those books which may have influenced his typography. Fewer of the French catalogues are annotated than the Club's English holdings, but there are some notable exceptions. One recent addition is the J. R. Abbey copy of the MacCarthy Reagh sale, held in Paris in 1815. Interleaved, and bound in four volumes, it contains notes on the opening bid, the underbid, and the final buyer.

The Club's collection of French booksellers' catalogues is far smaller than the auction catalogue collection. The earliest was issued by Philip

Borde, a bookseller of Lyon, in 1656. It lists a broad variety of books, some 8,000 in all, divided by fields and languages. Borde's work, like London's in English, sets a pattern for seventeenth- and eighteenth-century booksellers' catalogues, which were often bulky, polymathic compilations. In 1968 three hundred French catalogues of 1840 to 1870 were added, as well as an almost complete run of the seven hundred catalogues of the autograph dealer from Charavay. Notable additions to earlier areas of the French collection have continued to be made in the last fifteen years. The Club has representative files of twentieth-century French dealers, although not of the comprehensive scope of the English and American holdings.

Auction catalogues from Belgium, Holland, and Germany are another area that benefited a great deal from the labors of Wilmerding and Davis. The Dutch catalogues came almost entirely from the former, including the notable *Johannes Graevius Catalogus Bibliotheca Luculentissimae . . .* (Utrecht, 1703). This great collection, although prepared for auction, ultimately went intact to the University of Heidelberg. It was Davis, however, who contributed the earliest Dutch item to the Club: the catalogue of the scholar Theodore Granswinckel, published at The Hague in 1667. As with the French catalogues, the strength of the collection is after 1800, and there are few of the early Dutch catalogues mentioned by Pollard and Ehrman in *The Distribution of Books by Catalogue to A.D. 1800.* Nonetheless, it is certainly one of the stronger collections in America.

Among booksellers' catalogues from the Low Countries, the Club's most notable piece is a trade list issued in Amsterdam in 1681 by Daniel Elzevir. This lists thousands of books available from the printer-bookseller in every field, including Elzevir publications then in print. The catalogue of the bookseller Christopher Meisner, issued at Wolfenbüttel in two parts, in 1726 and 1728, is an equally interesting example from Germany; it contains over 20,000 entries in broad areas of learning. In these countries, however, most of the Club's holdings are catalogues published after 1850. During the 1960's, large runs of late nineteenth-century German dealers' catalogues were added.

Scattered material from Spain and Latin America (both notably difficult to collect), Eastern Europe and Russia, and Italy complete the collection. The dearth of material from Italy is probably the greatest gap in the
holdings, this category never having had the benefit of the angels who
built much of the rest of the collection. The weakness of these last areas is
only comparative, however, to the great holdings in English, American,
and French materials.

The book sales catalogues are a unique part of the Club's collections.
Although not the most valuable, they are certainly the part of the library
that would be the most difficult to replace. The general scarcity of early
booksellers' and auction catalogues is such that even a few items may
make an important holding. The collection at the Grolier Club, with the
range and comprehensiveness of its material, early and late, certainly ranks
as one of the best extant. Improvement is always possible, however, and
the Club looks to alert and generous members to help the catalogue collection grow in strength and usefulness.

# Private Library Catalogues

## WILLIAM P. BARLOW, JR.

I
N THE 1901 Grolier Club classification scheme, a number was assigned to "Private Libraries (includes libraries sold at auction)." The rapid accumulation of auction catalogues later required their separation from private libraries. Even so diminished, the collection remains second in size only to the auction and dealer catalogues. Prominently housed on nearly one hundred shelves in the librarian's office and the hall outside the library, the collection is much more inclusive than the title "Private Libraries" might indicate. It features, of course, catalogues of private libraries, but it also includes almost anything relating to a book collector and his collections. It thus encompasses biographies and autobiographies of collectors, descriptions of private libraries, exhibition catalogues, letters, and even reproductions of rare items from private libraries such as—in its most extravagant form—a run of the William Andrews Clark, Jr., Christmas books.

Even the term "private library catalogue" can embrace a range of objects originally serving widely different purposes. Manuscript lists, in acquisition order or alphabetical by author or subject, or printed catalogues, prepared during the collector's lifetime for the envy or edification of scholars and other collectors, are perhaps the "true" private library catalogues. But added to these are manuscript or printed inventories, prepared for inheritance purposes or the sale of the library, catalogues recording gifts of private libraries to institutions, and memorial volumes with lists of books and manuscripts owned.

It is not always clear, especially with early examples, in which category
a volume belongs. A particular problem exists with the printed inventories. Before the introduction of book auctions, which may date from as early as 1593 in Holland to as late as 1759 in Italy, the printed inventory was an accepted method of dispersing important collections. The famous *Bibliothecae Cordesianae catalogus* (1643) is of this type, while the equally famous *Bibliotheca Heinsiana* (1682) is an auction; and the rather hasty compilation of the *Catalogus Bibliothecae Thuanae* (1679) may have been by inventory listing, but may also have more closely resembled an auction. Perhaps the distinction is unimportant, but traditionally inventories have been regarded as private library catalogues and auctions as auctions. This tradition, to the extent the facts can be determined, has been followed in the Grolier Club library.

Until recent years, the Grolier Club collection of private library catalogues grew largely through gifts. As might be expected, a number of catalogues have been presented by the collectors themselves. The American collection has particularly benefited from such gifts, since the life of the Club coincides with the period in which most of these catalogues were produced, and the membership of the Club included many of the collectors producing the catalogues. Members in other countries have also contributed, and nonmember collectors have often thought it desirable to place copies of their catalogues in the Grolier Club library.

A larger number of catalogues—and, naturally, the older ones—have come from donors other than the compilers themselves. Among the early donors, the names of Samuel P. Avery, William Loring Andrews, and Leonard L. Mackall turn up with frequency on Club bookplates. Two significant later gifts were those of Waters S. Davis and Lucius Wilmerding.

In recent years, the private library collection has received more systematic attention, and purchases have predominated. Major plunges were taken at the sales of J. R. Abbey in 1966 and A. N. L. Munby ten years later. These purchases and others have in large part remedied the earlier desultory acquisition policy, but gaps are constantly being filled and remain to be filled.

Many private library catalogues have been printed in limited numbers and with even more limited special and large-paper issues; they have been subjected to unusual and even perverse distribution policies; and often they either have been poorly prepared or are of mediocre libraries. Gaps are inevitable, and completion of a collection of private library catalogues is neither possible nor practical.

In view of the interests of the Club's members and the large number of acquisitions obtained as gifts, it is not difficult to understand why American and British materials dominate the collection. These two groups together occupy about two-thirds of the shelf space, the British having a slight edge on the home team.

The early introduction of book auctions to England (1676), combined with barriers to the sale of family collections which lasted into the late nineteenth century, has left us with very few printed inventories of early English collections compared with those of France and Italy. Moreover, only a handful of English private library catalogues were compiled before the nineteenth century, when their publication became a bibliophilic pastime. Regretably, the Grolier Club does not own any of the half dozen or so known printed inventories of the eighteenth century and has only one of the similar number of private library catalogues of the same period: that of Robert Hoblyn of 1769.

To compensate, the Club has nearly one hundred British inventories in manuscript, and some are of significant or early collections. Most important are those of Arthur Capel, Earl of Essex, compiled from 1681 to 1683 by William Stanley; Marguerite, Countess of Blessington (1820); the Earls of Minto; Dawson Turner (only a part of his vast collection); and the fourth Earl of Ashburnham, in thirty-five small wedge-shaped volumes. Many others among these inventories in manuscript await research to determine their scholarly value, and some await even the identification of their owners.

The English section is completed with most of the best nineteenth- and twentieth-century private library catalogues, ranging from Dibdin's Spencer catalogues (1814–1823) to Wise's Ashley catalogues (1922–1936) and including a complete copy of the rare catalogue of Sir Thomas Phillipps's manuscripts. There are, as well, a large number of minor collections.

Here in the United States collecting habits tended to follow the British pattern. By the time there were any books to be sold in America, book dealers and auctions were well established in England, and the system was easily transferred. There is only one recorded example of an inventory sale in the eighteenth century, and in 1800 the first private library catalogue, that of Robert R. Livingston of Clermont, New York, was printed. It was apparently an isolated example. The earliest American private library catalogue in the Club's library is one of 1830, a thin catalogue of Arabic, Turkish, and Persian manuscripts belonging to William B. Hodgson. This also appears to be somewhat singular, since the craze (and indeed it became one) for privately printed catalogues does not appear to have taken hold until the 1870's.

Despite giving the British a half century head start, the Americans seem to have caught up. This section of the Club's collection is nearly as voluminous as the British and probably contains more titles. Once again, the great catalogues are here: Church, Hoe, Widener, Wrenn, Adam, Pforzheimer, and Arents, among others. The 1865–1866 catalogue of the John Carter Brown collection, most copies of which Brown had destroyed, is lacking, but the second edition of 1875–1882 is here.

The Grolier Club owns only a few American catalogues in manuscript, and this would seem to be a shortage members could rectify. Three early Grolier Club members are represented in the library by their own handwritten catalogues: William Loring Andrews, with a nicely painted title page; David Wolfe Bruce, in six volumes (the early printed books in this library were given to the Grolier Club); and Edwin Babcock Holden, in six volumes, with a cost code that begs to be broken.

The next largest group of catalogues is the French, but this section contains some of the collection's great rarities. Here are a dozen seventeenth-century inventories including an association copy from Prosper Marchand of the de Thou catalogue (1679), the very rare Bluet catalogue (1667), and the widow's copy of the inventory of Raphael Trichet du Fresne

(1662), which is officially signed on the last leaf by Colbert. The library also has some remarkable private catalogues, including that of Cardinal Le Tellier (1693), the scarce Hallée catalogue of 1730, and the catalogues of Claude Gros de Boze (1745), which may have been printed in twelve or fifteen or thirty-six or fifty copies, and Le Camus de Limare (1779). This last catalogue is supposed to be one of twenty-five, and the Club's copy is that of the owner, with eight pages of manuscript additions.

The French catalogues in manuscript are also choice and include a puzzling folio catalogue of Mme de Pompadour's library which does not compare with the 1765 sale catalogue, a 1676 inventory of the books of the historian Henry de Valois, and a catalogue of the Duchesse de La Vallière, mother of the great collector. A fascinating bibliophilic treasure with a Heber-Phillipps provenance is a twelve-page letter from the Abbé Desaunays to the Abbé Rive, dated 1777, with replies by the latter to questions about the Duc de La Vallière's library.

The German and Italian holdings are less numerous than the French but include a good representation of the early inventories and private catalogues as well as the major modern works. The *Uffenbachiana*, 1729–1731, may be found here. A special prize among the Italian catalogues is the 1787 inventory of the library of Maffeo Pinelli in six volumes with extensive notes on the flyleaves by the English collector Michael Wodhull. These notes apparently relate to the 1789 sale of Pinelli's books in London where Wodhull was a major buyer.

Spain, Portugal, the Netherlands, Russia, Switzerland, Hungary, and the Scandinavian countries are all represented with smaller but still very fine collections. Of particular interest among the Spanish catalogues is the very early printed inventory of Gabriel Sora (Saragossa, 1618).

It is not as easy to assess the relative importance of collections of private library catalogues as it is of collections of incunabula. For the earlier catalogues the list assembled by Archer Taylor (*Book Catalogues: Their Varieties and Uses*, Chicago, 1957) of catalogues recommended by mostly seventeenth- and eighteenth-century bibliographers is a useful guide. This list must be used judiciously, however. Of the 155 items listed, perhaps

fifty-five are private library catalogues or printed inventories. The re-
mainder are mostly auctions. Since all the bibliographers employed, except Dibdin, were Continental (even Dibdin's list was intended to be only of Continental catalogues), the bias is strongly against English catalogues. And the listing intentionally omits catalogues of manuscripts and specialized collections.

Qualifications aside, the Grolier Club owns just over half of these private library catalogues; not a bad percentage when perhaps 20 percent of the titles are virtually unobtainable. The Newberry Library probably has about 60 percent and the Library of Congress about 40 percent. No other institutional collection in this country appears to come close to these figures.

Whether the Grolier Club collection of private library materials is the best in this country, it is clearly the peer of the few which can claim to compete for that distinction. Moreover, arranged—as it is—together by country and by date, readily accessible and merged with related materials, and coupled—as it is—with the Club's remarkable auction and book-dealers' catalogues, it represents one of the outstanding facilities anywhere for the study of the history of book collecting. As a bonus for members, the collection serves as an attractive, conspicuous, and solemnly impressive reminder of the Grolier Club's noble heritage, not only of the past century, but of the past five centuries.

# Autograph Manuscripts

## HERBERT T. F. CAHOON

THE collection of autographs at the Grolier Club is small, but since letters and documents are by their nature unique, all have value for research. They represent a chronological span of over four hundred years. Nearly all are concerned with books and bookmen, and while many of them tell of routine matters of other times, many others have special significance in the Grolier Club collection because of the writer and content.

The cornerstones of the collection are two documents signed by Jean Grolier, on May 22, 1550, and November 3, 1563, both when he was treasurer general of France. The content of these documents is unexceptional (one an authorization for payment, one a receipt), but they are precious to us, for they represent in the bold upright J. GROLIER MANU PROPRIA SUBSCRIPSIT the spirit and the legacy of the man whose name we honor.

On September 11, 1574, Thomas Wotton, father of Sir Henry, the poet and ambassador to Venice, writes in a firm, large hand from Boughton Malherbe in Kent on matters concerning his family and estate, where he had entertained Queen Elizabeth the year before. Thomas Wotton, bibliophile, is known as the "English Grolier." Many books bound for his library are tooled in the interlaced style of those bound for Grolier and are lettered THOMAE WOTTONI ET AMICORUM.

Jacques Auguste de Thou inherited a fine collection of books from his father, who was a friend of Grolier, and he added many volumes bound

with his arms (and those of his wives) or in a fanfare style. Our de Thou
letter is written from Paris on January 15, 1583, to Antoine Loisel, scholar
and advocate for King Henri III in the province of Guyenne which, then
as now, had its lovers of fine books. The letter touches on history, politics,
and books (he had just received his patrimony); there was at this date a
lull in the religious wars, but de Thou considers the times uncertain and
fears the loss of his new fortune. Many of the letters of this future historian
and director of the royal library have survived, and all are prized for style
and content.

There is a document signed on July 25, 1621, by Jean de Chaumont,
librarian to Louis XIII (a monarch who had good books and manuscripts),
giving a quarter's payment of a pension to Paul Phelypeaux, seigneur de
Pontchartrain, secretary of state. Phelypeaux was then with the king at
the siege of Montauban, a Huguenot stronghold, where he died on October 21; this was probably the last payment he received.

Cardinal Mazarin, founder of the Bibliothèque Mazarine, is represented
by a signature on a marriage contract of February 22, 1661, two weeks
before his death.

Prominent among the autographs of the late seventeenth and part of the
eighteenth centuries are documents of booksellers and binders which are
of considerable historical interest. Robert Scott of London, in 1670, is
willing to allow Dr. Buck six pounds for his perfect copy of a seven-
volume set of the works of Saint Cyril of Alexandria, presumably that
published in Paris in 1638. John Starkey, in 1677, sends an invoice to Sir
George Jeffreys, soon to become the infamous chief justice of the King's
Bench. It includes plays by Ben Jonson, Dryden, Beaumont and Fletcher,
and a Shakespeare dated 1619 (quartos of Thomas Pavier?). The itemized
bill sent by Roger Warne is for books sold to Sir James Long or his widow
in the period 1691 to 1693; among them are controversial and pious
works, a few novels and plays, poems, and two runs of periodicals: *The
[Present] State of Europe* and *Works of the Learned*.

There is a list made by the celebrated actor of fops and coxcombs,
James William Dodd, who died in 1796, of a collection of about two

hundred and forty mainly pre-Restoration plays. Dodd was an omnivo-rous book collector, and his library was sold by Leigh and Sotheby in 1797 over a period of nine days. In addition to more than a thousand plays, he owned volumes of murder trials, scandals, erotica, demonology, and a variety of other curiously distinctive subjects. He also collected weapons of native Americans.

Christian Hartmann's invoice of 1699 asks payment for books he had bound for the Königliche und Churfürstliche Bibliothek in Dresden, and another binder, Joachim Hildebrandt, sends a bill in 1719 to the Royal Saxonian Library in Dresden for fifteen taler, one groschen, and six pfennige (less discount) for binding thirty-one books.

A splendid letter dated May 26, 1795, from Thomas Jefferson, when he was temporarily withdrawn from public life at Monticello, to Monsieur Froullé, bookseller in Paris, was printed in facsimile for the Club in 1971 on the occasion of the exhibition "Great American Book Collectors to 1800." Jefferson claims to have forgotten his French and writes in English in much detail of a shipment of books that took over a year to reach him. The box had been much wetted by salt water during a winter passage from Le Havre, and many of the books, especially some plate volumes of the *Encyclopédie*, are completely rotted. He asks the bookseller to replace them, for he is a subscriber and does not wish his set to be incomplete. A further list includes other replacements and some current and antiquarian books he needs. This time, he tells Froullé, pack them in a trunk and cover it with sealskin. He hopes Froullé has not suffered "by the civil storms which have been blowing over your head."

To round out the eighteenth century there is a letter from Isaiah Thomas in Worcester to Isaac Beers in New Haven, dated August 26, 1795, concerning a shipment of books; and one from the bookseller James Lackington of London, writing from his shop on Finsbury Square, his "Temple of the Muses," in May 1800, to his cousin George, to whom he had recently sold his share of the business. It was said of Lackington that his first object in life was to make money; as soon as he had acquired a fortune, he seems to have lost any love of books he may have had.

Historians of the book trade should take note of a small collection of autograph letters and invoices by twenty-one English booksellers and publishers of the second half of the eighteenth century and a similar group of sixteen American items of late eighteenth- to early nineteenth-century vintage. Though these documents are isolated examples of business papers, the names of William Strahan, Robert Dodsley, and Archibald Hamilton are worth noting, as are those of Hugh Gaine, James Rivington, and Valentine Nutter, New York bookbinder, among the Americans.

Thomas Frognall Dibdin has preserved, in sometimes questionable descriptions and ornate prose, the bibliographical and bookselling history of the first half of the nineteenth century. There are a number of his letters in the Club, including a series of thirty-seven written between 1826 and 1829 to the publisher William Pickering, for whom he was translating Thomas à Kempis. Dibdin was always in need of money, the "Mammon-Monster" as he calls it, and each letter contains an emotional plea for financial assistance. The Club's set of *The Bibliographical Decameron* (1817) is handsomely extra-illustrated and expanded from three volumes to twelve by the addition of engravings, drawings, and letters. It is the copy of George Henry Freeling, son of Sir Francis, the postal reformer, and is described by William A. Jackson in his study of Dibdin's publications.

In 1826 the young Count Guglielmo Libri (to give a short version of his name and title) knew that, for political reasons, he must leave Italy and his post as professor of mathematics in Pisa. Six letters written to him in that year from a Dr. Broval in Paris discuss the possibility of Libri's emigration to France, where he had been warmly received by fellow scientists during a visit two years before. These letters serve as prologue to his nefarious career as book thief that began in France some fifteen years later. A. N. L. Munby has written of Libri that "his reputation as a pillager of French public libraries has overshadowed his real claim to fame in the field of [mathematical] scholarship."

The Italian author and bibliographer Antonio Marsand acted as agent for Antoine Augustin Renouard, fecund writer on the history of books and manuscripts. In an undated letter he offers Renouard beautiful copies of two incunabula, the Lactantius printed in Subiaco in 1465 and a Cicero *De Officiis* printed in Rome in 1469.

On the first of July 1833, a year before he suddenly vacated his post as sublibrarian of the London Institution, William Upcott writes to a fellow collector, Thomas Thompson of Liverpool, about a common dilemma in this period of autographomania. Pursuit of autographs is on the increase, "but that *game* is growing scarce. Names that heretofore were as *common as carrots* rarely occur. . . ." He offers to trade autographs with provisioner Thompson for "one or two of his delicious hams."

After his return from America, John Camden Hotten commenced business as a bookseller and publisher. His signed lease from Cockburn, Campbell and Co., wine merchants, dated May 11, 1855, is for a small shop at 151 Piccadilly, where he remained for about ten years. His death in 1873 at the age of forty-one ended a publishing career that was not without irregularities. John Payne Collier, whose talents for scholarship were submerged by his Shakespeare forgeries, tells Mr. Brown, one of his copyists, in December 1869, "You *must* learn to spell."

At the end of his life, the American poet Fitz-Greene Halleck corresponded with Grolier founder William Loring Andrews about a new edition of Halleck's long poem *Fanny*, a satire on social climbers. Thirteen letters to Andrews in 1865 and 1866 discuss notes, illustrations, and a subscription list for the limited edition of seventy copies of the poem which first appeared in 1819.

There are three important groups of letters by and relating to bookmen, two of them Club members. Frederick Locker-Lampson, owner of the Rowfant Library, is represented by a group of letters, mainly from 1883, concerning an illustrated edition of his much-reprinted *vers de société* volume, *London Lyrics*, to be issued in 104 copies by the Book Fellows' Club of New York. There are also original drawings for this edition. A scrapbook kept by Locker-Lampson includes twenty lovely watercolors by Richard Doyle and fifteen by Ernest Griset as well as drawings by Kate Greenaway, Walter Crane, and Randolph Caldecott. A box of letters addressed to Locker-Lampson for the period of about 1887 to 1890 includes two from Greenaway, one from George Du Maurier, and many from American collectors.

Following the death of Beverly Chew in 1924, his brother presented to the Club letters written to that great collector by such friends as S. P. Avery, Robert Hoe III, John Kendrick Bangs, Charles Eliot Norton, Theodore Low De Vinne, and Harry Elkins Widener.

A box of papers surviving from the business career of Arthur Swann was purchased in 1978. They relate to events in his career as bookseller and in the auction business. There are letters from his employers such as John Anderson, Jr., and Cortlandt Field Bishop; one from T. J. Wise, in whom Swann retained an abiding faith; and many from other collectors and booksellers.

Fourteen letters from Elmer Adler, written from 1956 to 1958 to his sister Jean, tell of the early days of his *La Casa del Libro* in San Juan. There is also a childhood letter written in 1895 in which no clue to his later fine calligraphic hand can be discerned.

Finally, it should be stressed that the Grolier Club archives are a rich trove of autograph and typewritten materials covering a hundred years of activities. Not only members are included, but all persons who had dealings with the Club, especially in connection with membership, exhibitions, lectures, and publications. To choose some to list here would only slight others, but all await the curious researcher. By using the bibliography of publications and the list of exhibitions and lecturers printed in this book, as well as the complete list of members soon to follow, a student has a good working guide to the archives.

# The Print Collection

## PHILLIP D. CATE
## AND HERBERT D. SCHIMMEL

IN forming a print collection for the Grolier Club, early members at first sought representative examples covering the history of graphic art from the fifteenth-century woodcut to the photomechanical processes of their own day. A generation before print departments were formed in American museums, these Grolier *amateurs* hoped to extend the knowledge and enjoyment of members and the public by decorating the clubhouse with framed examples, by providing a research source for book and magazine illustration, and by sponsoring occasional exhibitions. Consequently, very few prints of master quality are present in the collection. After a brisk beginning in life, followed by a vigorous middle age, interest in the print collection gradually waned until very recently, as we shall see.

In addition to what was then termed "examples of printmaking from the earliest," nearly ten thousand items are present today in the Grolier's various iconographic collections. They include portraits of artists, printers, collectors, scholars, booksellers, and others allied with the book, as well as views of their habitats—libraries both domestic and institutional, printing houses, ateliers, bookshops, and binderies. The collections of ephemera are notable and include type specimens, paper sample books, prospectuses, and broadsides. Some original drawings and watercolors, particularly for Grolier Club publications, coexist happily with the print collections. All are now housed in archival-quality papers and boxes and are readily accessible.

Apart from some prints given after January 1884 to decorate the rooms of the Club's rented premises, the first gift recorded in the accessions book was a set of woodcuts by members of the American Society of Wood Engravers. These accessions books continue to the present day, listing artist, medium, subject, donor, valuation, and number. Thus, they too are part of the history of collecting taste and a record of changes in the marketplace.

By 1891 books in the library had a value of $6,000 and the gifts of prints at $2,679—a vivid indication of the interest in this aspect of the new Club's activities. The wood engravings were soon joined by a small selection of French prints and artists' portraits given by William Loring Andrews, J. Harsen Purdy, Beverly Chew, Charles Lang Freer, E. G. Kennedy, Marshall C. Lefferts, and Frederick Keppel. The generosity of Samuel Putnam Avery stands alone for the quantity and appropriateness of his innumerable gifts. He bought extensively for the Grolier during his frequent visits to Paris, at the same time building up the contemporary collection which became the cornerstone of the print room in the New York Public Library after his death in 1904.

By 1901 the 333 prints were valued at $5,886. After a card catalogue and storage cases were called for, proper solander boxes were secured, which are still in use, and a catalogue of portraits was launched. In that year, William F. Havemeyer doubled the portrait collection and again in 1902 tripled it with 1,400 additional gifts. Though admittedly many of them are cannibalized frontispieces, not a few are large and fine mezzotints and engravings in early states, then available in quantity on the market. Also in 1901, Edwin Babcock Holden gave a miscellaneous collection of 327 "European and American lithographs." Over several years, Avery and Kennedy gave numbers of French printers' and art dealers' trade cards and exhibition announcements—precious ephemera often incorporating original works. Their large gift of ephemera from the Paris Exposition of 1900 is particularly noteworthy for its time-capsule view of the art world of the time. In 1914 a group of members gave ninety handsome trade cards of English booksellers and binders of the period 1780–1830, the importance of which is being realized only late in the twentieth century. From 1925 through 1941 that incomparable collector of ephemera, Bella C. Landauer, made a series of appropriate gifts relating to the book trade over two centuries, and this from a woman, who in that period could not hope to become a member. In 1926, Frank Altschul presented several thousand "American engravings," a collection amassed by Warren C. Crane.

By 1920 the print collection had assumed its present shape and was the font for research in the graphic and typographic arts the founders envisioned through the 3,328 examples which had been gathered. In 1934 it was reported to the members that this number had doubled through gifts. In fact, only one reference to a purchase appears in the annual reports, a collection of portraits of "bookmen" bought in 1938.

The following year, the Society of Iconophiles, founded in January 1895 and housed in the present clubhouse since its completion in 1917, terminated and wound up its activities. Its members donated to the Grolier Club library the contents of its room, consisting of valuable pictures and maps, photographs of old New York, archives, proofs, and remainders of prints and publications. John T. Winterich in his 1967 history of the Grolier Club described the formation and activities of the Iconophiles: "Toward the end of 1894, William Loring Andrews, one of whose chief interests was in the field of New York historical prints, discussed with fellow-members the desirability of establishing a small and strictly intramural association whose purpose would be the issuance of reproductions of views of the city and of portraits of individuals who had been prominent in its history. . . . Its membership was to be limited to ten, drawn from the parent organization." They issued print series depicting New York City views and an occasional book of a lavishness almost inconceivable in today's world with all illustrations in the traditional media of engraving and lithography, deliberately bypassing the photograph and the photomechanical. The rich trove left by this amiable society of *dilettanti* has rested quietly here for forty years and only recently has been sorted, properly housed, and accorded the place it deserves in the Club's history

of interest in prints.

Drawings and watercolors are not present in quantity, but several groups deserve mention. One group, of course, consists of original works for Grolier publications, commencing with the delightful drawings for Irving's Knickerbocker *History* of 1886. There are single examples by American illustrators of the 1900 period, perhaps a reflection of the strong connection between the Grolier and the staff of *The Century Magazine*. Worth mentioning are drawings by Daniel Huntington, John Sloan, F. O. C. Darley (the gift of his widow), and typographic designs in ink by Bertram Grosvenor Goodhue, including the large original drawing for the cover of *The Knight Errant*, a short-lived aesthetic journal founded in 1892.

Around 1940, perhaps because of the war, a long hiatus in Grolier Club print acquisitions and activities set in. But since the formation of a print committee in January 1980, this traditional interest has been stirred up and the collection has at last been gone over piece by piece. Several small exhibitions have been held drawn entirely from our own collections, and a local university has begun print seminars here using original examples not available elsewhere in the city. Through sales at auction of small groups and single items deemed out of scope, money has been provided for a large steel print case, additional boxes, and liner papers of conservation quality.

The collection's goal was never to be able to demonstrate with masterpieces a full-scale history of printmaking, but to provide the means for teaching and for research as an iconographic source, or picture library. It stands readier than ever in the Club's history to contribute to the educational goals of the founders.

# Archives

## P. WILLIAM FILBY

THERE is always satisfaction in creating order, and the Grolier Club archives presented a notable challenge. For years these accumulated records were stored in a miscellany of old letter boxes and wooden, metal, and cardboard files. In preparing to organize them for easy access, the first order of business was to buy acid-free containers and folders of various types.

Beginning in 1976—in a bicentennial and therefore archival frame of mind—I moved to the exhibition hall balcony all the treasurer's folio journals and ledgers dating from 1884 to 1944 and the nineteenth-century alphabetical letter files. Correspondence relating to admissions, resignations, and transfers of this period were also shelved there, along with all material on exhibitions and publications. Remaining temporarily in the basement were yards of boxed correspondence, scrapbooks, several odd runs of Club ephemera, photograph albums of early members, the entire archives of the Iconophiles, complete and incomplete committee reports for years back, printed keepsakes, prospectuses, and files of journal and newspaper articles on printing and bibliography pasted on rotten cards. There was also the collection made by Walter Gilliss, elected in 1884, who until his death in 1925 saved all Club printing. He bequeathed it to the Club; similar collections came from S. P. Avery, Jr., C. W. McAlpin, Robert Jaffray, and others. Among more modern records were the special publications and ephemera relating to the Club's nine trips in the United States and abroad between 1959 and 1976, complete with many candid pictures of Club members.

Since the summer of 1982, shelving has been adequate to accommodate archives from all over the Club, with space for years of records to come. In this splendor, where it is now convenient to work, the final sorting and boxing continues, and a finding system is established. Now one can find, for instance, acceptances from the soon-to-be founders to attend the very first informal meeting in Robert Hoe's library to discuss organizing a Club in January 1884, or membership proposal letters for a hundred years, or lenders to exhibitions for a century.

Occasionally, work is enlivened by coming upon a gold nugget: a 1902 request to bring Bruce Rogers to the Club, his introduction to the Grolier; a letter informing the president that the Club had been dissolved and its charter forfeited for failing to file a "Certificate of Report and Existence" with the secretary of the state of New York (this in 1952), a letter from a supplier of books dated May 1912 reporting that it was probable that books en route to the Grolier were lost on the *Titanic*. Among many letters from Thomas J. Wise, there is one turning down his election to membership. He concludes: ". . . and it seems foolish to spend $70 a year to become a member of a club whose doors I may never enter!" This was written in 1922, twelve years before his unmasking. In another letter, Wise writes to Miss Granniss, the librarian, complimenting her on a Shelley catalogue but pointing out certain errors, ending "Be careful of fresh Shelley mss. There are a number of d . . . . d bad forgeries on the market. . . ." (Wise, we know from the archives, was proposed by A. Edward Newton and seconded by W. M. Elkins.)

Miss Ruth Shepard Granniss, assistant librarian for two years, then librarian from 1904 to 1944, was required to answer members' questions for forty-two years, along with other correspondence and regular duties. What a gem she was, so obviously patient and kind. At first she had no typewriter and from 1906 to 1916 wrote longhand on those infernal "Bushnell's Perfect Copying Book" tissues, then and now virtually unreadable. Until they are transcribed, the valuable information they contain will remain practically inaccessible. Many boxes contain the everyday business of the library in its hundred-year-old record of service to members and scholars; herein may be found letters from European, British, and American book people writing on all sorts of subjects. Even the correspondence about book purchases and the invoices from booksellers are of interest.

Perhaps of greatest interest are the publication and exhibition files, wherein still awaits a great deal of typographical and scholarly history. Sadly, the Club's extremely rich publication files are not 100 percent complete but are largely so. Ranging back to 1884, they should be used in combination with the card index to the Council's minutes and the monthly committee reports. They contain autograph and typed letters by a Who's Who of our authors, designers, printers, and chairmen (many of them of notably pungent personality), manuscripts, original art for illustrations such as the original paintings for the Knickerbocker *History* of 1886, Rudolph Ruzicka's wood blocks for the 1915 *New York*, and Bruce Rogers's drawings for the Dürer book and the *Champ Fleury*.

The files dealing with exhibitions (there have been well over six hundred of them since 1884) are also not absolutely complete but are nearly so after 1890. A casual look reveals the astonishingly rich collections owned by early members: Elizabethan quartos, Renaissance bindings, Old Master and Japanese prints, Blake watercolors, drawings, maps and views, and thousands of other treasures were duly marched to the clubhouse for exhibition and duly returned—with signed receipts to prove it. Only one notable example of our files as a resource is demonstrated by the records of our historic 1922 Degas exhibition of unique prints, drawings, and bronze dancers, which several times in recent years has drawn scholarly attention. This one exhibition alone shows all too clearly the change from that day, when nearly everything on loan came from private collectors, to the present time, when we rely so much on the good will of institutional lenders. But, after all, many of our members have been founders of libraries or museums, or major donors to them.

Interesting insights into the relationships among collectors, dealers, and librarians may be explored in voluminous files of letters proposing and seconding members. Even connections among cities are interesting: a remarkable number of Chicago residents were elected in the nineteenth century. This highly personal material is a small but rich vein of social and collecting history.

The House Committee files come vividly to life when one reads such mundane items as invoices for wine and liquor, for services such as gas and the installation of electricity in 1898 (for $583.65), and for the services of purveyors (most on handsome decorated bill heads—in themselves worth saving). Concerns of staff and wages (low until the 1960's), and, of course, members' complaints are constants. Of great interest are papers relating to the buildings and furnishings of our three clubhouses. In the case of the present house, designed by Bertram Grosvenor Goodhue, everything including deeds, fund-raising appeals, blueprints, and even drawings for hardware and chandeliers seems to be present.

Considerable as all this hundred years of record-keeping may seem, the Club's own archive is by no means the only archival collection in the house. Many other collections must at least be mentioned here.

The entire creative remains of that gifted and prolific book designer Frederic Warde (d. 1939) are in the Grolier Club. There are drawings, correspondence, picture references, sketches, notebooks, personalia such as army records, and the beginnings of Paul Bennett's projected book on Warde. Along with this came Warde's own collection of his books.

The surviving papers of our brother club, the Carteret Book Club of Newark, New Jersey, are here, along with a pristine set of its publications. Our own Iconophiles group gave us its files, proofs, printing plates, and remainder stock of prints when the group disbanded in 1930. The founding father of the Iconophiles, William Loring Andrews, bequeathed us his eight scrapbooks dealing with book matters of all sorts from the late nineteenth century until near his death in 1920. They record the busy collecting and social life of a New Yorker in the thick of cultural doings. Andrews had years of dealings with the artist-engraver Sidney L. Smith in the making of his many books. Art historians will get around to Smith some day and will find important records of his lifework here.

Printers and book artists have always enjoyed eating and drinking together. Among several groups of memorabilia we preserve from these informal organizations which waxed and waned during the past hundred years is that of The Aldine Club, comprising turn-of-the-century New Yorkers who in addition to enjoying themselves together also invited public men to their rites. Another informal but exceptionally lively group was The Stowaways who first gathered in 1909 and petered out in the late 1920's. In 1983 we bought their complete archive, still in a large trunk, of plentiful and witty ephemera and correspondence. It provides a delightful insight into the social world of the printing fraternity.

John S. Kebabian, Grolier member from 1959 until 1980, had a long career in the book trade. He has given us his file of library appraisals for private collections and estates—one being that of Henry Clay Folger. Certain restrictions are attached to the use of these files. In 1974 our member George M. Schieffelin, for many years corporate secretary at Charles Scribner's Sons, presented three steel files full of the correspondence of the now extinct but fondly remembered Scribner Rare Book Shop dating from 1946 to its dissolution, as well as the card files. A much smaller, but flavorsome, file of letters and catalogue materials relates to the final years of Wilfrid Voynich, the London bookseller of great intellectual distinction. This was the gift of H. P. Kraus and derives from the estate of Ethel L. Voynich, the novelist. Letters and galleys dealing with her later novels, after *The Gadfly*, are also present.

Kraus was also the donor of two other major gifts. The first was twelve folio volumes of stock and sale records from the eminent Paris bookselling firms of Morgand and Fatout, Damacène Morgand, and Edouard Rahir, ranging in date from 1877 to 1920. This gift is a vast mine of information about the purchases of French, British, and especially American bibliophiles in a fifty-year period. Kraus has also given us forty cloth boxes containing notes and fascimiles accumulated during the long career of Louis Polain (d. 1933), the Belgian scholar of incunabula.

In the world of bibliographical scholarship, perhaps our best known holdings are the important though incomplete run of ledgers from the Bowyer-Nichols firm of printers which range in date from 1710 to 1805. They were purchased in the John Gough Nichols sale at Sotheby's in 1929 and are presently on long-term deposit at the Bodleian Library. They form part of a "Future Publication" of The Bibliographical Society.

For one reason or another, collections of letters of and invoices to bibliophiles have not survived in any quantity. We have only a few such files, two of them very recent gifts from Christie's and the estates of the owners. They are papers concerning book-buying matters of Marjorie Wiggin Prescott of Greenwich, Connecticut, and Arthur Haddaway of Fort Worth, Texas. Two prominent book-collecting members have recently presented files of letters and invoices, to be used with discretion. We welcome such gifts in the Grolier library, for where else would such papers be preserved? May their number increase in the coming years, making the Grolier even more of a center of study for the art and mystery of book collecting.

The Grolier Club's own archives, and most of the other sources just discussed, are largely available to the qualified scholar making prior arrangements to use them. Restrictions on use and publication may be imposed on material deemed confidential Club matters by the Council or Library Committee. But speaking generally we are ready to welcome researchers in our second century.

# The Library as a Resource for the Collector and Scholar

## DOUGLAS F. BAUER

BOOKS, of course, have as many uses as they have readers. No, I may say without doubt their uses are many times that number. And the utility of books *about* books, or of books on the history and arts of book production and of making manuscripts—in short, the utility of the very books which the library of the Grolier Club has gathered since its earliest days—is correspondingly manifold. The unique virtue which our library has over comparable collections of such books may be somewhat less obvious, but it lies, I think, in the unsurpassed usefulness our collections offer to one class of reader in particular, whom I shall call the novitiate bibliophile. Sadly, he or she is the very reader who in the past has tended to be least aware of our resources and least inclined to use them—a special irony I can illustrate from personal experience. There is reason to hope, however, that growing awareness of our library's utility is now reversing this tendency.

But first, allow me a brief comment on the interdependence of book collecting and scholarship itself. For me it has become an article of faith that every book collector must be a dedicated student of the subject matter upon which his collecting focuses, and conversely that every scholar collects deliberately and of necessity those materials, usually books, which transmit the relevant knowledge of others and facilitate his own studies. Thus, collectors and scholars form a single species. Of course, conscious recognition of this mutuality of pursuits is not required of them, although the "bibliophile" might reasonably be defined to be a collector-scholar who not only recognizes the interdependence I am describing but who instinctively rejoices in it. Furthermore, if true scholarship is inseparable from thorough knowledge of the published literature upon which it is based, then it also seems inevitable that every bibliophile eventually discovers a need and develops a fondness for works on the making and collecting of books and manuscripts themselves, in addition, of course, to a continuing concern with the primary works on which his studies concentrate. He learns that the books about his books are as important, though not perhaps for the same reasons, as what he has chosen to accumulate or study for its own sake. Both the one and the other rank equally among the collector-scholar's basic tools.

Needless to say, quite a few other libraries today, public or private or in between, hold strong collections of books about books, and these largely duplicate one another. But for the serious bibliophile, for this special collector-scholar, whatever his degree of accomplishment, the library of the Grolier Club is extraordinarily valuable in at least two important respects. On the one hand, virtually all of the diverse collections here include extremely scarce or even unique materials. This is true of our books about books, bibliographical ephemera, and archives as well as of our many other special possessions highlighted in separate chapters of the present volume. Great care has been taken by the Club librarians for generations to seek rare items of these kinds, whereas most other libraries with similar interests have concentrated on building good collections of the principal works alone, acquiring an occasional rarity only by chance. On the other hand, the easy accessibility of nearly all materials here in the Club's library, even those available elsewhere, distinguishes it in a very practical sense from other collections. In larger and more comprehensive libraries particularly, where overcrowding either of books or of readers has become accepted as an inevitable condition of the times, there is no longer such ease, if ever there was. But although the Grolier Club's holdings may be far from complete in some areas, the deliberate narrowness of their scope and the comfortable arrangement of the books themselves within the close compass of our handsome clubhouse almost always offer the twin advantages of rapid retrieval and convenient comparison, while, like the proverbial bird in hand, this same ease of access usually compensates a reader for whatever inconvenience may be caused by omissions among the materials actually held by the Club. In short, our library deserves its special reputation both for its very scarce materials and because each of our holdings, whether scarce or not, waits here unusually ready to a reader's hand. Furthermore, these characteristics of scarcity and accessibility intersect in almost every collection within the Grolier library and naturally enhance each other.

The books of which I write have been assembled for Jean Grolier's honor in under a century by much industry and that happy coincidence of accident and miracle to which all great collections are indebted. Its founders never intended the Grolier library as an independent entity but rather conceived it only to serve immediate interests and needs of the membership, especially in the preparation of our Club's famous publications and exhibitions. Some of our earliest members gave the Club whole collections of their bibliographical reference materials, in part because they wished them to be more readily available to others for such purposes, and in part, to be sure, because little market demand or value attached to such items in those days. Yet one must never forget that, although its library is now equally available to nonmembers and members alike, the Grolier Club is and always has been principally an organization of quite private book collectors, and as changing times have inexorably altered the character and scale of private bibliophily, like changes have necessarily been reflected in the scope and intensity of the Club library's growth. When, for instance, many of the world's most important rare books and manuscripts were still in the hands of private owners just a few generations ago, our library was one of the few easily accessible places in America where the bibliographical resources for scholarly investigation of such books were being deliberately accumulated for their own sake and public use. Later, as bibliographical science continued maturing, and as institutional libraries multiplied and began to purchase the same general biblio-philic reference works on a much larger scale in order to complement the utility of their main collections, the ambitions of private collectors both within and without the Grolier Club were at the same time becoming more modest, more exacting, and more specialized, requiring these collectors to form their own bibliographical collections precisely focused upon their respective research requirements. These simultaneous pressures driving institutional and private libraries in diametrically opposite directions can be seen today in full force respectively in the ever-rising prices of older, general bibliophilic works and in the ever-growing demand for new and highly specialized bibliographical publications and periodicals. As a result, the collector-scholar for whom it was first conceived, whether member or not, now usually looks upon the Grolier library as his resource of last resort, consulting it only for works outside his customary interests or for the larger, older reference works he does not wish or cannot afford to own himself and has not found convenient to use elsewhere.

Some other consequences of the changing character of private book collecting should also be noted in any modern appraisal of our Club library. The more or less steady drift of rare books into institutional libraries and also the far greater number of such libraries today continue to swell demand for thorough bibliographical collections, and this in turn makes the expenditure of vast sums for the rarer of such materials that much easier to justify. Such formidable competition has of course required the Grolier Club in recent decades to withdraw from active pursuit of certain desirable materials in some areas relevant to its originally intended purposes, prompting concern among a few pessimistic members that the library as a whole may be moribund. At the same time, those Grolierites responsible for preparing our Club's official publications and for installing our exhibitions, whether large or small, usually have their own specialist knowledge and own reference resources available to them, and often need or prefer to use the research facilities of great institutional libraries rather than the Club's own. Such dependence upon public and private alternatives to the Grolier library, furthermore, has become so commonplace that our members frequently find it necessary to compete with their own Club in the acquisition of seldom-used bibliographic material, either on behalf of other institutions or for their own shelves, while the original advantage of cooperative ownership of a single copy thereof through the agency of the Grolier Club itself has been altogether forgotten. In addition, even if there were not already major gaps in the Club's collections and our reading room were full, it is now financially impossible for the Grolier or any similarly small institution to keep up with major public and university libraries, of which there are many in the immediate area, in acquiring the flood of new bibliographies or even such an immense *sine qua non* of bookish research as the recently completed *National Union Catalog* with its nearly eight hundred volumes.

Accordingly, the Library Committee, which shares responsibility with our resident librarian for overseeing and augmenting the Club's diverse collections and ensuring their utility, must reassess Grolier acquisition policies from time to time within the context of these shifting and often conflicting pressures. Cooperation with other libraries—including the loan and possible exchange of certain duplicate or out-of-field assets, and focusing in particular upon coordinated purchasing and microfilming plans to minimize competition and needless duplication among similar institutions—is regularly explored. The committee's deliberations range from identification of specific needs to philosophical analysis of the purposes served by particular collections or by our library as a whole. The committee continually weighs the expense of each proposed acquisition against realistic appraisals of its scholarly usefulness and relevance. But at each stage in our history, I believe it can be shown, the future direction of the library has been wisely determined not so much by considerations of the end we *ought* to be serving as by an informed acceptance of that course it is believed we *must* take in order to maximize the utility of what we actually have—the utility, that is, of whatever the Grolier Club's history and past policies have actually bequeathed us, including the rather limited funds available to augment that heritage. It is an irony of this improvisational development, rather than any fault of our custodians, that the library may be strongest today and capable of rendering the most valuable service in those areas of our holdings which have grown more by accretion of gifts than by deliberate purchase. This seems particularly the case within three main categories: our books about the history and techniques of book collecting itself; our many manuscript and printed catalogues of private and now mostly dispersed libraries; and our extraordinary runs of booksellers' and auction-house catalogues from all periods and countries. Yet even as I write, efforts are afoot under the able jurisdiction of the Library Committee to further enhance the usefulness of these strong suits and, to some extent, to define future acquisition policies *around* them for the benefit of the whole library.

In this connection, it may be appropriate to mention a related phenomenon: the large number of private bibliophiles today who passionately collect books about books and manuscripts as an end in itself. Their ubiquitous breed is, of course, alike in dignity with collector-scholars of older disciplines, for the literature of bibliophily is obviously as worthy of being gathered and preserved as any other class among the arts and sciences —the more so, perhaps, because it was relatively ignored until quite recent times. Today, most bibliophiles devote substantial effort to amassing a working group of such books for bibliographic reference, often without acknowledging that this too is an important aspect of their collecting. In fact, the steady proliferation of collectors and dealers who specialize in such books is further evidence of a growing recognition of the importance thereof for scholarship and suggests that the utility of the Grolier library, with one of the largest collections of this kind, should soon become more widely recognized than in the past. Spurring such interest, the Grolier Club itself has published numerous seminal works on books as *objets d'art*, along with related titles such as the centennial volume you are now holding that will lend weight to shelves around the world. Old notions that the study of books and manuscripts as physical objects is but a shabby handmaiden to the Muses have been so thoroughly refuted in the last generation that further argument of the point is no longer heard in well-read circles. But what still seems imperfectly recognized today is that such books about books are as indispensable a research tool for the collector-scholar who has made bibliophily his subject matter as they are for his cousin bibliophiles who choose to gather more traditional kinds of books or manuscripts. Unfortunately, members of this specialist breed all too often imagine that possessing their own private collections of books about books obviates the need to use a larger bibliographical reference library like the Grolier Club's, whereas paradoxically their enterprise could profit from such use at least as much as any other. In fact, if the scholarly potential of our collection here were ever fully appreciated by truly serious private collectors of books about books, not only their individual use but also their collective support of it would expand in a geometric hurry.

Earlier I mentioned two paramount respects in which our library is valuable to a bibliophile of whatever specialization: the scarcity of certain of its holdings, and the accessibility of them all. As to the former, virtues of some of the rarer or unique items at the Grolier Club are discussed in other chapters of the present volume. The scholarly uses of these otherwise unavailable historical materials are too obvious to justify recital and too numerous to permit anticipation. On the other hand, ease of access is a virtue of our collections deserving of careful attention here. The very compactness of the library commends it to anyone who has searched, perhaps in vain, throughout some gargantuan institution for the same resources dispersed among many departments. Due to their logical arrangement and convenient proximity, a reader surveying titles on the Grolier shelves for a particular book also sees at a glance related works, to be consulted later, that he might have forgotten or been ignorant of and, if he steps back but a foot or two, may behold on a single shelf those successive layers of scholarship upon which modern bibliography has been built. Were he estimating the relative rarity of an early book or attempting to identify its printer or its binder, or were he tracing the provenance of one volume or reconstructing an individual's entire library long after dispersal—to take these as just a few examples—then our reader would discover that his task is nowhere made easier than at the Grolier

Club. Or were he himself a printer or designer at work upon his newest book, as yet barely conceived, here too await models for his inspiration and instruction that he might not have found elsewhere. The Grolier must also be home base for anyone who intends seriously to study the history of book collecting, especially as practiced in America. And if casual browsing can play any role in his work, as it seems always to do in mine, there could be no more propitious place than our stacks. Serendipitous discoveries are particularly common among the Club's vast collection of booksellers' and auction-house catalogues, which at most other institutions are virtually neglected by readers due to their inaccessibility, but which are one of the Club library's most attractive features because of their neat arrangement, chronologically by country, on our open shelves.

Another aspect of accessibility to the Grolier library is equally important. Just as Jean Grolier himself ordered the gilded tomes in his own libraries to be inscribed with the Latin "et amicorum," indicating that that prince of bibliophiles considered these books common property to be shared unselfishly with his learned friends, so also the materials in our Club library have for nearly a hundred years been made available to the public without charge—in particular to properly accredited and experienced researchers and also to qualified students in relevant programs of study. In order to encourage the widest possible use of these materials by both members and nonmembers, every effort is made under the regulations of the Club to balance hospitality and helpfulness toward an individual reader against the obligation our Club has assumed to preserve its irreplaceable collections for future generations of scholars. Not only bibliographers receive a cordial reception here, but interdisciplinary trailblazers of many kinds utilize our resources, like the growing number of musicologists who have been consulting our catalogues over the last few years. A special welcome, of course, always awaits those whom earlier I dubbed novitiate bibliophiles, a term, incidentally, that should be understood to include not only the collector-scholar whose love's labor has just begun but also his more seasoned colleague who, know it or not, has something about his chosen subject yet to learn.

It is generally recognized that the Grolier had the first separate library in America devoted to books about books, aside from private collections like that of our first president, Robert Hoe III. Intended from its earliest days for use rather than ornament, the collection is arranged today according to a simple but practical system that divides the realm of bibliophily into some seventy provinces under a simple call system. These categories, it goes without saying, overlap on all sides, but the organizational plan as now implemented seems not to hinder the habitué and has proven of definite benefit to beginners. Complementing such order on our shelves is, of course, the Club's indefatigable librarian, whose full-time position dates back to 1898, when need for "an expert bibliographer in daily attendance" was first noted.

Completeness on the scale implied by such an organizational system is, of course, impossible, and our library is inevitably stronger in some areas than in others, one notable weakness being our holdings of relevant periodical literature. Because we are foremost a gathering place for book collectors, historical materials naturally take precedence here over the purely technical side of printing, although the latter is by no means neglected inasmuch as we recognize that what is technical today will have become historical by tomorrow. As with any library a century old, the Grolier also reflects the vicissitudes of thorough cataloguing done whenever there was time and of meager cataloguing when there was not. Furthermore, the Club must operate within a limited budget, and therefore conservation and physical maintenance of its materials as well as their security within the clubhouse are abiding problems as great as current accessioning and cataloguing. But one very positive asset that adds enormously to the usefulness of our library is the Club's "cabinet" of such collections as fine bindings from nearly all periods and representative incunabula from selected early printers—all serving to illustrate the various fields covered by the library and as good examples of what collectors collect. Our extensive archives, as yet barely even catalogued, are a further plus, as is the convenience of having several great institutional libraries nearby whose holdings are normally taken into account when new acquisitions for the Grolier library are being weighed.

With the foregoing as prologue, I should like to relate the personal experience referred to in my opening. I had already heard of the Grolier Club when I arrived in New York City as a young attorney, eager to begin the practice of law but already—so I imagined—quite a "serious" collector of books. That was, of course, long before I ever thought of becoming a member or had even met many other bibliophiles. There seemed no reason to use the library I knew the Club maintained, inasmuch as the vast riches of the New York Public Library were virtually across the street from me, Columbia's Butler Library only minutes farther, and other eminent college libraries, including my own alma mater's, within the diameter of a few hours by rail. Business took me on occasion also to Washington, where the Library of Congress became a second home during any spare hours. But the Grolier Club looked too forbidding and, yes, too private; anyway, there was no reason to go there. It took eight busy years in those other noble institutions to acquaint myself with the basic reference works in my field of bibliographical research. In tracking down some of the more arcane references that seemed relevant to my interests, I absorbed bibliophilic lore in snatches along the way, the hard way. Then it happened that I needed to trace the provenance of a volume of rare French republican pedagogical pamphlets by Jean-Baptiste Gail, and one catalogue of the nineteenth-century London auctioneer Thomas Thorpe, crucial for the project, had eluded me at every turn. My last alternative exhausted, I ventured finally into that little library on East 60th Street, and, *mirabile dictu,* was graciously welcomed. Never had I known even a Christmas morning so glorious! There on a single shelf were most of the bibliographies it had taken years to run to ground, some of them in better editions than I had found elsewhere; there scattered among them on the same shelf were like works, and better too, all unknown; and just over there seemingly countless tomes, of very uneven worth I later learned, on the philosophy of collecting which I would

99

never have discovered for myself in a hundred years. Passing shelf after neat shelf of unimagined inventories of dispersed libraries directly germane to my collecting, some of them in unique copies, I was shown to the Thorpes—all of them, bound in order and priced, mostly the annotated desk copies of the dealer himself. Years after, of course, I would recognize gaps in the collection—but that day the Grolier library was my heaven!

In conclusion, practical uses of our Club library are at least as numerous as the collector-scholars who would wish to visit if they but knew of its rich resources. I submit, however, that no reader could make *better* use of such a collection as I have described than the novitiate bibliophile mentioned earlier. Although more advanced scholars and specialists will always have need for the Grolier library, none could profit more from its very special advantages than the young amateur, that autodidact adrift as I was years ago, whose objectives and taste could be nurtured, whose knowledge and techniques could be further developed, and whose budding enthusiasm for books could be encouraged to flower and perhaps one day become a source of inspiration for still others, if he or she were just exposed to what is, very simply, the best working library for bibliophily anywhere today. The democracy of the intellect, to which men like me owe everything, comes from the printed book, and so to me it seems profoundly urgent that the Grolier Club, dedicated as it is to fostering a just appreciation for the book itself, should offer its own books about the arts and sciences of the book as a catalyst to promising and qualified novitiates, especially to those not already affiliated with other libraries. Although such readers almost never use the Club library now, it is they more than anyone else who can benefit from the extraordinary convenience its size and scope offer, and they who will mind less than more advanced specialists whatever occasional gaps are admittedly in the collections. Later, our library might even become a center for formal instruction in book-related arts, and it should continue as well to render traditional services. But for now we must acquaint that incipient lover of books with, and encourage free use of, the resources we offer here. One hopes that the present centennial volume has already begun to accomplish this. If so, new readers may soon delight in discovering for themselves the myriad uses of a resource such as ours. While so many libraries these days plead for more books, or more money to buy more books, we sound a different cry: Inspire new readers to use the wonderful collection of books we already have.

# Educational Uses
## of the Library

### TERRY BELANGER

THE founders of the Grolier Club wished to promote the arts of the book by establishing publication and exhibition programs and a library for bibliography, printing history, and books demonstrating excellent design, typography, illustration, binding, or innovative production techniques. The library quickly became the unique resource it continues to be, open to anyone who can benefit from its use.

There are, of course, larger research collections in New York, but to some persons the Grolier's smaller size is an advantage. Almost the entire collection is on open shelves, encouraging happy discoveries from looking at books instead of cards. The subject arrangement also facilitates use, for everywhere there is sufficient informality to allow common sense to prevail by putting like next to like, no matter what the rules say. Sets of periodicals and reference books and runs of catalogues are well ordered and generally complete. It may take an hour in the Grolier library to accomplish what might take a week in other libraries.

Since early in the twentieth century, library school classes have been welcome in the Grolier Club library. Henry Watson Kent, the Club's first professional librarian, appointed in 1900, was in Melvil Dewey's first class (1887). Ruth Shepard Granniss, librarian from 1904 to 1944, was a graduate of Pratt Institute's library school and very active in professional circles. Several succeeding librarians have been library school graduates;

all have encouraged the use of the library by graduate students, and untold numbers of papers have been written using the collection.

But until the 1970's, when the Grolier Club and the Columbia University School of Library Service established their mutually beneficial program, there had never been a formal arrangement between the Club and an educational institution as defined by the State of New York. The program described here has been a success, if only judging by the number of its graduates who are now members of the Grolier. It is also no coincidence that the development and strengthening of the graduate program at Columbia has gone hand in hand with a great increase in the use of the library by scholars and the book trade.

The program dates from 1971, when two students consulted me (then a professor in the library school) about their independent study projects. They had already talked with the Grolier's recently appointed librarian and learned that the collection of pre-1800 books was by contemporary standards inadequately catalogued. Discussion and examination revealed that there was indeed a great deal of work that needed doing. The only catalogue of the pre-1800 books was the shelflist arranged by subject, and that proved to be incomplete. Extensive cataloguing was obviously needed to make the collection useful and accessible. The two students were allowed to begin, but everyone concerned soon realized that the plan of having two persons working only one day a week was not a reasonable way to approach the problem. The Columbia School of Library Service and the Grolier Club therefore concluded that the project would become an ongoing one, with highly motivated students assigned to it as they emerged from an initial course on descriptive bibliography in the rare books program at Columbia, which was being established at that time.

At the start it was determined that the chief purpose of the Grolier Club Cataloguing Project (as it became known) was to forward the education of the students involved in it. The important by-product was, of course, the new and improved cataloguing of the Grolier collection of early books.

This significant principle enabled the project to proceed over the years in ways which few other libraries would have tolerated. The diversity of the Grolier holdings made it easy to find an area for students to work in no matter what their languages or bibliographical interest. The work was made interesting for everyone for two reasons. First, the books themselves are inherently worthwhile because of their subjects and age, being keystone books in the history of bibliography, library history, bookselling, paleography, graphic processes, and printing history down to the year 1800. Second, a calculated variation was made from merely clerical problems to those requiring advanced bibliographical skills. Each student was given a small number of books with which to work. If old catalogue cards did exist, they were matched up with the book. If no cards were found, a new record was made. Titles were then searched in standard catalogues such as those of the library of the British Museum and the Library of Congress. When available, LC cards were modified for our purposes as necessary. Otherwise, original cataloguing was done and the work given to me for revision. Finally, clean cards were typed and reproduced. Separate cards were made for author, title, subject, and special entries, and then all were filed. A rare book catalogue for the Grolier Club was underway. The pre-1800 collection was in a constant uproar by the mid-1970's as we forged ahead, learning as we went.

During the academic year of 1974–1975, the rare books program at Columbia assumed essentially its present form. In that year, the Book Arts Press, the bibliographical laboratory of the school, was fully incorporated into the curriculum. It was also the first year that we had a large number of students—some twenty. Seven asked to take part in the Grolier project; three are now Club members. As the project picked up speed and more students wished to take part, it became obvious that I could not continue unassisted to look after it properly. Relief in the person of Miss Marion Schild arrived in 1979. As recently retired principal descriptive cataloguer of the Library of Congress, her credentials ranged from a Ph.D. in Romance languages from Munich to many years of cataloguing the Lessing J. Rosenwald Collection, published by LC in 1977. Fortunately for us, she was now living in New York City, and she agreed to take over the primary responsibility for supervising the students. Upon application, the H. W. Wilson Foundation of New York generously agreed to provide financial support for her participation—the first outside funding the Grolier Club had ever received—and has continued it to the present.

All students participating in the project must write a description of their work. Comments about Miss Schild suggest how indispensable a part of the program she has become. One student wrote: "It is difficult to imagine that any other teacher could have imparted as much insight into the whys and wherefores of so many apparently arbitrary cataloguing rules, since few people can boast of Miss Schild's experience. Having herself been one of the brains behind the Anglo-American Cataloguing Rules, she has obviously devoted long and serious consideration to the problems of cataloguing and universal bibliographic control: her knowledge is therefore more than a matter of remarkable memory and an eye for detail. Above all, she knows how to share what she knows—she is an excellent teacher. It has been an unforgettable privilege to be able to work with her."

As the centennial year opens, a catalogue of pre-1800 books in the Grolier Club library is virtually complete. Additional helpful files, such as place of printing, chronological, and provenance (always of special interest to bibliophiles), are well under way.

Since 1971 more than one hundred Columbia University School of Library Service students have participated in the Grolier Club Cataloguing Project. The school is the nation's principal training ground for rare book and special collections librarians and it has produced many antiquarian booksellers as well. The Grolier project has been central to development and expansion of the program. The Club's willingness to allow students to use other parts of the collections, such as bookbindings, medieval manuscripts, and prints, has added an important element to their education, one available at no other library in the city. As Columbia's graduates go out to work in North America and elsewhere in the world, they remain in the debt of the Grolier Club, its librarian, and its library.

# The Clubhouse

## WENDELL GARRETT

HORACE WALPOLE'S frivolous attitude to politics and his serious attention to collecting made him the victim of Macaulay's reckless brilliance: "After the labours of the print-shop and the auction-room, he unbent his mind in the House of Commons. And, having indulged in the recreation of making laws and voting millions, he returned to more important pursuits, to researches after Queen Mary's comb, Wolsey's red hat, the pipe which Van Tromp smoked during his last sea-fight, and the spur which King William struck into the flank of Sorrel." All true bibliophiles have a bit of the antiquarian in them, and when the Grolier Club was established a century ago its founders set about furnishing the premises like a town house with some antiques and some new pieces in a revival of earlier styles. A certain amount was given and much was purchased, and over the years the clubhouse has been the happy recipient of portraits and busts, lamps and rugs, porcelains and tapestries, candlesticks and andirons, and tables and chairs donated by devoted members and thoughtful widows. The *Transactions* for 1894 report, "Some small additional expenditure was incurred in decoration, giving a homelike and cheerful appearance to the whole premises. . . . The furnishing of the club-house was done under the direction of the House Committee, Messrs. [Frederick A.] Castle, [Alexander W.] Drake, and [John Holme] Maghee. . . . The furniture purchased was plain but thoroughly good of its kind, and has stood the test of wear." Kipling once remarked that the atmosphere of a club "softens the ferocious, gives countenance to the meek and comfort to the solitary, educates the overlearned, silences the argumentative, and has been known to arrest the predestined prig on his downward path."

The membership of the Grolier Club has grown and the location has changed, but the spiritual and intellectual atmosphere, intentionally "homelike" and "cheerful," has remained the same ever since the days of gas lights and carriages and burnsides.

With clubs, as with the inn at Bethlehem, there is never enough room. The Grolier Club's first home was a two-and-a-half-story brick structure at 64 Madison Avenue, between 26th and 27th streets, in which it shared the ground floor with the Mott Memorial Library of medical books and anatomical skeletons. The upstairs rooms were let in the mornings to a kindergarten and in the afternoon to a ladies' fencing school, "and on some nights to one or more secret organizations." It soon became apparent that the Club would have to embark on an ambitious building program; a lot was purchased at 29 East 32nd Street and a three-story pressed brick and terra cotta Romanesque structure, designed by Charles W. Romeyn and Company, was completed in October 1889 and occupied the following month. The ground floor contained a lecture and exhibition hall; the second floor social, reading, and smoking rooms; and the top floor the library and council room. The *Transactions* for 1894 stated that "Before the building was finished a subscription was started to raise funds with which to furnish it. . . . The whole amount so raised together with additional sums from the Treasury as they have been needed, has been expended for furniture, and that now represents a total expenditure of $8,145.86." During the next few years the Club received, by gift from individual members, two notable acquisitions. One was the Dutch "Tapperij" kitchen or pub, presented by Edwin B. Holden (described and reported in the *Transactions* for 1899, and in *House Beautiful* in July 1897), and the other was *Aldus in His Printing Establishment at Venice, Showing Bindings to Grolier*, painted by François Flameng in 1890, commissioned and presented to the Club by Samuel P. Avery through his Paris agent, George A. Lucas, a member. In late 1899 Avery ordered, also through

Lucas, the Houdon bust of Franklin cast by Ferdinand Barbedienne that is now in the library.

There is little that is either Dutch (the model was a room in Cannes) or old about the "Tapperij" except the Delft tiles and a Friesland hanging clock; this "antiqued" interior still boasts a copper siphon for pumping beer and ale from Beefsteak John's, an old New York saloon.

This East 32nd Street building was the home of the Club for the next twenty-seven years, but all New York seemed to be moving uptown—the stores, the theaters, the clubs, even the residences. The old clubhouse, for all its hallowed associations, was no longer satisfactory for exhibitions, as a meeting place, or to house books. In 1913 a committee was appointed to search for a new site, and eventually 47–49 East 60th Street was purchased. Plans for the clubhouse were drawn by Bertram G. Goodhue, and the new clubhouse was opened in December 1917. When the members moved uptown, they brought the "Tapperij" and Flameng painting with them. The austere brick façade was decorated around the doorway with terra cotta from the New York Architectural Terra Cotta Works of Long Island City. Nineteen-seventeen might seem a bad year for building a new clubhouse, with the skies darkening across western Europe, but the members moved ahead with the true resolution of bibliomaniacs. "Nothing succeeds like excess," said the irrepressible Oscar Wilde, and an excess of talent was one ingredient in the success of the old Grolier.

Today one leaves a street congested with traffic for the calm serenity of the entry hall to face the venerable portraits and busts of some of the founders in burnsides, beards, the frock coat, and the boiled shirt: Alexander W. Drake by J. C. Johansen (1914), Robert Hoe, III, by J. W. Alexander (1889), and a plaster bust of Theodore Low De Vinne. A portrait of William Dean Howells by Frank Fowler (1903?) and the Flameng *Aldus* complete the art works in a room that conveys the prevailing scale of a private house. A fireplace, complete with brass andirons and French Empire mantel clock, and a Chippendale-style scroll-arm sofa add to the dignity and charm of the room. Beyond, in the small room leading into the exhibition hall, is one of the Club's curious relics—the master's chair from the Cauliflower Club, a high-seated ceremonial chair in the neoclassical style with a cauliflower carved in the cresting. It once was used in the club rooms of "The Free and Easy Counsellors Under the Cauliflower," a group of London booksellers who met regularly in the eighteenth century in a pub room in which a plaster cauliflower decorated the ceiling. To the rear on the ground floor, the exhibition hall—completely refurbished in 1954–1955 in preparation for the seventy-fifth anniversary, an inspiration of President Irving S. Olds—serves as the social center of the Club, tripling as a gallery, assembly room, and cocktail lounge. The spacious dimensions and serious purpose of the room are achieved by the ceiling that extends through the second floor, allowing for a gallery of periodicals around the upper level. Another step in the 1950's renovation was the alteration of the old mezzanine room into a combined Rare Book and Small Exhibition Room, where comfortable chairs, a handsome breakfront, tables, and an exquisite Heriz carpet give warmth. Over the mantel in this room hangs the 1850 portrait of Nathaniel Hawthorne by Cephas Giovanni Thompson, purchased from the author's son in 1908 by the New York Co-operative Society, an art firm, and given subsequently to the Club by Stephen A. Wakeman.

The heart of the clubhouse is the third floor, which houses the library and librarian's office, richly paneled in Georgian walnut and gracefully finished in plaster architectural details. A formidable trinity of Italian Renaissance poets in marble—Ariosto, Petrarch, and Tasso, given to the club in 1918 by De Vinne—and other sculptures gaze down sternly upon a massive reading table surrounded by a dozen mahogany Chippendale-style chairs with open-work splats in the form of a shell and nicely proportioned cabriole legs terminating in hairy paw feet. These handsome chairs in the French *rocaille* taste are nineteenth-century revivals of a mid-eighteenth-century English form fancifully carved with tracery, strapwork, and acanthus leaves. An original set of these chairs may be seen in the dining room of Stourhead, in Wiltshire, England. Other busts and statuettes include a terra cotta of Albrecht Dürer by Albert Ernest Carrière-Belleuse; a bronze reduction of Gutenberg from a statue in Strasbourg

109

by Pierre Jean David d'Angers; and a statue of Ambroise Firmin-Didot after the original at the Hôtel de Ville in Paris. Standing majestically at the end of the room is a mahogany tall-case clock, a finely proportioned specimen of pronounced architectural character, with works by Frans Dikhoff, a late eighteenth-century craftsman of Amsterdam.

Hanging on the walls of the clubhouse are some extraordinary portraits of literary figures and topographical views. In the librarian's office, over a massive turned chair given to De Vinne in 1886 by the Century Company, hangs an oil portrait of Henry Wadsworth Longfellow painted by Thomas Buchanan Read in Rome in 1869, while upstairs in the sixth-floor council room is a hauntingly beautiful grisaille oil on composition board of James Russell Lowell painted in London in 1881 by Francis Lathrop. And among the many pictures of literary interest and association that decorate the Club are a pair of watercolors by Alexander Jackson Davis: *City Hall, New York* (1826) and *City Hall Park, New York* (1827). In the course of the years, institutions like individuals "live and learn" about mistaken attributions in their holdings, and the Grolier Club is no exception. The portrait long thought to be of John Dryden (and published as such) is now known to be by the English portraitist Mary Beale, of her husband in costume. The Ben Jonson portrait long thought to be a copy after Gerrit van Honthorst is now believed to be a copy after Abraham Blyenberch; and the Alexander Pope is now attributed to the studio rather than the hand of Sir Godfrey Kneller.

The Club has always maintained an adequate supply of silver flatware and Sheffield plated silver candelabra and candlesticks for setting a properly appointed table for small dinners. But in addition to this household silver, there are on the premises some remarkable pieces of considerable rarity. There is a Queen Anne silver salver made by William Gamble in London in 1712, engraved with the arms of the Bertie family and an inscription of 1918 to William Loring Andrews from the Society of Iconophiles. A set of three George III silver-gilt standing salts in the Elizabethan style are marked by William Fountain of London in 1808. Much used and somewhat abused are three pieces of an American Empire tea service made by John Targee of New York in 1825. And in the revival spirit of the Club, there is a generous silver tankard made by the Meriden Britannia Company after a Jeremiah Dummer Boston tankard of 1700.

On the fifth floor of the clubhouse, at the rear of the building, one may savor the aesthetic tastes of the late nineteenth century. Comfortably furnished with generous armchairs in the arts and crafts style of William Morris, a heavily tufted sofa, and golden oak tables *en suite* (one carved on the stretcher *G.C. 1889*), the room properly reflects the *fin de siècle* fascination with Japanese exoticism. Over the fireplace is *The Strife of Good and Evil* in ink and colors by Utagawa Kuniyoshi (1798–1861) which was presented to the Club by Heromich Shugio, a Japanese member elected in 1884. Massive brass andirons on the hearth have large bulbous standards decorated with fleurs-de-lis supported on winged horses rising out of claw-and-ball feet. Blue and white Oriental porcelains harmoniously combine with a bronze portrait medallion of George A. Lucas, the art agent for Samuel P. Avery and others in Europe. On the walls hang a pair of paintings by Howard Pyle, both of 1902: *Friar Roger Bacon in His Cell* and *William Caxton at His Press*. They were used as two of the frontispieces in T. F. Dibdin's *Bibilomania*, published in four volumes by The Bibliophile Society in 1903. Scattered around the room are half a dozen late nineteenth-century chairs in the neoclassical style identical to some of the dining room chairs at The Century Association, reaffirming the close relationship between these two temples on the Parnassus of this American Athens.

As the Lord looked back upon His creation and saw that it was good, so may we mortals who occupy this serene clubhouse on East 60th Street look back on the creation of something unique and wonderful by our predecessors one hundred years ago.

# Publications

## C. WALLER BARRETT

FROM its beginning the Grolier Club has been deeply interested in the publication of books on the book arts, collecting, bibliographical works, and autobiographical works of prominent bookmen. Although the original and continued objective of the Club, "the literary study and promotion of the arts pertaining to the production of books," did not provide for their publication, it seems clear that this was an aim prominent in the minds of the founders. By 1889 authorization of publication became official in the Club constitution. One can hardly promote the book arts without producing visible examples of desired effects. Over the last century some 145 major publications have been issued by the Club, each a contribution to typography, scholarship, or both.

The first members of the Committee on Publications were all founders of the Club, men admirably suited to achieve the objective of beautifully produced, scholarly works. William Loring Andrews, a trustee of the Metropolitan Museum of Art and New York University, was already involved in the production of bibliographical, iconographical, and historical monographs. Theodore Low De Vinne was a master printer and author of *The Invention of Printing* (1876). He had made graphic arts history with the redesigning of *The Century Magazine*, and was the first president of the United Typothetae of America. Alexander W. Drake was the art director of *The Century Magazine* and a prime mover in the development of the illustrated magazine. Albert Gallup was a distinguished lawyer and later New York Parks Commissioner. Edward S. Mead was a partner of

Dodd, Mead, the publishers and antiquarian booksellers. Rounding out the committee were the two great collectors Robert Hoe, Jr., and Beverly Chew.

This redoubtable group lost no time in beginning operations. Less than six months after the official organizational meeting of the Club the committee voted to issue the first Club publication, *A Decree of Star Chamber Concerning Printing, Made July 11, 1637*. This was reprinted from the original printing made in London by Robert Barker in 1637. To establish a precedent of limited editions, 150 serially numbered copies were printed. Two copies besides these were printed on vellum and were sold at auction for $45 and $36 respectively. The second copy was presented to the Club library, where it shares a slipcase with copy 1 of the paper copies, each of the latter bearing the signature of the nine founders. Since the printed limitation was violated by the production of the two vellum copies, copies 149 and 150 were officially burned in the Club fireplace. This first publication elicited favorable comments from the press. Robert Hoe added his modest commendation in a letter to a journalist: "The Publications Committee of the Club thinks it a pretty nice specimen of printing." The Star Chamber volume was designed and printed by Theodore Low De Vinne, with an introduction. It was the first of some sixty books printed by De Vinne for the Grolier Club up to 1917. Walter Gilliss of the Gilliss Press also produced many Grolier books in the period between 1894 and 1924. During the past hundred years the talents of many other celebrated designers and printers have been enlisted, including Bruce Rogers, William Edwin Rudge, John Henry Nash, Thomas Maitland Cleland, Carl Purington Rollins, Frederic and Bertha Goudy, Joseph Blumenthal, P. J. Conkwright, Peter Beilenson, Elmer Adler, and Roderick Stinehour. The presses include Merrymount, A. Colish, Harbor, Stinehour, George Grady, Overbrook, Spiral, Anthoensen, Plimpton, Country Life, Chiswick, and the university presses of Princeton, Oxford, and Cambridge.

In a list of publications of such virtually uniform excellence as those I call the Grolier Hundred and Forty-Five, it is difficult to place the accolades on individual books. After its propitious beginning, the committee immediately continued to produce a flow of volumes worthy of Grolier standards. By the turn of the century a total of twenty-eight books had been published, an average of two a year. In 1888 a news report stated that "the Grolier Club in its three years of existence has by its own publications done much to raise the standards of taste for well-made books." Perhaps the two most impressive publications of this period were *A History of New-York* by Diedrich Knickerbocker, in two volumes priced at $20, and Richard de Bury's *Philobiblon* in three volumes at $25. A magnificent set of this latter title is in the Club library, bound by The Club Bindery. The single work of fiction in this pre-1900 period was a handsome new edition of *Peg Woffington* by Charles Reade. During the period around the turn of the century the committee benefited from the labors of Samuel Putnam Avery, Bayard Tuckerman, William F. Havemeyer, Charles F. Chichester, and Richard Hoe Lawrence.

In this early period the Club had a contract with the publications committee whereby all profits on books printed would accrue to the Club but all losses would be assumed by the individual members. Although this contract was abandoned in later years, it should be said that Grolier books have continued to sell well, and few have shown a serious loss.

During this century the committee has continued its successful career. It added to its roster a number of distinguished members, such as publisher Arthur H. Scribner and architect Bertram Grosvenor Goodhue, who drew the plans for the present clubhouse. Frank Altschul, the philanthropist and founder of the Overbrook Press; Carroll Atwood Wilson, the legendary collector; William M. Ivins, Jr., curator of prints at the Metropolitan Museum; Wilmarth S. Lewis, the Walpole collector; Monroe Wheeler, mover and shaker at the Museum of Modern Art; and Frederick B. Adams, Jr., a former president of the Club, all served with distinction. It is interesting to glance at the results of their efforts in the new century. Even during the years of the two World Wars, noteworthy books such as *Of the Just Shaping of Letters: From the Applied Geometry of Albrecht Dürer* were issued. It came out in 1917. *The United States Navy 1760 to*

*1815*, of 1942, was an appropriate title for the time. In the twentieth century up to the present, one hundred and sixteen books have been published.

It is always enlightening to consider which of the Grolier Club publications are the most notable. Three works establishing lists of important works have become often-cited references. These are *One Hundred Books Famous in English Literature* (1902), with Henry W. Kent's *Bibliographical Notes on One Hundred Books Famous in English Literature* (1903); *One Hundred Influential American Books Printed Before 1900* (1947); and Harrison D. Horblit's *One Hundred Books Famous in Science* (1964). The 1908 Club edition of Hawthorne's *The Scarlet Letter*, illustrated by George H. Boughton, was the Club's second essay of a new edition of a classic novel. Two works on engravings and etchings suggest a prevailing interest of the Club in earlier years. *The Etched Work of Whistler* by Edward G. Kennedy, issued in 1910, was the most expensive work published by the Club to that time, costing $75. Together with three additions, it was the last word in Whistler scholarship for that time. *New York: A Series of Wood Engravings in Colour and a Note on Colour Printing* by Rudolph Ruzicka was issued in 1915. In the history of books and book design there was the Albrecht Dürer book already mentioned, *Book Decorations by Bertram Grosvenor Goodhue* (1931); *Fra Luca de Pacioli of Borgo S. Sepolcro* (1933) by Stanley Morison; and George B. Ives's edition of *Champ Fleury* by Geoffroy Tory, issued in 1927. Gabriel Austin's research in establishing the titles and former owners of books once in our patron's possession resulted in the 1971 publication of *The Library of Jean Grolier: A Preliminary Catalogue*. *The Truthful Lens*, a 1980 survey of books illustrated by original photographs by Lucien Goldschmidt and Weston J. Naef, was yet another of our pioneering works in bibliography. Most recently, two quite different but appropriate books were selected to help mark the centennial: Joseph Blumenthal's typographic memoir and the catalogue of the great bibliography exhibition of 1981.

An area of publication which has always been of particular interest to the membership are books relating to the Grolier Club and its activities.

The autobiography of Henry Watson Kent, *What I Am Pleased to Call My Education*, includes the period he was librarian of the Club. *Grolier 75: A Biographical Retrospective to Celebrate the Seventy-fifth Anniversary of the Grolier Club* gave biographical sketches of seventy-five members of note. John T. Winterich's *The Grolier Club, 1884–1967: An Informal History*, is a succinct account of the Club's record to that point. *The Grolier Club Iter Italicum* (1963) and *The Grolier Club Iter Germanico-Helveticum* (1973) chronicle two of the Club's European trips.

One cannot look at the history of Grolier publication only in the major works. The steady stream of meticulously edited and admirably designed individual exhibition catalogues which commenced in 1886 deserve special mention. There are also notices of meetings and exhibitions and the *Yearbooks*. One of the most felicitous of undertakings was the casting of medallion portraits in bronze of eminent American writers from 1892 to 1911. On all of these the committee imposed high standards of design and artistry. Finally, some mention should be made of the now revived *Gazette*, of special importance in preserving the annals of the Club.

This survey of Grolier Club publications mentions only a small fraction of the whole. The entire bibliography, with all details of bibliographical interest, is included in this volume. It reveals in full the impressive record of publishing the Grolier Club established in its first hundred years.

# Publications of
# the Grolier Club, 1884–1983

## ALLEN ASAF

THE most recent comprehensive list of Grolier Club publications was issued by the Club in 1948, a list based upon the one in parts no. 5 & 6 (1947) of the series *Selective Check Lists of Press Books*, edited by Will Ransom. The centenary of the Grolier Club is a fitting moment at which to produce a new and complete list of the Club's publications. The entries in this list are based on an examination of the books themselves, with additional details from the 1948 list as well as from descriptions published in the *Yearbook* from 1884 through 1967. The *Yearbook* descriptions sometimes provide information not given here (for example, title transcriptions showing line endings). The numbers preceding entries in the present publication are for reference purposes only; they do not appear in the publications, nor do they match those of previous lists.

The list is divided into four parts. Part I describes the publications authorized by the Committee on Publications as examplars of "the arts pertaining to the production of books," as well as offprints and keepsakes published for distribution to members (except for exhibition handlists, recorded in Part II). In each entry, the first paragraph transcribes the wording, but not necessarily the punctuation, of the title as it appears on the title page. The next paragraph begins with the dimensions of the leaf, measured to the nearest $\frac{1}{8}$ of an inch, height followed by width. Pagination is counted from the first printed page to the last, including all blanks that fall between them (blanks preceding and following printed pages are not counted); unnumbered pages not part of a numbered sequence are counted and shown in square brackets. Plates not part of a pagination sequence are counted and the total number of them listed. When available, information on typefaces, edition size, paper, binding, and publication price complete this part of the description. The name of the printer (and occasionally the names of others associated with the production of the book) and the year of publication are listed on the next line. Further notes about the book may be given in a final paragraph. In years in which more than one book was published, the entries are listed in order of publication. Every item in the list was published by the Grolier Club of the City of New York. Details of joint or multiple imprints are given in the notes paragraph.

Part II records handlists for visitors to exhibitions. Information in each entry is given in the following order: a short descriptive or summary title not including words such as "A catalogue of an exhibition . . ."; dimensions of leaf (when other than 7 x 4⅜ inches); pagination; plates (if any); printer (when available); year. All were published in printed wrappers.

Part III describes the periodical publications of the Club. The arrangement of entries for a given periodical title is similar to that already described for entries in Part I or Part II.

Part IV lists medallions: subject depicted, size, designer, founder, number cast, material, issue price, year.

Except for ephemeral printing, such as invitations, announcements, and prospectuses, all known publications of the Club through 1983 have been included.

1   A Decree of Star Chamber Concerning Printing, Made July 11, 1637.
Reprinted by The Grolier Club from the First Edition by Robert
Barker, 1637.

> 9 x 6; [93]p.; 148 copies on Holland paper with Japan paper wrappers, 2 copies
> on vellum with vellum wrappers; gilt-stamped with a design after a Roger
> Payne binding. $2.00 by subscription, $4.00 after publication.
>> *Printed by the De Vinne Press.*                                    1884
>> Introduction and notes by members of the Club.

2   Rubáiyát of Omar Khayyám, the Astronomer-Poet of Persia. Ren-
dered into English Verse by Edward FitzGerald.

> 9 x 6; xx, [2], 62, [2]p.; head-pieces printed in gold and colors from Persian
> models in Owen Jones's *Grammar of Ornament*; 150 copies on Japan paper, 2
> copies on vellum; Japan paper wrappers printed in blue and gold from a design
> in *Outlines of Ornament* by William James Audsley and George Ashdown
> Audsley. $3.00.
>> *Printed by the De Vinne Press.*                                    1885
>> Reprinted from the edition of Bernard Quaritch, London, 1879.

3   A History of New-York From the Beginning of the World to the
End of the Dutch Dynasty: Containing, Among Many Surprising and
Curious Matters, the Unutterable Ponderings of Walter the Doubter,
the Disastrous Projects of William the Testy, and the Chivalric Achievements of Peter the Headstrong—the Three Dutch Governors of New
Amsterdam, Being the Only Authentic History of the Times That
Ever Hath Been Or Ever Will be Published, by Diedrich Knickerbocker [Washington Irving]; A New Edition, Containing Unpublished Corrections of the Author, with Illustrations by Geo. H. Boughton, Will H. Drake, Howard Pyle, and Etchings by Henry C. Eno
and F. Raubicheck.

> 2 volumes, 9 x 6; vol. 1.: [16], 312p., frontispiece etching in 3 states and 1 plate;
> vol. 2: [6], 275, [1]p., frontispiece in 3 states and 4 plates (1 folded); head- and

tail-pieces and section illustrations printed in brown; Elzevir type; 175 sets on Holland paper, 2 sets on vellum; orange boards. $20.00.

*Printed by the De Vinne Press.* 1886

Includes a subscribers list at end of vol. 2; a cancel title-page for vol. 1 was provided at end of vol. 2, with instructions to the binder.

4   A Lecture on Bookbinding as a Fine Art, Delivered Before the Grolier Club, February 26, 1885, by Robert Hoe.

10 x 8; [6], 36, [2]p., 63 plates reproduced by the Bierstadt process; 200 copies on Holland paper; cream-colored boards with matching linen spine and corners, top edge gilt. $7.50.

*Printed by the De Vinne Press.* 1886

5   Historic Printing Types: A Lecture Read before The Grolier Club of New-York, January 25, 1885, with Additions and New Illustrations, by Theo. L. De Vinne.

10 x 8; [2], 110, [1]p.; illustrated with type facsimiles throughout text; 200 copies (190 for subscription) on Holland paper, 2 copies on vellum; cream-colored boards with matching linen spine and corners. $3.00.

*Printed by the De Vinne Press.* 1886

6   Peg Woffington, by Charles Reade.

2 volumes, 7 x 4½; vol. 1: [10], 183p.; vol. 2: [6], 220, [2]p.; 250 copies on Holland paper, 2 copies on vellum; white linen gilt-stamped with an overall leaf and flower pattern; endpapers printed with a design of lace. $4.50.

*Printed by the De Vinne Press.* 1887

Decorations and initials, in the style of the early 18th century, designed by Charles M. Jenckes.

7   Christopher Plantin and the Plantin-Moretus Museum at Antwerp, by Theo. L. De Vinne, with Illustrations by Joseph Pennell and Others.

10 x 7; 98, [1]p.; 300 copies on paper, 3 on vellum; wrappers printed with a facsimile of a Plantin title-page in black and red. $2.50.

*Printed by the De Vinne Press.* 1888

8   Ricardi de Bury: Philobiblon ex Optimis Codicibus Recensuit Versione Anglica Necnon et Prolegomenis Adnotationibusque Auxit An-

dreas Fleming West in Collegio Princetoniae Professor, Pars Prima Textus.

[Vol. 2]: The Philobiblon of Richard de Bury: Edited From the Best Manuscripts and Translated into English with an Introduction and Notes by Andrew Fleming West, Professor in Princeton College. Part Second, English Version.

[Vol. 3: title as in vol. 2]: Part Third, Introductory Matter and Notes.

3 volumes, $7\frac{5}{8}$ x 6; vol. 1: 130, [2]p.; vol. 2: 145, [2]p.; vol. 3: 173, [1]p.; frontispieces and plates; black-letter type specially cast for vol. 1, printed in black, red, and gold; 297 sets on L. L. Brown paper, 3 sets on vellum; bound by William Matthews in parchment, with de Bury's seal in gold on the upper covers, endpapers printed in a black, red, and gold diaper pattern. $25.00.
*Printed by the De Vinne Press.*                                  1889

9   Modern Bookbinding Practically Considered: A Lecture Read Before The Grolier Club of New-York, March 25, 1885, with Additions and New Illustrations, by William Matthews.

10 x 8; [2], 96p.; frontispiece, decorations, and 8 plates of facsimiles printed in color; 300 copies on Holland paper, 3 copies on vellum; cream-colored cloth with the Club arms gilt-stamped on the upper board, top edge gilt. $3.50.
*Printed by the De Vinne Press.*                                  1889

10  Areopagitica: A Speech of Mr. John Milton for the Liberty of Unlicensed Printing to the Parliament of England, with an Introduction by James Russell Lowell.

$6\frac{1}{2}$ x $4\frac{1}{2}$; lvii, [3], 189, [1]p.; frontispiece portrait, etched by G. Mercier after an engraving by Faithorne, and facsimiles; 325 copies on Holland paper, 3 copies on vellum; blue boards with printed spine label. $6.00.
*Printed by the De Vinne Press.*                                  1890

11  Aldus in His Printing Establishment at Venice Showing Grolier Some Bookbindings. An Etching by Léopold Flameng.

Plate: 18 x $18\frac{7}{8}$; image: 14 x $15\frac{3}{4}$; 300 copies on Japan paper, 3 on vellum; signed by the painter and the etcher. $10.00.

*Printed by Salmon of Paris.*                                      1891
The etching is made after the painting by François Flameng, presented
to the Club by Samuel Putnam Avery.

12  Washington Irving: A Sketch, by George William Curtis.

9 x 6; [8], 115, [2]p.; 2 wood-engravings by Richard G. Tietze of Matilda
Hoffman and Washington Irving, one line drawing of the Cockloft Hall
Summer House by Arthur B. Davies from a watercolor by W. E. McDougall; 344 copies on hand-made paper, 3 copies on vellum; bound under the
supervision of William Matthews in full red morocco with Club arms gilt-
stamped on upper board. $8.00.
*Printed by the De Vinne Press.*                                   1891

13  Effigies of the Most Famous English Writers from Chaucer to Johnson.

9 x 6; 78p.; two portraits reproduced by Edward Bierstadt: Ben Jonson as
engraved by Vaughan and Thomas Killigrew as engraved by Faithorne; 200
copies on hand-made paper; cream-colored wrappers with title printed in red
and black. $2.00.
*Printed by the De Vinne Press.*                                   1891
A large-paper printing of Exhibition Handlist no. 14, with additions and
corrections.

14  Barons of the Potomack and the Rappahannock, by Moncure Daniel
Conway.

9 x 6¼; xvii, [1], 290, [2]p.; frontispiece, 6 plates, 3 facsimiles; types imitating
those used by the Elzevirs of Leyden; 360 copies on Italian hand-made paper
with watermarks of the Grolier Club arms and name, 3 copies on vellum;
light blue-green Lallanne paper boards with Fairfax family arms gilt-stamped
on both boards. $10.00.
*Printed by the De Vinne Press.*                                   1892

15  Catalogue of An Exhibition of Illuminated and Painted Manuscripts,
Together with a Few Early Printed Books with Illuminations—Also
Some Examples of Persian Manuscripts—With Plates in Facsimile
and an Introductory Essay.

9 x 6¾; xxxiii, [1], 64p.; frontispiece and 21 plates reproduced by the Bier-

stadt process; 350 copies on Holland paper; olive green cloth with title and Club arms gilt-stamped on upper cover. $5.00.

*Printed by the De Vinne Press.*                                                           1892

16  Catalogue of Original and Early Editions of Some of the Poetical and Prose Works of English Writers from Langland to Wither, with Collations & Notes, & Eighty-seven Facsimiles of Title-pages and Frontispieces, Being a Contribution to the Bibliography of English Literature.

$9\frac{3}{4}$ x $6\frac{7}{8}$; xiii, [1], 240, [1]p.; 10 plates of facsimiles reproduced by the Bierstadt process, plus additional facsimiles in text; 400 copies on Van Gelder hand-made paper, 3 copies on vellum; light brown linen sides with reddish brown leather spine, Club arms gilt-stamped on both boards. $10.00.

*Printed by the De Vinne Press.*                                                           1893

A completely revised and expanded version of Exhibition Handlist no. 20.

17  Facsimile of the Laws and Acts of the General Assembly for their Majesties Province of New-York, Etc., Etc., at New-York, Printed and Sold by William Bradford, Printer to their Majesties King William and Queen Mary, 1694: Together with an Historical Introduction, Notes on the Laws, and Appendices, by Robert Ludlow Fowler, Counsellor-at-Law.

$11\frac{3}{4}$ x $7\frac{3}{4}$; [12], clxiii, [1]p.; [4], 84, 3, [1], 4, [6], 11, [2]p. in facsimile; 3 headpieces and a plate (showing William Bradford's tomb) etched by Max Rosenthal; 312 copies on English hand-made paper imitating the original, 3 copies on vellum; limp white vellum binding with the royal arms blind-stamped on the sides. $15.00.

*Printed by the De Vinne Press.*                                                           1894

Includes a bibliographical note on the first edition by Charles R. Hildeburn.

18  A Classified List of Early American Book-plates, with a Brief Description of the Principal Styles and a Note as to the Prominent Engravers, by Charles Dexter Allen.

9 x $6\frac{1}{4}$; 88p. including frontispiece and 26 plates; 350 copies on Italian hand-made paper with watermarks of the Grolier Club arms and name, 3 copies on vellum; gray wrappers with title printed in black and red. $1.50.

*Printed by the De Vinne Press.*      1894

A large-paper printing of Exhibition Handlist no. 24 with additional material.

19    The Catalogue of Books from the Libraries or Collections of Celebrated Bibliophiles and Illustrious Persons of the Past with Arms or Devices upon the Bindings, Exhibited at The Grolier Club in the Month of January 1895.

$9\frac{3}{8}$ x $6\frac{7}{8}$; xiii, 75, [2]p.; frontispiece and 23 plates; type pages within ruled lines; 350 copies on Holland paper, 3 copies on vellum; dark greenish blue cloth gilt-stamped with title and Club arms on upper cover. $4.50.

*Printed by the De Vinne Press.*      1895

20    Catalogue of the Engraved Work of Asher B. Durand.

9 x 6; [2], 103, [1]p.; frontispiece portrait and 1 plate; 350 copies on Van Gelder paper; cream-colored wrappers. $2.00.

*Printed by the Gilliss Press.*      1895

A large-paper issue of Exhibition Handlist no. 27; introduction by Charles Henry Hart.

21    A Description of the Early Printed Books Owned by The Grolier Club, with a Brief Account of Their Printers and the History of Typography in the Fifteenth Century.

$11\frac{3}{4}$ x $7\frac{3}{4}$; 77, [1]p.; frontispiece, facsimiles, and decorations; 400 copies on English hand-made paper, 3 copies on vellum; tan cloth with brown calf spine. $5.00.

*Printed by the De Vinne Press.*      1895

A large-paper edition of Exhibition Handlist no. 25 with the addition of facsimiles and translations of their texts by Dr. Nelson Glenn McCrea of Columbia College.

22    The Poems of John Donne, from the Text of the Edition of 1633 Revised by James Russell Lowell, with the Various Readings of the Other Editions of the Seventeenth Century, and with a Preface, and Introduction, and Notes by Charles Eliot Norton.

2 volumes, $6\frac{7}{8}$ x $4\frac{3}{8}$; vol. 1: xxxviii, [2], 253, [3]p.; vol. 2: x, [2], 282,

[6]p.; frontispiece portraits; Scotch types; 380 copies on German hand-made paper, 3 copies on vellum; grayish green cloth gilt-stamped with Donne's arms on both covers. $12.00.

*Printed by the De Vinne Press.* 1895

23 Catalogue of an Exhibition Illustrative of a Centenary of Artistic Lithography, 1796–1896: with 244 Examples by 160 Different Artists. Illustrated with 20 Photo-engravings, from the Originals by Bonington, Cassatt, Chauvel, Daumier, Decamps, Engelmann, Fantin-Latour, Gavarni, Hanfstaengl, Homer, Jacque, Jacob, Millet, Newsam, Otis, Prout, Raffet, Vernet, and Wagenbauer.

9 x 6¼; [2], 83, [2]p.; frontispiece portrait and 22 leaves of plates; 400 copies on Italian hand-made paper with watermarks of the Club name and arms, 3 copies on vellum; printed gray wrappers. $2.50.

*Printed by the De Vinne Press.* 1896

A large-paper edition of Exhibition Handlist no. 29, with additional entries and illustrations.

24 The Charles Whittinghams Printers, by Arthur Warren.

9¾ x 6⅞; [6], vi, 353, [2]p.; frontispiece portrait, plates, and facsimiles; 385 copies on specially made French hand-made paper, 3 copies on vellum; dark green morocco spine with light green boards printed with the Whittingham device. $16.00.

*Printed by the De Vinne Press.* 1896

25 A Chronological Catalogue of the Engravings, Dry-Points and Etchings of Albert Dürer, as Exhibited at The Grolier Club, Compiled by S. R. Koehler.

12¼ x 9; [10], lxi, [3], 103, [1]p.; 5 photogravures, 1 artotype, and 1 illustration in text; 400 copies on Van Gelder hand-made paper; bluish green cloth gilt-stamped with a facsimile of Dürer's initials on both covers. $10.00.

*Printed by the De Vinne Press.* 1897

26 Two Note Books of Thomas Carlyle, from 23d March 1822 to 16th May 1832, Edited by Charles Eliot Norton.

8 x 5; [6], xiii, [1], 304, [1]p.; portraits and facsimiles; 387 copies on special

hand-made Holland paper, 3 copies on vellum; brown morocco spine and corners, with green paper sides blind-stamped with a stylized thistle, top edge gilt. $5.00.
*Printed by the De Vinne Press.*                                    1898

27  Portrait of Benjamin Franklin, An Etching by Henri Lefort.
Plate: 20½ x 15⅜; image: 16⅛ x 12¼; 387 copies on Japan paper, 4 copies on vellum. $10.00.                                    1898
The etching is taken from the painting by J. S. Duplessis.

28  The Life of Charles Henry Count Hoym, Ambassador from Saxony-Poland to France and Eminent French Bibliophile, 1694–1736, Written by Baron Jérôme Pichon for the Society of French Bibliophiles and Translated into English for the Grolier Club, with a Sketch of the Life of the Late Baron Pichon.
10¾ x 7; 309, [1]p.; 2 portraits, 8 plates, initials, and decorations; 303 copies on French hand-made paper watermarked "Grolier," 3 copies on vellum; orange brocaded silk sides with maroon morocco spine and corners. $16.00.
*Printed by the De Vinne Press.*                                    1899

29  A Translation of Giovanni Boccaccio's Life of Dante, with an Introduction and a Note on the Portraits of Dante by G. R. Carpenter.
8½ x 6¾; 186, [1]p.; frontispiece portrait, 1 folded plate, decorations and initials; Renner type; 300 copies on Italian hand-made paper watermarked "Grolier," 3 copies on vellum; full vellum over boards, embossed with a design on orange ground (signed "EE") by E. B. Edwards, Jr., decorative printed endpapers matching color of cover. $10.00.
*Printed by the De Vinne Press.*                                    1900

30  Catalogue of an Exhibition of First and Other Editions of the Works of John Dryden (1631–1700), Together with a Few Engraved Portraits and Two Oil Paintings—Commemorative of the Two Hundredth Anniversary of His Death.
9 x 6; [2], 101p.; frontispiece portrait: photogravure after Kneller; 200 copies on Van Gelder hand-made paper; gray boards gilt-stamped with title, red leather spine label. $2.00.

*Printed by the De Vinne Press.* 1900

A large-paper printing of Exhibition Handlist no. 42 with additions. The original oil portrait on which the frontispiece is based was bequeathed to the Grolier Club by Beverly Chew in 1924 in the belief that it represented Dryden by Kneller. It has been reattributed to the Restoration painter Mary Beale and the sitter identified as her husband Charles.

31 Catalogue of Etchings and Dry Points by Rembrandt, Selected for Exhibition at the Grolier Club of the City of New York April–May 1900.

9 x 6¾; 49, [1]p.; frontispiece portrait; 310 copies (25 reserved) on Van Gelder hand-made paper; maroon cloth with Club arms and title gilt-stamped on upper cover. $1.50.
*Printed by the De Vinne Press.* 1900

32 Framed Paintings, Water-colors, and Prints.

9½ x 7; pp. 57–68, [1]; cream-colored printed wrappers.
*Printed by the Gilliss Press.* 1900
An offprint from the *Transactions*, Part III, 1899, with a special title page, listing framed pictures hanging in the clubhouse at this date.

33 Title-Pages as Seen by a Printer, with Numerous Illustrations in Facsimile and Some Observations on the Early and Recent Printing of Books, by Theodore Low De Vinne.

9½ x 6½; xix, [1], 370, [1]p.; about 300 facsimiles, some in color, plus decorations and initials; Renner type; 325 copies (14 reserved) on Fabriano hand-made paper; red straight-grain morocco spine and corners, gray boards with the Club arms stamped in dark green. $18.00.
*Printed by the De Vinne Press.* 1901

34 Catalogue of an Exhibition of Selected Works of the Poets Laureate of England.

9 x 6; xix, 81p.; frontispiece portrait: mezzotint of Ben Jonson engraved by A. Arlent Edwards after the painting then attributed to Honthorst; 300 copies on Van Gelder hand-made paper; gray boards, gilt-stamped with title, red leather spine label. $2.50.

*Printed by the De Vinne Press.*
A large-paper printing of Exhibition Handlist no. 44.

35   The History of Helyas, Knight of the Swan, Translated by Robert Copland from the French Version Published in Paris in 1504: A Literal Reprint in the Types of Wynkin de Worde after the Unique Copy Printed by Him upon Parchment in London, MCCCCCXII.

$8\frac{7}{8}$ x $6\frac{3}{4}$; xviiip., [150]p. in facsimile; 325 copies (14 reserved) on Whatman hand-made paper, 3 copies on vellum; full pigskin stamped in brown with facsimile taken from the final leaf displaying the devices of William Caxton and Wynkyn de Worde on both covers, brass clasps with the Caxton device; chemise backed with brown pigskin, leather slipcase stamped as the covers. $20.00.

> *Printed by the De Vinne Press.*                    1901
> Includes a Historical Preface by Robert Hoe, then owner of the original. The type was specially made by Sir Charles Reed's Sons, after the original font by de Worde.

36   A Tentative Scheme of Classification for the Library of the Grolier Club.

$6\frac{5}{8}$ x 4; 20p.; light brownish gray printed wrappers.
> *Printed by the Gilliss Press.*                    1901
> An offprint from the *Yearbook* for 1901, with a special title page. See also Publication no. 51. The scheme was devised by Henry Watson Kent and Richard Hoe Lawrence.

37   One Hundred Books Famous in English Literature, with Facsimiles of the Title-pages and an Introduction by George E. Woodberry.

$10\frac{3}{4}$ x 7; lii, 200, [2]p. including 100 facsimiles; 305 copies (6 reserved) on French hand-made paper watermarked "Grolier," 3 copies on vellum; blue hand-made paper over boards with vellum spine and tips. $17.00.
> *Printed by the De Vinne Press.*                    1902

38   Bibliographical Notes on One Hundred Books Famous in English Literature, Compiled by Henry W. Kent.

$10\frac{3}{4}$ x 7; xxii, 227, [1]p.; 305 copies (6 reserved) on French hand-made paper watermarked "Grolier," 3 copies on vellum; blue hand-made paper over boards with vellum spine and tips. $13.00.

*Printed by the De Vinne Press.* 1903

39 Catalogue of the Engraved Portraits of Washington, by Charles Henry Hart.

12 x 9; xxv, [1], 406, [1]p.; frontispiece portrait and 20 plates; 425 copies (14 reserved) on American hand-made paper with a watermark of the Club initials; blue boards gilt-stamped with the Club arms, with vellum spine and tips; blue dust jacket with paper label, slipcase covered in blue paper. $25.00.

*Printed by the De Vinne Press.* 1904

Three copies were accompanied by portfolios containing separate impressions of the photogravure plates on India paper, and an impression of the mezzotint frontispiece portrait in color.

40 Catalogue of an Exhibition of Original and Early Editions of Italian Books Selected from a Collection Designed to Illustrate the Development of Italian Literature.

9¼ x 6; xxxvi, 99, [1]p. including 20 facsimiles of title pages; 306 copies (6 reserved) on Van Gelder hand-made paper; gray boards gilt-stamped with title, red leather spine label. $2.50.

*Printed by the De Vinne Press.* 1904

A large-paper printing of Exhibition Handlist no. 48; includes text of an address by F. Marion Crawford.

41 The Boston Port Bill as Pictured by a Contemporary London Cartoonist, by R. T. H. Halsey.

10¼ x 6½; xxix, [1], 333, [1]p.; including frontispiece portrait, 10 plates, and decorations; 325 copies (12 reserved) on American hand-made paper with a watermark of the Club arms, 3 copies on vellum; gilt-stamped full calf; dust jacket with spine printed in gold. $30.00.

*Printed by the Gilliss Press.* 1904

42 Catalogue of Original and Early Editions of Some of the Poetical and Prose Works of English Writers from Wither to Prior, with Colla-

tions, Notes, and More than Two Hundred Facsimiles of Title-pages and Frontispieces.

3 volumes, 9¾ x 6⅞; vol. 1: xiii, [1], 271, [1]p.; vol. 2: ix, [1], 249, [1]p.; vol. 3: ix, [1], 335, [1]p.; 400 sets on Holland paper, 3 sets on vellum; brown linen covers gilt-stamped with the Club arms, reddish brown morocco spine. $30.00.

*Printed by the De Vinne Press.* 1905

43  First Editions of the Works of Nathaniel Hawthorne, Together with Some Manuscripts, Letters, and Portraits: Exhibited at The Grolier Club from December 8 to December 24, 1904, with Frontispiece Portraits, Additions to Text, and Index.

9 x 6; xi, [1], 77, [1]p.; frontispiece portrait (in 3 states) and 1 plate; 40 copies on Van Gelder hand-made paper; dark gray boards gilt-stamped with title, red leather spine label.

*Printed by the De Vinne Press.* 1905

A large-paper printing of Exhibition Handlist no. 52, with additions, privately printed for the author, J. C. Chamberlain, over the Club's imprint.

44  The Grolier Club of the City of New York, Lists of Publications, 1884–1905, Exhibition Catalogues, 1886–1905.

6¾ x 4⅛; pp. [2], 107–165, [2]; light brownish gray printed wrappers.

*Printed by the Gilliss Press.* 1906

An offprint from the *Yearbook* for 1906, with a special title page.

45  American Engravers Upon Copper and Steel, by David McNeely Stauffer. Part I: Biographical Sketches, Illustrated; Part II: Check-list of the Works of the Earlier Engravers.

2 volumes, 9½ x 6¼; vol. 1: [2], xxxi, [1], 391, [1]p., 43 plates; vol. 2: x, 566, [1]p.; 350 sets (27 reserved) on specially made imported mold-made paper, 3 sets on Imperial Japan paper; dark gray-green boards printed with the Club arms, gray buckram spine, green leather spine labels; chemise for each volume covered in dark gray-green paper with red leather spine labels; slipcase. $18.00.

*Printed by the De Vinne Press.* 1907

46   Researches Concerning Jean Grolier, His Life and His Library, with a
Partial Catalogue of His Books, by A.-J.-V. Le Roux de Lincy,
Edited by Baron Roger Portalis, Translated and Revised by Carolyn
Shipman.

11½ x 8¼; xlv, [1], 386, [1]p., 14 plates; 300 copies (3 reserved) on Arnold
unbleached hand-made paper, 3 copies on Imperial Japan paper; cream-
colored boards with blue morocco spine and corners.
*Printed by the De Vinne Press.*                                           1907
The plates were printed in Paris by the firm of Léopold Carteret.

47   The Grolier Club of the City of New York, List of Books and Articles Relating to Bookbinding to be Found in the Library.

6⅝ x 4; pp.[4], 117–184, [1]; light brownish gray wrappers.
*Printed by the Gilliss Press.*                                            1907
An offprint from the *Yearbook* for 1907, with a special title page.

48   The Scarlet Letter, by Nathaniel Hawthorne, Illustrated by George
H. Boughton.

11 x 7½; [10], 325, [1]p.; 13 plates (each in two states: color and black-and-
white); 300 copies on French hand-made paper with a watermark of the
Club arms, 3 copies on Imperial Japan paper; cream-colored boards, embossed
with a letter "A" in scarlet and gold on upper board, brown linen spine.
$50.00.
*Printed by the De Vinne Press.*                                           1908
Includes the preface to the second edition. The plates were printed in
Paris by the firm of Léopold Carteret.

49   The Etched Work of Whistler, Illustrated by Reproductions in Col-
lotype of the Different States of the Plates, Compiled, Arranged and
Described by Edward G. Kennedy, with an Introduction by Royal
Cortissoz.

3 portfolios and 1 volume of text; text volume: 12¼ x 9; xxxvii, [1], 167,
[1]p.; portfolio mounts: 14⅞ x 12; over 1000 reproductions on 495 mounts;
402 sets on Old Stratford paper, 2 sets on Italian hand-made paper; brown
boards gilt-stamped with the Club arms, brown linen spine (text volume).
$75.00 by subscription, $100.00 after publication.

*Printed by the De Vinne Press.*                                  1910
An additional plate was discovered, reproduced, and sent to subscribers
after publication. See also Publications nos. 57, 71, 75 for Additions.

50   Notable Printers of Italy During the Fifteenth Century, Illustrated
with Facsimiles from Early Editions and with Remarks on Early and
Recent Printing, by Theodore Low De Vinne.

12½ x 9½; [4], 210, [1]p. including 41 facsimiles; 397 copies (97 reserved for
the author) on American paper, 3 copies on Imperial Japan paper; cream-
colored boards gilt-stamped with the title and Club arms on upper board,
brown linen spine. $15.00.
*Printed by the De Vinne Press.*                                  1910

51   The Classification Used in the Library of the Grolier Club.

6⅝ x 4; pp. [4], 125–145, [1]; brownish gray printed wrappers.
*Printed by the Gilliss Press.*                                   1910
An offprint from the *Yearbook* for 1910, with a special title page; a
revised version of the *Tentative Scheme* (Publication no. 36).

52   Depositio Cornuti Typographici: That Is, A Comical or Mirthful
Play Which Can Be Performed Without Any Offence, at the Recep-
tion and Confirmation of a Journeyman Who Has Learned Honestly
the Noble Art of Book-Printing, and by Means of Which Also in
Future Times Young Men Can Be Named, Confirmed, and Received
as Journeymen Printers, at the End of Their Apprenticeship, Written
in Good Faith in Compliance with Friendly Request and Particular
Desire, Likewise to the Imperishable Honour of the High and Greatly
Renowned Art of Book-Printing, by John Rist, Originally Printed at
Lüneburg: Reprinted as Acted at The Grolier Club, January 28,
1909.

9⅛ x 5⅞; vii, [1], 34, [3]p.; Caslon type; 250 copies on Glaslan paper;
brownish gray boards with green cloth spine. $5.00 (sold with no. 53 below).
*Printed by Daniel Berkeley Updike at the Merrymount Press.*       1911

53   Reading a Poem, by Wm. Makepeace Thackeray.

9⅛ x 5⅞; ix, [1], 48, [3]p.; decorations after sketches by Thackeray, redrawn by W. A. Dwiggins; Scotch type; 250 copies; gray boards with blue cloth spine. $5.00 (sold with no. 52 above).

*Title page and colophon designed by W. A. Dwiggins, printed by Daniel Berkeley Updike at the Merrymount Press.* 1911

This play was performed by members of the Grolier Club at the Annual Meeting held 27 January 1910.

54  A Catalogue of the First Editions of the Works of Alexander Pope (1688–1744), Together with a Collection of the Engraved Portraits of the Poet and of His Friends.

9 x 6; [2], vii, [1], 85p.; frontispiece portrait, 3 plates, and 2 leaves in facsimile; 200 copies on Van Gelder hand-made paper; gray boards gilt-stamped with title, red leather spine label. $3.00.

*Printed by the De Vinne Press.* 1911

A large-paper printing of Exhibition Handlist no. 69 with illustrations added.

55  A Short List of Microscopic Books in the Library of The Grolier Club, Mostly Presented by Samuel P. Avery.

6⅝ x 4; pp. [4], 121–151, [1]; brownish gray printed wrappers.
*Printed by the Gilliss Press.* 1911

An offprint from the *Yearbook* for 1911, with a special title page.

56  Catalogue of an Exhibition Commemorating the Hundredth Anniversary of the Birth of William Makepeace Thackeray (1811–1863).

9 x 6; xii, 141, [1]p. including 10 plates, frontispiece portrait; 260 copies on Van Gelder hand-made paper; gray boards gilt-stamped with title, red leather spine label. $4.00.

*Printed by the De Vinne Press.* 1912

A large-paper printing of Exhibition Handlist no. 71 with illustrations, introduction, and index.

57  A Series of Six Reproductions of Additional States of Whistler's Etchings Supplementing the Club's Catalogue and Reproductions of

the Etched Work of Whistler, Compiled and Described by Edward
G. Kennedy.                                                                    1912

> Issued with descriptive text only to the subscribers of the original set
> (no. 49). See also Publications nos. 71, 75. $2.00.

58  The Writers of Knickerbocker New York, by Hamilton Wright
Mabie, Illustrations Engraved by Walworth Stilson.

7¼ x 4⅜; vii, [1], 121p.; 300 copies on French hand-made paper, 3 copies on
roman vellum; green cloth blind-stamped on both covers with an oval frame
of leaves and scrolls and the Grolier arms in the center; all edges gilt. $8.00.
*Printed by the De Vinne Press.*                                              1912

59  Catalogue of an Exhibition of the Works of Charles Dickens, with
an Introduction by Royal Cortissoz.

9 x 6; xxvi, 230, [1]p.; 9 reproductions, including a color frontispiece portrait; 300 copies on Van Gelder hand-made paper; gray boards gilt-stamped
with title, red leather spine label. $5.00.
*Printed by the De Vinne Press.*                                             1913
A large-paper printing of Exhibition Handlist no. 73 with revisions,
introduction, and index.

60  Baziliωlogia: A Booke of Kings, Notes on a Rare Series of Engraved
English Royal Portraits from William the Conquerer to James I,
Published Under the Above Title in 1618 by H. C. Levis.

10½ x 8; [1], xviii, 188, [1]p.; 68 portraits and facsimiles; 300 copies on
Japan vellum; cream-colored boards with tan cloth spine and printed paper
spine label. $10.00.
*Printed by the Chiswick Press.*                                             1913

61  Catalogue of an Exhibition of Works by John Leech (1817–1864),
Held at The Grolier Club from January 22 until March 8, 1914, with
an Introduction by Stanley Kidder Wilson.

9 x 6; xxii, [2], 187, [1]p.; color frontispiece portrait and 2 facsimiles; 240
copies on Van Gelder hand-made paper; gray boards gilt-stamped with title,
red leather spine label. $5.00.
*Printed by the De Vinne Press.*                                             1914

62 Franklin and His Press at Passy: An Account of the Books, Pamphlets, and Leaflets Printed There, Including the Long-lost "Bagatelles," by Luther S. Livingston.

9¼ x 6¼; xii, [2], 216, [1]p.; frontispiece portrait, 44 facsimiles and type specimens; Fry, Brimmer, and Oxford types, some cast from the original matrices; 300 copies on Van Gelder hand-made paper, 3 copies on Alton Mill hand-made paper (with the frontispiece in a different state); marbled boards with dark blue cloth spine; slipcase covered in dark blue cloth. $18.00.

*Designed by Bruce Rogers, printed by the Riverside Press.* 1914

63 First Editions of the Works of Robert Louis Stevenson, 1850–1894, and Other Stevensoniana Exhibited at The Grolier Club from November 5 to November 28, 1914.

9 x 6; xxiii, [5], 87p.; color frontispiece and 4 facsimiles; 180 copies on Van Gelder hand-made paper; gray boards gilt-stamped with title, red leather spine label. $5.00.

*Printed by the De Vinne Press.* 1915

A large-paper printing of Exhibition Handlist no. 74 with introduction, addenda, and index.

64 New York: A Series of Wood Engravings in Colour and a Note on Colour Printing by Rudolph Ruzicka, with Prose Impressions of the City by Walter Prichard Eaton.

11¼ x 7½; xxi, [1], 120, [1]p.; 10 full-page illustrations and 20 head- and tail-pieces, all in color; 250 copies on French hand-made paper, 3 copies on Imperial Japan paper with progressive states of the engravings in folding cases; blue boards with cream-colored cloth spine and dark blue leather spine label. $25.00.

*Printed by the De Vinne Press.* 1915

The full-page illustrations were printed in Paris by the firm of Emile Fequet.

65 Wood-Engraving: Three Essays, by A. V. S. Anthony, Timothy Cole, and Elbridge Kingsley, with a List of American Books Illustrated with Woodcuts.

9 x 5¾; [10], 84, [1]p.; 260 copies (10 copies reserved); cream-colored wrappers. $3.00.

> *Printed by the Gilliss Press.*                                                1916
> The list of books, compiled by Ruth S. Granniss, is of an exhibition held at The Grolier Club, April 8 – May 8, 1915.

66    Catalogue of an Exhibition Illustrative of the Text of Shakespeare's Plays, as Published in Edited Editions, Together with a Large Collection of Engraved Portraits of the Poet.

9 x 6; xiv, 115, [1]p.; 25 halftone portraits; 207 copies (7 reserved) on Van Gelder hand-made paper; gray boards gilt-stamped with title, red leather spine label. $5.00.

> *Printed by the De Vinne Press.*                                              1916
> A large-paper printing of Exhibition Handlist no. 75 with additional entries.

67    A Catalogue of Books Illustrated by Thomas Rowlandson, Together with a Collection of Original Drawings by Him Exhibited at the Grolier Club, in November 1916.

9 x 6; xx, 124, [1]p.; title vignette and 4 reproductions in color; 200 copies on Van Gelder hand-made paper; pinkish boards with a green paper spine label. $6.00.

> *Printed by the De Vinne Press.*                                             1916
> A large-paper printing of Exhibition Handlist no. 76 with 67 additional entries and an appendix.

68    A Catalogue of Books in First Editions Selected to Illustrate the History of English Prose Fiction from 1485 to 1870.

9 x 6; xix, [1], 149, [2]p.; 32p. of plates; 250 copies on French hand-made paper; light brown boards blind-stamped with Club arms, brown leather spine label. $6.00.

> *Printed by the De Vinne Press.*                                             1917
> A large-paper printing of Exhibition Handlist no. 77 with the addition of illustrations.

136    69    List of Publications and Exhibition Catalogues, 1884–1916.

7⅝ x 4¾; [8], 88, [1]p.; 1000 copies; blue printed wrappers.
*Printed by the Gilliss Press.*
An offprint from the *Yearbook* for 1917, with a special title page.

1917

70   Of the Just Shaping of Letters: From the Applied Geometry of Albrecht Dürer, Book III.

12¼ x 8½; [4], 40, [4]p.; facsimiles reproduced from the first edition of 1525; Centaur type; 215 copies on Kelmscott hand-made paper; 145 copies in marbled paper boards with vellum spines; 70 copies in brown butcher paper boards with vellum spines; 3 copies on vellum, full niger morocco. $12.00.
*Designed by Bruce Rogers, printed under his personal supervision at the Mall Press of Emery Walker and Wilfred Merton, Hammersmith, London.* 1917
This version by R. T. Nichol is the first published English translation.

71   Second Set of Additions to The Grolier Club's Catalogue and Reproductions of the Etched Work of Whistler, Compiled and Described by Edward G. Kennedy.

Descriptive text and 4 reproductions; also includes descriptions of 4 additional states not reproduced.                                                           1919
See also Publications nos. 49, 57, 75.

72   Notes and Journal of Travel in Europe, 1804–1805, by Washington Irving, with an Introduction by William P. Trent, and Title-page and Illustrations in Aquatint Designed and Engraved by Rudolph Ruzicka.

3 volumes, 6⅞ x 4¼; vol. 1: xliv, 167p.; vol. 2: [8], 188p.; vol. 3: [8], 199, [1]p.; Oxford type; 257 copies (7 reserved) on rag paper, 3 copies on Japan vellum; dark blue cloth with a gilt border of leaves on covers and gilt bands on spines, top edges gilt. $30.00.
*Printed by Daniel Berkeley Updike at the Merrymount Press.*          1921

73   A Bibliography of William Blake, by Geoffrey Keynes.
10⅞ x 8¾; xvi, 516, [1]p.; 44 illustrations, including 4 color lithographs; 250 copies (25 for the author) on specially made paper; dark blue cloth with morocco spine, top edge gilt. $50.00.
*Printed by the Chiswick Press.*                                           1921   137

74 Quattrocentisteria: How Sandro Botticelli Saw Simonetta in the
Spring, by Maurice Hewlett.

12 x 8½; [4], v, [1], 19p.; Cloister Old Style type made especially for this
volume; 300 copies on special Van Gelder hand-made paper; Morris paper
boards (marbled) with light brown cloth spine and paper spine label.

*Designed and printed by John Henry Nash.* 1921
This is the first of six publications making up the Printer's Series. Each
one was the independent work of an American printer/designer whose
only restriction was the length of the work chosen and its cost of production. The six volumes sold as a group for $30.00. The other books in
the series are Publications nos. 77–81.

75 Third Set of Additions to The Grolier Club's Catalogue and Reproductions of the Etched Work of Whistler, Compiled and Described
by Edward G. Kennedy.

Descriptive text and 5 reproductions. $5.00. 1922
See also Publications nos. 49, 57, 71.

76 A Descriptive Catalogue of the First Editions in Book Form of the
Writings of Percy Bysshe Shelley, Based on a Memorial Exhibition
Held at The Grolier Club from April 20 to May 20, 1922, by Ruth
S. Granniss.

9 x 6¼; xx, 133, [1]p.; frontispiece and 29 facsimiles of manuscripts; 350
copies (50 reserved for presentation to libraries) on Van Gelder hand-made
paper; blue boards with paper spine label. $7.50.

*Printed by the Gilliss Press.* 1923

77 The Culprit Fay and Other Poems, by Joseph Rodman Drake.

9 x 5¾; xv, [1], 49, [1]p.; frontispiece portrait and 2 illustrations by Edward
Everett Winchell; Elzevir type; 300 copies on English hand-made paper;
light brown Japan paper boards with parchment paper spine.

*Printed by Walter Gilliss.* 1923
A volume in the Printer's Series. See note to Publication no. 74.

78 The Pierrot of the Minute, by Ernest Dowson.

7 x 4½; 49p.; Deberny Elsevir Ancien roman and italic types; text enclosed

in red-printed borders of ornaments after Fournier; 300 copies on Dutch
Antique paper; marbled boards with wraparound paper label; yellow slipcase
with spine label.

> *Designed by Bruce Rogers, printed by William Edwin Rudge.* 1923
> A volume in the Printer's Series. See note to Publication no. 74.

79 A Lodging for the Night: A Story of Mediæval Paris, by Robert
Louis Stevenson.

8 x 5¼; [6], 50p.; Caslon type; 300 copies on Worthy Aurelian (Mittineague)
paper; blue boards with red cloth spine and paper label.

> *Designed and printed by Carl Purington Rollins.* 1923
> A volume in the Printer's Series. See note to Publication no. 74.

80 The Compromise of the King of the Golden Isles, by Lord Dunsany.

11 x 8; 25, [1]p.; Garamond italic type; 300 hand-numbered copies on Eltham
hand-made paper; gold-sprinkled brown boards, black cloth spine.

> *Designed and printed by Thomas Maitland Cleland.* 1924
> A volume in the Printer's Series. See note to Publication no. 74.

81 Three Essays: I. Book-Buying, II. Book-Binding, III. The Office of
Literature, by Augustine Birrell.

11½ x 8¼; [4], xxvi, [1]p.; Goudy type; 300 copies on special paper with a
watermark of the Club arms; blue-gray boards with gray cloth spine.

> *Designed and printed by Frederic and Bertha Goudy.* 1924
> This volume was printed on the Albion hand press used by William
> Morris to print the Kelmscott Chaucer. A volume in the Printer's Series.
> See note to Publication no. 74.

82 A Descriptive Catalogue of an Exhibition of Japanese Figure Prints
from Moronobu to Toyokuni, by Louis V. Ledoux.

9 x 6; xiv, 89, [1]p.; color frontispiece and 28 plates; 300 copies on Van Gelder
hand-made paper; gold-flecked cream-colored boards with paper spine label.
$15.00 (sold with no. 83 below).

> *Printed by the Gilliss Press.* 1924
> An illustrated edition (reset) of Exhibition Handlist no. 83.

83  A Descriptive Catalogue of an Exhibition of Japanese Landscape, Bird, and Flower Prints, and Surimono from Hokusai to Kyōsai, by Louis V. Ledoux.

9 x 6; xii, 93, [1]p.; color frontispiece and 12 plates; 300 copies on Van Gelder hand-made paper; gold-flecked tan boards with paper spine label. $15.00 (sold with no. 82 above).
*Printed by the Gilliss Press.*                                        1924

84  A Dissertation Upon English Typographical Founders and Founderies, by Edward Rowe Mores with Appendix by John Nichols, &c. &c., Edited by D. B. Updike.

9½ x 6; xl, [2], 103, [2]p.; portrait, facsimiles, and a fold-out pedigree chart; 250 copies on Vidalon paper; marbled cloth with paper spine label. $15.00.
*Printed by Daniel Berkeley Updike at the Merrymount Press.*       1924
Includes a ten-page memoir of Mores by Richard Gough.

85  The Grolier Club: The Library.

7 x 4½; 8p.; blue printed wrappers.                                    1925
Later given the series title: Library Pamphlet, no. 1.

86  Recollections of The Gilliss Press and Its Work During Fifty Years, 1869–1919, by Walter Gilliss.

9 x 5⅞; xx, [2], 134, [1]p.; frontispiece portrait, 12 plates, and 2 illustrations in text; 300 copies on Eltham hand-made paper; blue Ingres paper boards with dark blue French calf spine, top edge gilt. $7.50.
*Printed by the Country Life Press, Garden City, N.Y.*              1926

87  Gazette Française: A Facsimile Reprint of a Newspaper Printed at Newport on the Printing Press of the French Fleet in American Waters During the Revolutionary War, with an Introduction by Howard M. Chapin.

12½ x 8¼; 12, [4]p., 15p. in facsimile; 300 copies on Arches hand-made paper; cream-colored boards with blue cloth spine and paper spine label. $7.50.
*Printed by Douglas C. McMurtrie.*                                     1926

88 Belles-Lettres Repository: Devoted to Polite Literature, the Fine Arts, &c. Founded by Samuel Woodworth. Vol. II, no. 1, Saturday, May 29, 1926.

11½ x 8⅞; 4p.; 525 copies; issued unbound in stiff blue wrappers with paper label on cover. Sent to members of the Club, none for sale.

*Designed and printed by Carl Purington Rollins.* 1926
The *Belles-Lettres Repository* was a periodical published in New Haven, the only known copy of which is vol. I, no. 7, 1808. This "issue" of it is "printed as nearly as may be in the manner of the original." It includes a reprint of Ruth Shepard Granniss's essay "The New York Printers and the Celebration of the French Revolution of 1830" (which was her contribution to *Bibliographical Essays: A Tribute to Wilberforce Eames*) and a bibliography of Samuel Woodworth.

89 Notes on the American Press at the End of the Eighteenth Century, by Bernard Faÿ.

14¼ x 10¾; [10], 29p.; 26 full-sized facsimiles of newspapers, folded; Caslon Old Face type; 325 copies (5 for the author) on rag paper; green boards with paper labels on spine and upper board; slipcase. $16.50.
*Format and typesetting by Carl Purington Rollins at the Sign of the Chorobates.* 1927
A gift from Frank Altschul allowed 3 copies to be extra-illustrated with original 18th-century newspapers in cover pockets.

90 Champ Fleury, by Geofroy Tory, Translated into English and Annotated by George B. Ives.

12⅜ x 8½; [6], xxiii, [1], 208, [1]p.; reproductions of illustrations from the first edition of 1529; Centaur type; 390 copies on rag paper, 7 copies on larger hand-made paper; paste-paper boards with a diaper pattern of fleur-de-lys and thistles, vellum spine. $75.00.
*Designed by Bruce Rogers, printed by William Edwin Rudge.* 1927
Illustrations and diagrams redrawn by Bruce Rogers.

91 List of Publications and Exhibition Catalogues Issued by the Grolier Club, 1917–1927.

6⅝ x 4⅛; pp. 135–152.

*Printed by the Gilliss Press.*                                     1928
An offprint from the *Yearbook* for 1928, with the section title leaf serving
as cover title.

92  Catalogue of Work of the De Vinne Press: Exhibited at the Grolier
Club on the Occasion of the One Hundredth Anniversary of the
Birth of Theodore Low De Vinne, December 25, 1828, with Ad-
dresses by Ira Hutchinson Brainerd and John Clyde Oswald.

9½ x 6; xii, 89, [1]p.; frontispiece portrait and reproduction of the Typothetae Gold Medal; Garamond type; 300 copies (50 reserved for J. W. Bothwell) on Kinkora paper; brown flexible boards gilt-stamped with title. $7.50.
*Printed under the supervision of J. W. Bothwell by the A. W. Stevens
Printing Company, Brooklyn.*                                      1929

93  Catalogue of the Works of Rudyard Kipling Exhibited at The Grolier Club from February 21 to March 30, 1929.

9½ x 6¼; xi, [1], 201, [2]p.; frontispiece portrait and 34 collotype plates;
325 hand-numbered copies on Fabriano paper; light blue-gray Ingres paper
boards with Club arms gilt-stamped on upper board, light brown linen spine
with paper label, top edge gilt. $15.00.
*Printed by the Plimpton Press.*                                    1930

94  A Summary of the Work of Rudyard Kipling, Including Items As-
cribed to Him, Compiled by Lloyd H. Chandler.

9½ x 6¼; xxvii, [1], 465p.; 325 hand-numbered copies (50 reserved for the
author) on Milton white laid paper; light blue-gray Ingres paper boards with
Club arms gilt-stamped on upper board, light brown linen spine and paper
label, top edge gilt. $15.00.
*Printed by the Plimpton Press.*                                    1930

95  Catalogue of an Exhibition of the Private Papers of James Boswell
from Malahide Castle Held at the Grolier Club, New York, December Eighteenth, 1930 to February Seventh, 1931.

9¼ x 6¼; [218]p.; 600 copies; light brown wrappers.
*Printed by William Edwin Rudge.*                                  1930
Written by Frederick A. Pottle.

96   The Colonial Printer, by Lawrence C. Wroth.

10⅛ x 6¾; xvii, [1], 271, [2]p.; 15 plates, and tables in text; Mountjoye type; 300 copies on rag paper; marbled cloth sides with blue cloth spine, top edge gilt. $27.50.

*Designed and printed by Daniel Berkeley Updike at the Merrymount Press.*

1931

97   Book Decorations by Bertram Grosvenor Goodhue.

11 x 8½; [82]p.; frontispiece portrait and approximately 300 reproductions; Cheltenham type; 400 copies on unbleached Arnold hand-made paper; gray boards with white paper spine. $15.00.

*Designed by Ingalls Kimball at the Cheltenham Press, printed by William Edwin Rudge.*   1931

Introduction by Ingalls Kimball.

98   A List of Paintings and Prints Now Displayed on the Walls of The Grolier Club, Compiled by Edward G. Kennedy.

7 x 4½; 60p.; blue printed wrappers.
   *Printed by the Harbor Press.*   1931
Library Pamphlet no. 2.

99   The Study of Incunabula, by Konrad Haebler, Translated from the German by Lucy Eugenia Osborne, with a Foreword by Alfred W. Pollard.

9¼ x 6¼; xvi, [2], 241, [1]p.; 350 hand-numbered copies on antique wove rag paper; red cloth with Club arms gilt-stamped on upper board. $15.00.
   *Printed by the Harbor Press.*   1933

100   Fra Luca de Pacioli of Borgo S. Sepolcro, by Stanley Morison.

12¼ x 8¼; [2], vii, [3], 105, [1]p.; 390 copies on Batchelor's hand-made paper, Italian patterned paste-paper boards with vellum spine, top edge gilt, slipcase; 7 copies on large paper, full vellum. $25.00.

*Designed by Bruce Rogers, printed by the Cambridge University Press.* 1933

101   The Duchess of Portland's Museum, by Horace Walpole, With an Introduction by W. S. Lewis.

143

10 x 7; viii, 15, [2]p.; 3 illustrations; 450 copies on Rives Les Bibliophiles paper; light green boards printed with shells, green cloth spine. Published by the Club and Mr. Lewis as a gift to members (stated in a presentation slip laid in).

*Designed and printed by Edmund Burke Thompson at Hawthorn House.*

1936

No. 11 in Lewis's series of *Miscellaneous Antiquities*.

102   John Evelyn: A Study in Bibliophily & a Bibliography of His Writings, by Geoffrey Keynes.

10 x 7⅞; xvii, [3], 308, [2]p.; frontispiece portrait, 25 plates, and facsimiles; 300 copies on laid paper, of which 130 were for the Grolier Club; black cloth with Evelyn's mystic pentacle gilt-stamped on upper board, top edge gilt; blue-gray printed dust jacket. $15.00.

*Printed by Walter Lewis at the Cambridge University Press.*   1937

Jointly published with the Cambridge University Press; 170 copies have the Cambridge University Press imprint on the title page.

103   A Catalogue of an Exhibition of Renaissance Bookbindings, Held at The Grolier Club from December 17, 1936 to January 17, 1937, with an Address Delivered by Lucius Wilmerding.

8¾ x 5¾; 68p.; frontispiece and 15 collotype plates; 200 copies on rag paper; stiff tan printed wrappers. $2.00.

*Designed by Frederic Warde, printed by the Morrill Press.*   1937

104   Early American Sport: A Chronological Check-list of Books Published Prior to 1860, Based on an Exhibition Held at The Grolier Club, Compiled by Robert W. Henderson, with an Introduction by Harry T. Peters.

9¼ x 6; [4], xvii, [1], 134, [2]p.; illustrated title page and 12 collotype facsimiles; 400 copies on Archer paper; tan cloth with red leather labels on upper cover and spine. $5.00.

*Designed by John Fass, printed by the Harbor Press.*   1937

Title page illustration signed by Betty Babcock.

105   Daniel Berkeley Updike and the Merrymount Press.

8 x 5½; 47, [9]p.; reproductions and decorations; Linotype Fairfield type;

150 copies on machine-made paper; cream-colored boards with brown cloth spine; colophon signed by D. B. Updike. $2.00.

*Designed and printed by Elmer Adler at the Pynson Printers.* 1940

850 copies were published as American Institute of Graphic Arts Keepsake no. 61. These copies were unsigned in tan wrappers.

Contains addresses by Royal Cortissoz, David T. Pottinger, Lawrence C. Wroth, and D. B. Updike, with a checklist of Updike's writings by Karl Küp. Decorations by Mary J. Newell, W. A. Dwiggins, John Howard Benson, Rudolph Ruzicka, and T. M. Cleland.

106 Six Hundred Years of Sport: A Catalogue of an Exhibition Held at The Grolier Club December 12, 1940 through February 4, 1941.

8⅜ x 5⅝; ix, [1], 37p.; frontispiece; Baskerville type; 500 copies; brownish gray printed wrappers. $1.00.

*Printed by Daniel Berkeley Updike at the Merrymount Press.* 1940

107 Plant Illustration Before 1850: A Catalogue of an Exhibition of Books, Drawings, and Prints, Held by the Garden Club of America and The Grolier Club, from February 20 to March 31, 1941.

8⅜ x 5⅝; xiii, [1], 33p.; frontispiece; 600 copies; green printed wrappers. $1.00.

*Printed by Daniel Berkeley Updike at the Merrymount Press.* 1941

108 Library of The Grolier Club: Demonstration Plate, Drawn, Etched, and Printed in a Little Over Two Hours at The Grolier Club, March 9, 1941, by John Taylor Arms.

Plate: 4 x 6; image: 3⅞ x 5⅞; 100 copies, signed in pencil by the artist. $5.00.
1941

The sketch, plate, and two proofs were presented to the Club.

109 The United States Navy, 1776 to 1815, Depicted in an Exhibition of Prints of American Naval Engagements and American Naval Commanders, Held at The Grolier Club, November 19, 1942 to January 17, 1943.

11 x 8; xi, [1], 158, [2]p.; frontispiece and 14 plates; Janson type; 700 copies;

blue boards gilt-stamped with title and printed illustration of the U.S. frigate *Constitution* on the upper board. $3.00.

*Printed by the George Grady Press.* 1942

110  The Grolier Club and Its Exhibitions Held From Time to Time: An Address by Ruth Shepard Granniss, October 21, 1943.

7 x 4⅛; 31, [1]p.; Bembo type; 450 copies; white printed wrappers. Distributed to members as a keepsake for the Club's 60th anniversary.

*Printed by the George Grady Press.* 1944

111  The Grolier Club and Its Iconographic Collections: An Address by Henry Watson Kent, November 18, 1943.

7 x 4¼; 28, [2]p.; Bembo type; 450 copies; white printed wrappers. Distributed to members as a keepsake for the Club's 60th anniversary.

*Printed by the George Grady Press.* 1944

112  Aubrey Beardsley: Catalogue of Drawings and Bibliography, [by] A. E. Gallatin.

9⅛ x 6⅛; [8], 141, [6]p.; frontispiece portraits by Frederick Hollyer and 7 collotype plates; 300 copies; blue cloth, with title gilt-stamped on upper cover. $6.00.

*Printed and bound by the George Grady Press.* 1945

Includes advertisement for other books by A. E. Gallatin.

113  Letter-book of Mary Stead Pinckney, November 14th, 1796 to August 29th, 1797, With an Introduction by Donald Mugridge, Edited by Charles F. McCombs.

8 x 5¼; [6], vii, [1], 116, [2]p.; Caslon Old Face type, hand-set; 300 copies on Rives Liampre paper; reddish orange cloth, author's name and title gilt-stamped on upper cover. $10.00.

*Printed by the Overbrook Press.* 1946

114  One Hundred Influential American Books Printed before 1900, Catalogue and Addresses, Exhibition at The Grolier Club, April eighteenth · June sixteenth MCMXLVI.

6¼ x 9¼; 139, [1]p.; 7 gravure facsimiles; Monotype Fournier type; 600

copies on all-rag Fabriano Capuleti wove paper; red cloth with white cloth spine, top edge gilt. $10.00 for members, $15.00 for nonmembers.

> *Designed by Elmer Adler, printed by the Press of A. Colish.* 1947
> Essays by Frederick B. Adams, Jr., John T. Winterich, and Thomas H. Johnson.

115 The Engraved & Typographic Work of Rudolph Ruzicka: An Exhibition.

$5\frac{3}{4}$ x $8\frac{1}{2}$; 36, [3]p.; illustrated title page and 7 illustrations, some in color; Fairfield type; 500 copies; paste-paper wrappers designed by Veronica Ruzicka; colophon signed by Rudolph Ruzicka. $3.50 for members, $5.00 for nonmembers.

> *Designed by Rudolph Ruzicka, printed and bound by the George Grady Press.* 1948
> Introduction by Walter Muir Whitehill.

116 List of Publications, Exhibition Catalogues and Other Items Issued by The Grolier Club, 1884–1948.

$9\frac{3}{8}$ x $6\frac{1}{8}$; 24p.; 1500 copies; gray printed wrappers. $1.00.

> *Designed by Fred Anthoensen, printed by the Anthoensen Press.* 1948
> For further information, see the introduction to this list.

117 What I Am Pleased to Call My Education, by Henry Watson Kent, Edited by Lois Leighton Comings.

9 x $5\frac{7}{8}$; xiii, [3], 208, [1]p.; 8 plates; Baskerville and Bulmer types; 1025 copies on Worthy Dacian 75 percent rag laid paper; blue cloth. $5.00 for members, $7.50 for nonmembers.

> *Designed by Joseph Blumenthal, printed by the Spiral Press.* 1949

118 The Grolier Club, 1884–1950: An Informal History, by John T. Winterich.

9 x 6; 36, [2]p.; 4 plates; English Aldine Bembo type; 1250 copies on Arches all-rag paper; green boards with Club arms gilt-stamped on upper board. $2.00.

> *Designed and printed by the Press of A. Colish.* 1950
> See also revised edition, Publication no. 133.

119 Two Addresses Delivered to Members of The Grolier Club: I. Trollope's America, by Willard Thorp on October 18, 1949. II. The Lawyers of Anthony Trollope, by Henry S. Drinker on November 15, 1949.

8⅞ x 5⅞; 47, [1]p.; 750 copies; light gray boards with paper label on upper board. $2.00.

*Designed by Jan van Krimpen, printed by Joh. Enschedé en Zonen, Haarlem, Netherlands.* 1950

120 Freedom of the Press and L'Association Mensuelle: Philipon versus Louis-Philippe, by Edwin De T. Bechtel.

9 x 11¾; [6], 40, [55]p. including 24 plates; Linotype Janson; 750 copies on Art Mat paper; gray cloth with gilt-stamped title on spine and upper cover. $12.50.

*Designed by Elmer Loemker, printed and bound by the George Grady Press.* 1952

121 Catalogue of Printed Works by and Memorabilia of Antoine Laurent Lavoisier, 1743–1794, Tuesday, February 19 through Sunday, March 30, 1952, Exhibited at The Grolier Club.

8½ x 5½; 79, [1]p.; 1000 copies; light blue printed wrappers. $2.00.
*Printed and bound by the George Grady Press.* 1952
Written by Denis I. Duveen and Herbert S. Klickstein.

122 Fifteenth Century Books and the Twentieth Century: An Address by Curt F. Bühler, and a Catalogue of an Exhibition of Fifteenth Century Books Held at The Grolier Club, April 15 – June 1, 1952.

10 x 7; 57, [2]p.; 8 collotype plates; Weiss type; 1000 copies on Curtis rag paper; gray-and-white decorated boards with red cloth spine, title gilt-stamped. $3.00.

*Designed and printed by Peter Beilenson, illustrations printed by the Meriden Gravure Company, bound by the Russell-Rutter Company.* 1952

123 William Blake's Illuminated Books: A Census, Compiled by Geoffrey Keynes and Edwin Wolf 2nd.

10¾ x 8½; xviii, [2], 124, [3]p.; 8 leaves of collotype plates; Monotype Bell type; 400 copies on Titanium Cartridge paper; blue cloth, title gilt-stamped on spine, top edge gilt. $10.00.

*Designed and printed by the University Press, Cambridge (Brooke Crutchley, University Printer), illustrations by the Chiswick Press.* 1953

124   Authors at Work: An Address Delivered by Robert H. Taylor at the Opening of an Exhibition of Literary Manuscripts at The Grolier Club, Together with a Catalogue of the Exhibition by Herman W. Liebert and Facsimiles of Many of the Exhibits.

11 x 8½; 52, [2], [48 collotypes], [4]p.; Granjon type; 750 copies; blue cloth, title gilt-stamped on spine. $10.00.

*Designed and printed by Peter Beilenson, collotypes printed by the Meriden Gravure Company, bound by the Russell-Rutter Company.* 1957

125   An Exhibition Celebrating the Seventy-fifth Anniversary of the Grolier Club, with Addresses by C. Waller Barrett and Alexander Davidson, Jr. Delivered at the Opening of the Exhibition March 17, 1959.

9 x 6; [2], 44p.; text in Waverly and display in Sistina type; 1000 copies; pink wrappers. Sent to all members.

*Designed and printed by Peter Beilenson.* 1959

126   Grolier 75: A Biographical Retrospective to Celebrate the Seventy-fifth Anniversary of the Grolier Club in New York.

10½ x 6¾; [16], 240, [3]p.; Baskerville type with Bulmer and Perpetua for display; 1000 copies on Curtis rag paper; cream-colored buckram spine with reddish buckram sides, gilt-stamped leather spine label; slipcase with paper sides printed with an overall pattern of the Grolier Club arms, paper spine label. $15.00.

*Designed by Joseph Blumenthal, printed by the Spiral Press.* 1959
Calligraphic "75" on title page and spine label by Philip Grushkin.

127   Catalogue of an Exhibition of Historical and Literary Americana, from the Collections of Thomas W. Streeter and C. Waller Barrett, Together with Additions from the American Antiquarian Society

and the Yale University Library, Held in the Exhibition Hall of The Grolier Club, September 1959.

9½ x 6¼; 47, [1]p.; English Monotype Bell; 1000 copies; brown printed wrappers. Sent to all members.

*Designed and printed by the Thistle Press.*　　　　　　1960
Errata slip sent to all members.

128　Italian Influence on American Literature: An Address by C. Waller Barrett and a Catalogue of an Exhibition of Books, Manuscripts and Art Showing This Influence on American Literature and Art, Held at The Grolier Club, October 17 to December 10, 1961.

10 x 7; 131, [2]p. including 31 plates; Bodoni type; 850 copies on Curtis rag paper; 100 copies bound in Italian Bertini decorated paper boards with black goatskin spine; slipcase covered in same paper, none for sale. 750 copies bound in dark gray Roma hand-made paper boards, the Club arms gilt-stamped on upper board with a natural buckram spine, gilt-stamped black leather spine label; slipcase, paper sides and cloth. $10.00.

*Designed by Joseph Blumenthal, text printed by the Spiral Press, illustrations printed by the Meriden Gravure Company, bound by the Russell-Rutter Company.*　　　　　　1962

129　The Grolier Club Iter Italicum, Edited by Gabriel Austin.

9⅜ x 6⅜; xxi, [3], 298, [2]p.; 18p. of photographs; Bembo type; 750 copies (250 reserved for the Italian hosts and the travelers) on Curtis rag paper; light brown cloth with Club arms blind-stamped on upper board, yellow dust jacket of hand-made Fabriano paper printed in black and red. $10.00.

*Designed by Roderick Stinehour, text printed by the Stinehour Press, illustrations printed by the Meriden Gravure Company, bound by J. F. Tapley Co.*　　　　　　1963

130　Elmer Adler in the World of Books: Reminiscences of Frederick B. Adams, Jr., John T. Winterich, Lawrance Thompson, Kneeland McNulty, Al Hine, David Jackson McWilliams, Edward Naumburg, Jr., Philip C. Duschnes, Elmer Adler, Edited by Paul A. Bennett.

7 x 4½; ix, [3], 114, [2]p.; 32p. of plates; Caledonia and Bulmer types; 800 copies on SN Text paper; black cloth sides and gray cloth spine.

*Designed by P. J. Conkwright, printed by the Princeton University Press and the Meriden Gravure Company, bound by J. F. Tapley Co.* 1964
Other contributions are by Virginius Cornick Hall, Jr., Alexander Dallas Wainwright, and P. J. Conkwright. Also published over the following imprints: Friends of the Princeton University Library (750 copies), the Typophiles (400), La Casa del Libro, San Juan, Puerto Rico (150). Each imprint was published in a different color binding; boxed sets of the four variant imprints and bindings were available.

131   One Hundred Books Famous in Science: Based on an Exhibition Held at The Grolier Club, by Harrison D. Horblit.

11 x 8; [8], 449, [2]p. including 220 leaves of plates; Bembo type; 1000 copies on Curtis rag paper; blue cloth spine and gray cloth sides, with title and Club arms gilt-stamped on spine, top edge gilt; slipcase with gray paper sides, blue cloth head and tail. $37.50 for members, $50.00 for nonmembers.
*Designed by Roderick Stinehour, set by the Stinehour Press, printed by the Meriden Gravure Company, bound by J. F. Tapley Co.* 1964

132   Robert Frost and the Lawrence, Massachusetts, "High School Bulletin": The Beginning of a Literary Career, by Edward Connery Lathem and Lawrance Thompson.

11¾ x 9½; 94, [2]p.; title page portrait; 1200 copies; blue boards printed with a facsimile of the cover of the Lawrence High School Bulletin, gilt-stamped blue cloth spine, top edge gilt. $15.00 for members, $20.00 for nonmembers.
*Designed and printed by the Stinehour Press, facsimiles of the "Bulletin" printed in two colors by the Meriden Gravure Company, bound by J. F. Tapley Co.* 1966

133   The Grolier Club, 1884–1967: An Informal History, by John T. Winterich.

9½ x 6⅜; 49, [2]p.; 8p. of plates; 2000 copies on Curtis rag paper; gray boards printed with the Club arms in an overall pattern, gilt-stamped gray linen spine; slipcase of gray cloth and the patterned paper. $15.00 for members, $20.00 for nonmembers.

*Designed by Joseph Blumenthal, text printed by the Spiral Press, illustrations
printed by the Meriden Gravure Company, bound by the Russell-Rutter
Company.* 1967
A revised edition of Publication no. 118.

134 Fifty-five Books Printed before 1525 Representing the Works of
England's First Printers: An Exhibition from the Collection of Paul
Mellon, January 17 – March 3, 1968.

10 x 7; xiii, [1], 62, [3]p.; 6p. of plates; 1650 copies on Curtis rag paper;
1500 copies bound in tan cloth, 150 copies in tan wrappers.

*Designed and printed by the Anthoensen Press, illustrations printed by the
Meriden Gravure Company, bound by Robert Burlen & Son.* 1968

135 Eighteenth-Century Studies in Honor of Donald F. Hyde, Edited
by W. H. Bond.

$10\frac{1}{2}$ x $6\frac{3}{4}$; xv, 424, [1]p.; 4 leaves of plates; Baskerville type; 1650 copies;
black cloth spine with brown cloth sides, the Club arms gilt-stamped on
upper cover; slipcase covered in gray paper printed with an overall pattern of the Club arms, black cloth on head and tail. $35.00.

*Designed by Joseph Blumenthal, printed by the Spiral Press, illustrations
printed by the Meriden Gravure Company.* 1970

136 The Library of Jean Grolier: A Preliminary Catalogue, by Gabriel
Austin, with an Introductory Study, "Jean Grolier and the Renaissance" by Colin Eisler.

11 x $8\frac{1}{2}$; viii, 137p.; frontispiece and 9 plates; Bembo type; 1000 copies on
Curtis rag paper; blue cloth spine and gray cloth sides, upper cover gilt-
stamped showing both sides of the 1558 jeton marking the "Reunion du
Royaume de France," title gilt-stamped. $35.00.

*Designed by Greta Franzen, set by William Clowes & Sons, Ltd, printed by
the Halliday Lithograph Corporation, bound by A. Horowitz & Son.* 1971

137 John Donne, 1572–1631: A Catalogue of the Anniversary Exhibition of First and Early Editions of His Works Held at The Grolier
Club, February 15 to April 12, 1972, Compiled by Robert S. Pirie.

9 x 6; xv, [1], 41, [2]p.; frontispiece portrait and 4 plates; Baskerville type;

500 numbered copies (plus 150 for the compiler): 350 copies in wrappers decorated with type ornaments, 150 copies in boards covered with the same decorated paper. $10.00 in boards, $7.50 in wrappers.

*Text printed by the Stinehour Press, illustrations printed by the Meriden Gravure Company.* 1972

138 Early Books and Manuscripts: Forty Years of Research, by Curt F. Bühler.

$9\frac{3}{8}$ x $6\frac{1}{8}$; xxi, [3], 659, [2]p.; 20 plates; 510 copies; blue cloth with a monogram combining "P.M." and "G" gilt-stamped on upper cover. $50.00.

*Designed by P. J. Conkwright, printed by the Princeton University Press, illustrations printed by the Meriden Gravure Company.* 1973

A joint publication of the Grolier Club and the Pierpont Morgan Library; includes list of subscribers.

139 The Maya Scribe and His World, [by] Michael D. Coe.

11 x 17; 160p.; 6p. of color plates, numerous black-and-white illustrations throughout; Helvetica type; 1000 copies; blue cloth with orange stamping on spine and upper cover. $50.00.

*Designed by Norman Ives, printed by the Meriden Gravure Company.*

1973

A second printing of 500 copies was made in 1977.

140 The Grolier Club Iter Germanico-Helveticum, Compiled from the Travelers' Notes by Robert Nikirk.

$9\frac{3}{8}$ x $6\frac{3}{8}$; viii, [4], 100, [2]p.; 2 plates, 1 fold-out map drawn by Fritz Kredel; Bembo type; 300 copies, of which 150 were reserved for hosts and travelers; orange cloth. The endpapers illustrate the Johann Gutenberg–Jean Grolier Medal commissioned from Leonard Baskin (see Medallions, no. 6). $10.00.

*Printed by Universitätsdruckerei H. Stürtz AG, Würzburg, Germany.*

1973

A record of the Grolier Club trip to Germany and Switzerland in May 1970.

141 The Truthful Lens: A Survey of the Photographically Illustrated Book, 1844–1914, [by] Lucien Goldschmidt and Weston J. Naef.

11 x 8½; xii, 241, [2]p. including 172 photographs; Baskerville type; 1000 copies on specially made paper from the Curtis Paper Company; black cloth with the Club arms gilt-stamped on upper cover, red leather spine label gilt-stamped; slipcase covered in gray paper with printed label on spine and upper side. $75.00 for members, $125.00 for nonmembers.

*Designed by Peter Oldenburg, text printed by the Stinehour Press, illustrations printed by the Meriden Gravure Company.*     1980

Includes list of subscribers.

142    Typographic Years: A Printer's Journey Through a Half Century, 1925–1975, by Joseph Blumenthal.

9¼ x 6; [12], 153, [2]p., with 18 unnumbered pages bound in following p. 6; 8p. of illustrations; Baskerville type; 300 copies; gray boards printed with the Club arms in an overall pattern and dark red cloth spine; slipcase covered with same printed paper on sides with cloth on head, tail, and fore-edge, with printed paper label. $75.00.

*Designed by Joseph Blumenthal, text printed by the Stinehour Press, illustrations printed by the Meriden Gravure Company.*     1982

Includes list of subscribers; the chapter "The Grolier Club and the Spiral Press," introduced by Roderick D. Stinehour, includes 14 illustrations (bound in following p. 6); first Centennial publication.

143    BR Today: A Selection of His Books with Comments.

8⅛ x 4⅞; xiv, 41, [2]p.; 450 copies; light brown boards and gray-brown cloth spine, with BR's thistle device printed on the upper board and the Grolier Club arms designed by BR in 1927 on the lower board. $8.50.

*Designed by Bert Clarke, printed by the Press of A. Colish.*     1982

144    Bibliography, its History and Development: Catalogue of an Exhibition Held at the Grolier Club from April 21 to June 6, 1981, to Mark the Completion of the National Union Catalog Pre-1956 Imprints, by Bernard H. Breslauer and Roland Folter.

9 x 6; 224p.; 14 plates; Bembo type; 600 copies. $37.50.

*Designed by Philip Grushkin, printed by the Press of A. Colish.*     1984

Foreword by David A. Smith, Head of the National Union Catalog Publication Project; second Centennial publication.

# PART II: EXHIBITION HANDLISTS

1   Modern Bookbindings: French, English, and American. 16p.
    *The De Vinne Press.*                                         1886

2   Drawings by Edwin A. Abbey for *She Stoops to Conquer* by
    Oliver Goldsmith. 7⅞ x 5¼; 12p. *Gilliss Brothers and Turnure,
    Art Age Press.*                                               1886

3   Early Printed Books. 16p. *The De Vinne Press.*               1887

4   Turner's Liber Studiorum. 8⅞ x 5⅞ and 7 x 4⅜; 40p.
    *The De Vinne Press.*                                         1888

5   Early Printed Books Related to America. 7⅜ x 4½; 20p.
    *The De Vinne Press.*                                         1888

6   Etchings of Alphonse Legros. 16p. *The De Vinne Press.*       1889

7   Japanese Prints and Illustrated Books. 44p. *The De Vinne Press.*
                                                                  1889

8   Books and Prints Illustrating the Origin and Rise of Wood
    Engraving. 8p. *The De Vinne Press.*                          1890

9   Modern Wood Engraving: Works of the Society of American
    Wood Engravers. 16p.                                          1890

10  Illustrated Bill Posters. 12p. *The De Vinne Press.*          1890

11  Recent Bookbindings, 1860–1900: Executed by American,
    English, and French Bookbinders. 61p. *The De Vinne
    Press.*                                                       1890

12  Works on Alchemy and Chemistry. 32p. *The De Vinne Press.*
                                                                  1891

13  The Fan in All Ages: A Brief History of its Evolution to
    Accompany an Exhibition of Fans, Mostly French, of the
    XVIIIth Century, Illustrating the Decorative Art of That

Period as Applied to Fans. 6¾ x 4⅝; 21p. *The De Vinne
Press.*                                                                    1891

14   Engraved Portraits, Being the Effigies of the Most Famous English
Writers from Chaucer to Johnson. 69p. *The De Vinne Press.*
See Publication no. 13.                                                    1891

15   Etchings by Ph. Zilcken. 19p.                                          1892

16   Line Engravings Designed to Illustrate the History of the Art
During the Past Four Centuries. 28p. *The De Vinne Press.*     1892

17   Portraits Engraved by William Faithorne. 38p. *The De Vinne
Press.*                                                                    1893

18   Medals and Plaques Exhibited at the Monthly Meeting of The
Grolier Club, April 6, 1893. 11p. *The De Vinne Press.*        1893

19   Books Printed by William Bradford and Other Printers in the
Middle Colonies. 100p.; 1 facsimile. *The De Vinne Press.*     1893

20   Old English Books from Langland to Wither Designed to Illustrate
Bibliographically the Poetical and Prose Works of English
Writers. 37p. *The De Vinne Press.*                           1893
See Publication no. 16.

21   Editions of *The Complete Angler.* 26p. *The De Vinne Press.*
                                                                           1893

22   Portraits in Pastel by J. Wells Champney. 5⅜ x 4⅛; 8p.     1894

23   Commercial Bookbindings: An Historical Sketch, with Some
Mention of an Exhibition of Drawings, Covers, and Books. 23p.
*The De Vinne Press.*                                                      1894

24   Early American Bookplates. 38p.; 21 plates. *The De Vinne Press.*
See Publication no. 18.                                                    1894

25   Early Printed Books. 33p.; frontispiece portrait. *The De Vinne
Press.*                                                                    1894
See Publication no. 21.

26   Engraved Portraits of Women Writers: Sappho to George Eliot.
     24p. *The Gilliss Press.*                                      1895

27   The Engraved Work of Asher B. Durand. 103p. *The Gilliss
     Press.*                                                        1895
     See Publication no. 20.

28   Engraved Portraits of French Authors to the Close of the
     Eighteenth Century. 16p. *The De Vinne Press.*                 1895

29   A Centenary of Artistic Lithography, 1796–1896. 73p.
     *The De Vinne Press.*                                          1896
     See Publication no. 23.

30   Japanese Prints. 23p. *The De Vinne Press.*                    1896

31   A Chronological List of the Works of Alfred, Lord Tennyson,
     with Some Items of Tennysoniana and a Series of Portraits
     of the Poet Laureate. 24p. *The De Vinne Press.*               1897

32   Plans and Views of New York City, 1651–1860. 38p.
     *The De Vinne Press.*                                          1897

33   Etchings and Drawings by Charles Méryon. 54p.; frontispiece
     and 1 plate. *The De Vinne Press.*                             1898

34   Engraved Titles and Frontispieces Published in England During
     the Sixteenth and Seventeenth Centuries. 42p. *The De Vinne
     Press.*                                                        1898

35   English Literary Portraits. 28p. *The De Vinne Press.*         1898

36   Decorated Early English Bookbindings. 32p. *The De Vinne Press.*
                                                                    1899

37   Sketch of the Life of Charles Balthazar Julien Févret de Saint-Mémin
     Issued to Accompany an Exhibition of His Engraved Portraits
     [by F. Weitenkampf]. 10p. *The De Vinne Press.*                1899

38   Portraits of Lincoln. 66p. *The De Vinne Press.*               1899

39   Original Editions of the Works of Edmund Spenser. 19p.
     *The De Vinne Press.*                                          1899

40  Engraved Portraits of Washington. 51p. *The De Vinne Press.*
1899

41  Works of Geoffrey Chaucer. 45p. *The De Vinne Press.*    1900

42  Works of John Dryden. 88p. *The De Vinne Press.*    1900
See Publication no. 30.

43  Engravings by Ferdinand Galliard. 17p. *The De Vinne Press.*
1900

44  Works of the Poets Laureate of England. xv, 80p.; errata slip
inserted. *The De Vinne Press.*    1901
See Publication no. 34.

45  Engravings, Etchings, and Lithographs by Women. 118p.
*The De Vinne Press.*    1901

46  Mosaic Bookbindings. 53p. *The De Vinne Press.*    1902

47  Etchings, Dry-Points, and Mezzotints by Sir Francis Seymour
Haden. xi, 112p. *The De Vinne Press.*    1902

48  Italian Books. 84p. *The De Vinne Press.*    1902
See Publication no. 40.

49  Silver, Embroidered, and Curious Bookbindings. xi, 86p.
*The De Vinne Press.*    1903

50  Dramatic Folios of the Seventeenth Century. 25p. *The De Vinne
Press.*    1903

51  Etchings and Dry-points by Whistler. 88p. *The De Vinne Press.*
1904

52  First Editions of the Works of Nathaniel Hawthorne. vii, 69p.
*The De Vinne Press.*    1904
See Publication no. 43.

53  Works of William Blake. xvii, 147p. *The De Vinne Press.*
1905

54  Eighteenth Century French Engravings. 19p. *The De Vinne Press.*
1905

55  Selected French Almanacs from a Complete Collection (1694–1883) Illustrative of French Binding During this Period. 28p. *The De Vinne Press.*  1905

56  The Two Hundredth Anniversary of the Birth of Benjamin Franklin. 100p. *The De Vinne Press.*  1906

57  Some of the Latest Artistic Bindings Done at The Club Bindery. 47p. *The De Vinne Press.*  1906

58  Engraved Portraits of Actors of Olden Times. vi, 46p. *The De Vinne Press.*  1907

59  Medals and Plaques by Victor D. Brenner. 33p. *The De Vinne Press.*  1907

60  Lithographs by Whistler. vi, 15p. *The De Vinne Press.*  1907

61  Ornamental Leather Bookbindings Executed in America Prior to 1850. xiii, 106p. *The De Vinne Press.*  1907

62  Early American Engraving Upon Copper, 1727–1850. viii, 100p.; frontispiece. *The De Vinne Press.*  1908

63  Etchings and Dry-points by Cameron. 46p. *The De Vinne Press.*  1908

64  Etchings by Joseph Pennell. 23p. *The De Vinne Press.*  1908

65  Tercentenary of the Birth of John Milton. vi, 116p.; 2 plates. *The De Vinne Press.*  1908

66  Bronzes and Paintings by Antoine-Louis Barye. 20p. *The De Vinne Press.*  1909

67  Engraved Work of Edwin Davis French. vii, 48p. *The De Vinne Press.*  1909

68  Johnson Bicentenary. viii, 106p.; frontispiece incorporating six portraits. *The De Vinne Press.*  1909

69  First Editions of Alexander Pope. vii, 85p. (including addenda). *The De Vinne Press.*  1911
See Publication no. 54.

70  Angling Books Together with a Number of Manuscripts, Angling
Book-plates, Prints, Medals, etc. viii, 59p. *The De Vinne Press.*
1911

71  Works of William Makepeace Thackeray. viii, 105p. *The De Vinne
Press.*  1912
See Publication no. 56.

72  War of 1812: Naval Prints. 14p. *The De Vinne Press.*  1912

73  Works of Charles Dickens. 220p. *The De Vinne Press.*  1913
See Publication no. 59.

74  Works of Robert Louis Stevenson. vi, 74p. *The De Vinne Press.*
See Publication no. 63.  1914

75  Shakespeare's Plays. vi, 114p. *The De Vinne Press.*  1916
See Publication no. 66.

76  Books Illustrated by Thomas Rowlandson. xiv, 109p. *The De Vinne
Press.*  1916
See Publication no. 67.

77  English Prose Fiction, 1485–1870. ix, 149p. *The De Vinne Press.*
See Publication no. 68.  1917

78  Chronological Exhibition of Mezzotints from Von Siegen to
Barney. xii, 78p.; frontispiece. *The De Vinne Press.*  1918

79  Angling Book Plates. viii, 84p.; frontispiece. *The De Vinne Press.*
1918

80  Works of William Blake. vii, 12p. *The Gilliss Press.*  1919

81  One Hundred Illustrated Books, 1472–1896. vi, 17p. *The Gilliss
Press.*  1921

82  Prints, Drawings, and Bronzes by Edgar Degas. 14p. *The Gilliss
Press.*  1922

83  Japanese Figure Prints. ix, 83p. *The Gilliss Press.*  1923
See Publication no. 82.

84  Etched Work of Charles A. Platt. 31p.  1925

85  Type Specimen Books and Broadsides Printed Before 1900. [12]p.
    *The Harbor Press.* 1926

86  Seventeenth Century Line Engraved Portraits. 9⅜ x 6⅜; 11p.
    *Edward Stern & Co.* 1935

87  Aubrey Beardsley: Drawings and Books. [4]p. 1945

88  A Descriptive Guide to the Exhibition Commemorating the Death
    of Nathaniel Hawthorne, 1804–1864. 8 x 5⅜; v, 17p.; 1 fold-out
    map. *Field & Beattie Division of Chas. P. Young Co.* 1964

89  American Illustrated Books, 1945–1965. 8⅝ x 5⅜; [12]p.
    *The Spiral Press.* 1965

90  Europe in 1776: A Bicentennial Exhibition of Books, Maps,
    Engravings, Drawings. 9¾ x 6¾; 14p. 1976

# PART III: PERIODICALS

1  [The Yearbook of the Grolier Club]: Officers, Committees, Constitution and By-Laws, Members, Reports of Officers and Committees for
   the Year . . . (varies slightly).

   6⅝ x 4¼ (varies slightly). Published annually 1884–1978, except none published 1885–1886; biannually since 1979. Binding varies—1884–1917: tan-
   colored boards with vellum spine, "Grolier Club" gilt-stamped on upper
   boards; 1918: grayish brown wrappers with printed title; 1919–1931: tan-
   colored boards printed with the Club arms; since 1932: tan-colored wrappers,
   printed with the Club arms.

161

2  Transactions of The Grolier Club.

Part I: From Its Foundation, January 1884, to July 1885.

$9\frac{1}{2}$ x 7; 65p.; 740 copies on laid paper; Lalanne charcoal-colored wrappers over loose boards.

*Printed by Gilliss Brothers and Turnure, the Art Age Press.*        1885

Part II: From July Eighteen Hundred and Eighty-Five to February Eighteen Hundred and Ninety-Four.

$9\frac{1}{2}$ x 7; 156p.; head- and tail-pieces, initials, and illustrations throughout; 750 copies on hand-made paper; cream-colored wrappers over boards, title gilt-stamped on spine and upper board, the Club arms gilt-stamped on lower board. $4.00.

*Printed by the Gilliss Press.*        1894

Part III: From February Eighteen Hundred and Ninety-Four to July Eighteen Hundred and Ninety-Nine.

$9\frac{1}{2}$ x 7; 227, [3]p.; frontispiece, 12 full-page portraits, head- and tail-pieces, initials, and illustrations throughout; 470 copies on American hand-made paper, cream-colored wrappers over flexible boards. $7.50.

*Printed by the Gilliss Press.*        1899

Part IV: From July Eighteen Hundred and Ninety-Nine to December Nineteen Hundred and Nineteen.

$9\frac{3}{4}$ x 7; xi, [1], 178, [3]p.; frontispiece, 16 full-page illustrations, head- and tail-pieces; 404 copies on Blandford wove paper; cream-colored wrappers over boards, title gilt-stamped on spine and upper board.

*Printed by the Gilliss Press.*        1920

3  The Gazette of The Grolier Club.

[Vol. I], no. 1–11 /12, May 1921 – June 1929.

7 x $4\frac{1}{2}$; 273p.; issued stapled, without wrappers.
Caption title.

Vol. II, no. 1–8, May 1931 – May 1949.

7 x $4\frac{1}{2}$; 304p.; issued stapled, without wrappers.
Caption title.

New Series, no. 1–33 /34, June 1966–1981 /82.

$8\frac{1}{8}$ x $5\frac{3}{8}$; various page lengths; various colored printed wrappers (nos. 1–16).

8¾ x 5½; various page lengths, cream-colored, illustrated wrappers (nos. 17–33/34).

Still in publication.

*Printed by Clarke and Way, Inc. (nos. 1–13), The Press of A. Colish (nos. 14–20/21), The Stinehour Press (nos. 22/23–33/34).*

4   The News Sheet of The Grolier Club.

No. 1, Dec. 10, 1941; [4]p.

11 x 8½.

*Designed by Bruce Rogers, printed by the Harbor Press.*

New Series:

Vol. I, no. 1, May 1, 1978; 6p., ill.

Vol. II, no. 1, April 1979; 8p., ill.

Vol. II, no. 2, June 1979; 8p., ill.

Vol. II, no. 3, September 1979; 8p., ill.

Vol. II, no. 4, December 1979; 8p., ill.

Vol. III, no. 1, March 1980; 8p., ill.

Vol. III, no. 2, July 1980; 8p., ill.

Vol. IV, no. 1, November 1980; 8p., ill.

Vol. IV, no. 2, March 1981; 8p.

Published irregularly.

# PART IV: MEDALLIONS

1  Portrait of Nathaniel Hawthorne.

   Circular, 7 in. diameter. Modeled by Désiré Ringel d'Illzach. 173 copies in
   bronze, 3 in silvered bronze. $10.00.                                    1892

2  Portrait of James Russell Lowell.

   Circular, 7 in. diameter. Modeled by Charles Calverley, cast by John Williams.
   372 copies in bronze, 3 in silvered bronze. $10.00.                      1896

3  Portrait of Edgar Allan Poe.

   Circular, 6¾ in. diameter. Modeled by Edith Woodman Burroughs, cast by
   the "cire perdue" process. 277 in bronze (limited to number of subscribers
   plus 3 additional for the Club), 3 in silver. $8.00.                     1909

4  Portrait of Ralph Waldo Emerson.

   Circular, 7¼ in. diameter. Modeled by Victor David Brenner, cast by John
   Williams. 300 copies in bronze, 3 in silver. $10.00.                     1909

5  Portrait of Henry Wadsworth Longfellow.

   7½ x 5¾. Modeled by John Flanagan, cast by the A. Griffoul & Bros. Co.
   300 copies in bronze, 3 in silver. $10.00.                               1911

6  The Johann Gutenberg–Jean Grolier Medal.

   Circular, 3 in. diameter. Obverse: imaginary portrait representation of Jean
   Grolier, with his arms; reverse: imaginary portrait representation of Johann
   Gutenberg. Modeled by Leonard Baskin, cast by Medallic Art Company. 100
   copies in bronze, 1 in silver. $50.00.                                   1970

       Commissioned to commemorate the Iter Germanico-Helveticum, May
   1970.

# Exhibitions

## G. THOMAS TANSELLE

THE central place that exhibitions have occupied in the life of the Grolier Club is suggested by the fact that the story of those exhibitions begins with the first regular meeting of the Club. On May 1, 1884—just three months and eight days after the nine founding members had gathered to propose the formation of the Club—some thirty members attended a reception to inaugurate the rooms redecorated for the Club's use at 64 Madison Avenue and to view a display of etchings, which in fact (according to the *Tribune*) nearly covered up the newly painted walls (of "a subdued tint shade of buff"). The *World*, reporting the event the next day, recognized its social side before getting down to the business of commenting on the assembled objects: "The tastefully and artistically decorated club-room was well filled soon after 8 o'clock with the members who smoked, chatted and examined with quiet interest an unusually rare and interesting collection of some one hundred and sixty etchings and many specimens of fine paper, printing and other elements in the making of books." The evening was widely, and favorably, noted in the press (and not only in New York), but no account surpassed in comprehensiveness the article in the May number of *The Art Age*. It is not surprising that this publication offered a relatively detailed listing of the exhibits and printed a summary of President Hoe's remarks and a transcript of the secretary's statement, for the journal was edited by Arthur B. Turnure, the Club's first secretary. Part of what he said that evening is important in the history of the Club: "With a view to extending the influence of the club in relation to the arts entering into the production of books—its object as defined by the constitution—it is the intention that this exhibition, which is more in the nature of an informal opening, shall be followed at regular intervals by other collections of a special character to both illustrate and instruct in various branches of bookmaking." He proceeded to define the scope of the Club as encompassing "not only the interests of the typefounder, the printer, the lithographer, the engraver, the bookbinder, the paper maker, and the publisher, but that of the amateur and collector and of every designer who contributes in any way to the making of a book."

To the present-day reader, a conspicuous omission from these agenda (if anything can be considered missing, since "the interests of . . . the amateur and collector" could be all-embracing) is any reference to first editions or books notable for their place in intellectual history. The initial focus of the Club, and perforce of its exhibitions, was on the artistry of books, not their content. Perhaps the founders might have been expected to acknowledge first-edition collecting more explicitly, for they (or some of them) were not unaware of the new movement that was to produce as its first monument Buxton Forman's *A Shelley Library* two years later. (The less elaborate *Longfellow Collectors' Handbook* of 1885, the first American author bibliography, was by Beverly Chew, one of the earliest members of the Club.) In any case, it was natural that they did not at first think of such material in connection with exhibitions. Although some prominent book displays with a historical emphasis had recently been mounted (at the Centennial Exhibition in Philadelphia in 1876 and the Caxton Celebration in South Kensington in 1877), books were still not often regarded as appropriate pieces for exhibition. The displaying of visual art, on the other hand, was of course a well-recognized activity, even if there were not many places where one could go for such displays; and the early exhibitions of the Grolier Club should be thought of as a manifestation of the period that saw the founding of art museums in several major American cities and the development of other places (as at the Union League Club in New York) for viewing art. That the Club's exhibitions helped satisfy a need is indicated by the ready audience they found: each of the first two exhibitions, of etchings and of illuminated manuscripts, attracted over six hundred people in its three days, as the report on the first fifteen months of the Club proudly announced, even though no public notices had been released and tickets of admission were available only from members.

The emphasis on art in the Club's exhibitions did not mean, however, that traditional subjects would necessarily be adhered to; and the shows of the next few years confirmed the Club's interest in contemporary as well as earlier work—for instance, modern American wood engravings (on three occasions, in 1886, 1888, and 1890) and drawings by Edwin A. Abbey (1886, the first Club exhibition devoted to a single figure and Abbey's first one-man show). The heavy implications of these choices were suggested in the New York *Times* on June 19, 1887, scarcely more than three years after the Club's first exhibition, in an article by David Gamut on "The Grolier Club's Work," declaring that its members "have to be severe judges of themselves because the world is looking at them, and perhaps they will be held to account for the artistic taste of their country." Of the twenty-two exhibitions held during the six years in which the Club occupied the Madison Avenue rooms, fifteen focused on art, three on printing, and two on binding. The two remaining shows, in May and December of 1888, were the first Club exhibitions to involve subject collecting. The first (and most original of the lot) displayed manuscripts of eighteenth- and nineteenth-century authors and was therefore the first Club exhibition to have a literary subject and to be concerned with something other than the artistry of the items selected. The *Mail & Express* recognized it as "the most complete and interesting of its kind that has ever been seen in New York" (though one must doubt that there had been many "of its kind" for comparison). The other, showing early printed books relating to America, represented a recognized field of interest, but one that placed subject matter ahead of other considerations.

The pattern set by this sequence of exhibitions continued when the Club moved to its new house at 29 East 32nd Street, where the first show in the ground-floor exhibition hall (in January 1890) dealt with the beginnings of book illustration. Improved facilities encouraged more exhibitions, and the next four years, rounding out the Club's first decade, saw twenty-eight exhibitions, all but six of them dealing with art (French posters, in 1890, and Daumier, in 1892, are not surprising choices, but eighteenth-century fans, in 1891, seem somewhat removed from the arts of the book). Of those six, two were of bindings (1890, 1893), and the other four deserve special notice as forerunners—in their various ways—of kinds of shows that would become more common in later years: in January 1891, books on alchemy and chemistry, a pioneer exhibition relating to the history of science; in April 1893, books printed in the middle colonies, with an address by the authority on the subject, Charles R. Hildeburn; in May 1893, English authors up to Wither, the second literary exhibition, resulting in one of the Club's major publications; and in December 1893, the works of Izaak Walton on the 300th anniversary of his birth, the first of what was to become a distinguished series of single-author exhibitions celebrating significant anniversaries.

The Club remained in the 32nd Street house for twenty-four more years, through late 1917, presenting in it 117 more exhibitions. The bulk of them (73) continued to display art, ranging from Dürer (1897) and Rembrandt (1900) to Leech (1914) and Pennell (1908), with two timely shows on Japanese prints (1889, 1896) and eight (between 1905 and 1913) on William F. Havemeyer's great collection (presented to the Club) of portraits of book collectors, printers, publishers, authors, engravers, and binders. If printing (with four shows) and binding (with nine) were underrepresented during this period, there were outstanding efforts in each category, such as the exhibition on Gutenberg (1900), really innovative ones on commercial bookbindings (1894) and early American bindings (1907), and one on mosaic bindings (1902), which drew 1500 visitors and was—according to the president, Howard Mansfield—the first American exhibition of its kind. The most distinctive aspect of the exhibition program in these years was the marked increase in the number of literary shows. There were twenty, largely devoted to single authors—Keats

(1895), Tennyson (1897), Spenser (1899), Chaucer (1900), Dryden (1900), Hawthorne (1904), Blake (1905), Franklin (1906), Milton (1908), Johnson (1909), Pope (1911), Thackeray (1912), Dickens (1913), Stevenson (1914), Shakespeare (1916). In 1903, the Club's twentieth year, two literary exhibitions of unusual interest were held. One was a remarkable gathering of seventeenth-century dramatic folios—which nevertheless seemed to confirm the view that literature had less drawing power than art, for President Mansfield was moved to chide the members, in his annual address, for their "comparative indifference" toward this show. The other was perhaps the best-known show the Club has ever held, "One Hundred Books Famous in English Literature." The printed record of this exhibition has since been cited in innumerable dealers' catalogues and has become a landmark in collecting history. John Carter, the most perceptive commentator on taste in book collecting, called the selection "admirable" but found the list, as used by later collectors, "marmoreal rather than stimulating." One must agree that lists, when followed slavishly by those who wish to avoid thinking, are not a positive influence; the constructing (rather than following) of lists, on the other hand, requires knowledge and discernment and is therefore a natural outgrowth of the activity that characterizes collecting at its best.

As New York moved uptown, so did the Grolier Club; the present building, with its spacious two-story exhibition hall, was formally opened in December 1917 with an exhibition of books and manuscripts from Persia and the Levant. Since that time (to the end of 1983), 320 shows have been held in that hall, many of them attracting considerable attention and constituting important statements on their subjects. The principal trend over these years has been a shift away from pictorial shows and toward exhibitions of literary and historical material and of books linked by subject matter. In the first decade after the move, art still dominated, though it accounted for a smaller proportion of the total number of shows than had been the case in the previous clubhouse (40 percent rather than 60 percent). But from then through the end of World War II, only about 30 percent of the shows took art as their major feature, whereas shows of books and manuscripts organized by subject—such as polar exploration (1932), sport (1937, 1940), or tobacco (1941)—amounted to nearly 40 percent, and if the strictly literary shows are added the figure rises to over 50 percent. In the quarter century since then, the trend is more noticeable still, with art representing under 20 percent of the total, literature shooting up to more than 30 percent, and other categories of subject-collecting amounting to about 35 percent (the other arts of the book, such as printing, typography, and binding, filling out the remaining 15 percent or so). Some exhibitions can of course be classified in more than one way, but the change in emphasis is nevertheless unmistakable: exhibitions with themes referring to the content of the books and manuscripts displayed have come to overshadow, in quantity at least, those concerned with what the founders in 1884 called "the arts pertaining to the production of books."

Those arts, however, have continued to inspire outstanding shows, among them some exhibitions that have perhaps been accorded more attention than any others: an exhibition on the beginnings of printing in Europe (1968), commemorating the 500th anniversary of Gutenberg's death and including—remarkably—three copies of the 42-line Bible (with this show the exhibitions committee, in the words of Gordon Ray's report as president, "reached the high point of its history"); a display of Mayan calligraphy (1971), the first to emphasize its quality as calligraphic art; and "The Truthful Lens" (1974), the first major exhibition dealing with photographs as book illustrations. The great tradition of literary shows celebrating anniversaries associated with major authors—well launched in the old clubhouse—has continued unabated, running from Keats (1921), Shelley (1922), and Byron (1924) in the twenties to Proust (1972) and Joyce (1982) in recent years. The early show of "One Hundred Books Famous in English Literature" has also had its progeny: "One Hundred Illustrated Books, 1472–1896" (1921), "One Hundred Influential American Books, 1640–1900" (1946), and Harrison Horblit's "One Hundred Books Famous in Science" (1958), the latter two now nearly as conspicuous in catalogue references as their progenitor. A new, and welcome, tradition was established in 1968, with the showing of treasures from the John Carter Brown Library; since then, selections have been presented from the holdings of seven other institutions, introduced in each case with a talk by the director of the institution or someone closely associated with it. From the earliest days of the Club, distinguished speakers have addressed the monthly gatherings on topics related (usually) to the exhibitions then on view, and the success with which this honorable practice has been maintained can be suggested by a sampling of names and subjects from a mere two decades: Col. Ralph Isham and Frederick A. Pottle on the Boswell papers (1930–1931), Stanley Morison on writing and lettering books (1933), John Carter on "Certain 19th-century pamphlets" (1935), William A. Jackson on Dibdin (1935), Wilmarth Lewis on Horace Walpole (1936), Frederick B. Adams, Jr., on radical literature (1938), Robert Frost on contemporary poetry (1939), Archibald MacLeish speaking as Librarian of Congress (1944), Millicent Todd Bingham on Emily Dickinson (1945), W. H. Auden on Henry James (1946), Allen Tate on "little magazines" (1948), Alfred A. Knopf on American type designers (1948), Marianne Moore (speaking during an exhibition on American women writers) on "Humility, Concentration, and Gusto" (1948), and Malcolm Cowley on Edgar Allan Poe (1949). It should be added that exhibitions held since February 1955 have had the advantage of a renovated exhibition hall, with more effective and considerably larger display cases. The completion of this renovation, the first major reconstruction of the house, was fittingly celebrated with an exhibition offering "A Retrospective View of Notable Grolier Club Exhibitions." On one earlier occasion, for the sixtieth anniversary of the Club, the past exhibitions were themselves the subject of an exhibition (October 1943); the address, published in pamphlet form as *The Grolier Club and Its Exhibitions Held from Time to Time* (1944), was a skillful account by Ruth Shepard Granniss, who had become the Club's librarian in 1905 and knew the subject more intimately than anyone else.

Another job of renovation in the clubhouse plays a role in the history of the Club's exhibitions. For the seventy-fifth anniversary, the mezzanine room was made into a Rare Book Room and was provided with cases so that it could also house small exhibitions. The librarian at the time, Alexander Davidson, Jr., asked H. Bacon Collamore to select some of his books (American poetry and Beatrix Potter) for display there; and this exhibition, in 1959, became the first of what was announced as "a series of such informal exhibits." The next year Paul Mellon, Norman Strouse, and Donald Stralem showed books in the room (costume books, Victor Hammer imprints, and American literature, respectively). And in September 1961 President Donald Hyde created a Committee on Small Exhibitions, with H. Bradley Martin as its first chairman. Each of the small exhibitions was to represent a single member's collection—in contrast to the public exhibitions, which draw from many sources inside and outside the membership and which never attach lenders' names to individual items. The president's report of 1962, noting that these shows have an appealing intimacy, predicted—correctly, it turns out—that they are "destined to be increasingly important to us." (At one earlier period in the Club's history a series of small "supplementary exhibitions" was held concurrently with the major exhibitions: during four years, 1920–1923, eight such exhibitions were mounted, largely of prints in the Club's possession.) From the fall of 1961 to the end of 1983, 109 small exhibitions were held (in addition to a few exhibitions placed on view briefly for special occasions and interpolated between the regularly scheduled shows; some further displays in the mezzanine corridor, provided in recent years by the Print Subcommittee when those cases were not required for the small exhibitions; and a series of nineteen shows, mostly of private presses, mounted in the lobby by the Committee on Modern Fine Printing between 1971 and 1977). The emphases of these shows correspond fairly closely with those of the public exhibitions held in the same period; that is, the largest number of shows were on literary figures (over 35 percent of the total), with nonliterary books collected for their subjects closely following (30 percent) and with book illustrations and prints in a distant third place (about 16 percent). Bindings (five shows) and fine printing (eleven shows) have also been represented splendidly if less frequently. A

glance at the roster of small exhibitions reveals that it amounts to an honor roll of great American collectors active in the past quarter century. These exhibitions, and the pleasant receptions with which they open, have been a valuable addition to the Club's activity and are now as firmly fixed among the Club's traditions as those of much greater age.

To say that some six hundred exhibitions of all kinds have been held within the various walls of the Grolier Club during the past century, and that a third of them have featured pictorial art and a quarter of them belles lettres, would be true but would be less meaningful—as the foregoing suggests—than to examine the shifts in emphasis as the years passed. What influence this long succession of exhibitions has had is a question not easily answered. As early as 1903 Samuel Putnam Avery dedicated the Columbia catalogue of his binding collection to the Club "in recognition of the stimulating effect its exhibitions and publications have exerted upon bookbinding as a fine art." Many of the exhibitions appear to have been the first or most comprehensive of their kind or to have been held at strategic moments. (One thinks of the seven shows devoted to Whistler between 1890 and 1910, four of which fell in the years just after his death, when his reputation was in decline.) Catalogues or other forms of published description accompanied, or emerged from, about a quarter of the exhibitions, increasing the possibilities for influence. To determine the precise place of each Grolier show in the history of its subject would require extensive research, though the undertaking would not be without its rewards for the cultural historian. Whether the exhibitions that pointed new directions have outnumbered those that reflected their times is perhaps less significant finally than the sustained excellence that the exhibitions collectively represent. They began at a time when few exhibitions were held, and their continuing presence, their repeated demonstration of intelligence and taste, must surely have played a role in the development of the exhibition as a form for the dissemination of knowledge, particularly in the field of books and manuscripts.

Exhibitions, now taken for granted, flourish in numerous institutions, the Grolier Club among them, despite increasing distractions. It is not merely amusing to notice the reason given by R. T. H. Halsey, reporting in 1911 for the Committee on Arrangements, for declining attendance at exhibitions: "The crowded life of our modern New York has left little time to many of our members for devotion to things bookish; and the great attractions of the drama, opera and lecture hall have removed us far from the influence of the life in the old Knickerbocker Town when the meetings of the literary and historical societies took precedence over all social gatherings." Three years later the president, Edward G. Kennedy, took up the theme: "Since those early days, conditions in New York have altered. Places of entertainment have multiplied enormously—drama, concert, opera, the circus and other varied entertainments have their attractions. Besides, all sorts of performances or entertainments are organized for the benefit of various charities—some of them deserving enough —and then the automobile! This takes both money and, what is still more valuable, time. Everything is quite kaleidoscopic and bewildering compared to thirty years ago." (These comments, by the way, show why one can do no better, for a history of the exhibitions and their social context, than to read the annual reports of the president and the chairman of the Committee on Arrangements—as the committee responsible for exhibitions and addresses was called until renamed "Committee on Public Exhibitions" in 1972.) The president of 1914 went on to say that because of these distractions "our quiet exhibitions are passed over" by many who might otherwise see them. Every generation thinks its life more harried than that of the one preceding, and with less time for "quiet exhibitions." Nevertheless, exhibitions at the Grolier have not been superseded by the dozens of simultaneous exhibitions or the scores of competing entertainments. As that reporter for the *World* a hundred years ago understood, they are social as well as intellectual events. They provide occasions on which like-minded individuals can gather to salute, and learn from, instances of the connoisseurship that makes collecting and scholarship a single enterprise. The Grolier exhibitions begin their second century holding a position as special as they held at the beginning of their first.

# Exhibitions and Meetings, 1884–1983

## ALLEN ASAF

IN THE following list, each entry for an exhibition begins with the month of opening, followed by the title or a brief description of the exhibition and then, on the next line, by the name of the speaker or speakers who talked on a topic related to that exhibition. When an exhibition was the subject of more than one meeting with a talk, the months of the meetings are attached to the speakers' names; when a speaker talked on a subject unrelated to the exhibition then on view, such meetings are listed on a separate indented line, with the title or topic indicated.

References in square brackets are to publications associated with the exhibitions, ranging from full catalogues to brief handlists, from complete texts of speakers' remarks to short summaries. For separate publications of the Grolier Club, these references are keyed by entry number to the list of the Club's publications in the present volume, a prefixed "P" referring to Part I of the list and "H" to the record of handlists (Part II). References to articles in Grolier Club periodicals begin with "T" (for *Transactions*) or "G" (for *Gazette*). For independently produced items, not published by the Club, the references take the form [Place: publisher, date], though the record of such items is probably not complete.

A few exhibitions, displayed very briefly in conjunction with another special event, are not included here nor are the Annual Meetings (fourth Thursday in January) when they did not open an exhibition or present a speaker. But with those exceptions, this list is a record of all Grolier Club exhibitions and all speakers at openings and monthly meetings. 175

# 1884

MAY   Miscellaneous etchings [T, pt. 1]
Speakers: Robert Hoe, III, Arthur Turnure

NOVEMBER   Illuminated manuscripts [T, pt. 1]

# 1885

JANUARY MEETING   Address by Theodore Low De Vinne, "Historic Printing Types." [T, pt. 1; P 5]

FEBRUARY MEETING   Address by Robert Hoe, III, "Artistic History of Bookbinding." [T, pt. 1; P 4]

MARCH MEETING   Address by William Matthews, "Modern Bookbinding Practically Considered." [T, pt. 1; P 9]

MAY   Original drawings for book illustrations [T, pt. 1]

NOVEMBER   Specimens of photomechanical processes
Speaker: Charles F. Chandler

# 1886

JANUARY   Wood-engravings by the Society of American Wood Engravers
Speaker: Elbridge Kingsley

FEBRUARY   Bookbindings executed previous to 1800

MARCH MEETING   Address by William I. Knapp, "Thierry Martens and the Early Spanish Press." [T, pt. 2]

MAY   Modern bookbindings—French, English, and American—executed since 1800 [H 1]

NOVEMBER   Specimens and reproductions of wood-engravings of the 15th and 16th centuries
Speaker: W. J. Linton

DECEMBER   Drawings by Edwin A. Abbey for Oliver Goldsmith's *She Stoops to Conquer* [H 2]

# 1887

JANUARY   Etchings by Charles Storm van 's Gravesande
176   Speaker: Richard A. Rice

FEBRUARY  Drawings and etchings for book illustrations by George Cruikshank

MARCH  Early printed books [H 3]
Speaker: Brayton Ives

MAY  Japanese and Chinese bookmaking
Speaker: Heromich Shugio

NOVEMBER  Early English portrait engravings

NOVEMBER MEETING  Address by Andrew Fleming West, "The Philobiblon."

# 1888

JANUARY  J. M. W. Turner's *Liber Studiorum* [H 4]
Speaker: Russell Sturgis [T, pt. 2]

MARCH  Modern wood engravers in America
Speaker: W. Lewis Fraser

APRIL  American illustrated books

MAY  Manuscripts of 18th- and 19th-century authors

NOVEMBER  A selection of etchings by Jules Jacquemart

DECEMBER  Early printed books relating to America [H 5]
Speaker: George Hannah

# 1889

JANUARY  Etchings by Alphonse Legros [H 6]
Speaker: Howard Mansfield

APRIL  Japanese colored prints and illustrated books [H 7]

# 1890

JANUARY  Books and prints illustrating the origin and rise of wood-engraving [H 8]
Speaker: William C. Prime

FEBRUARY  Modern wood-engraving—works by the Society of American Wood Engravers [H 9]

MARCH  Lithographs by Paul Gavarni

APRIL  James McNeill Whistler—etchings, drawings, and paintings

NOVEMBER   French bill posters [H 10]

DECEMBER   Etchings by Paul Rajon

DECEMBER   Recent bookbindings, 1860–1890, executed by American,
English, and French bookbinders [H 11]

## 1891

JANUARY   Works on alchemy and early chemistry [H 12]
Speaker: H. Carrington Bolton

FEBRUARY   Etchings by, and portraits of, Bracquemond, Buhot, Flameng,
Haden, Jacques, Legros, Lalanne, Rajon, and Whistler
Speaker: Frederick Keppel [T, pt. 2]

FEBRUARY   Etchings by Rembrandt, with an original painting, *The
Bohemian Girl*

> MARCH MEETING   Address by Irving Browne, "The Pursuits of the
> Book Worm."

APRIL   Fans, mostly French, of the 18th century [H 13]

> MAY MEETING   Address by John Stockton-Hough, "Research on the
> Library of Demetrius Canevarius, 1559–1625."

NOVEMBER   Etched portraits by Léopold Flameng

DECEMBER   Engraved portraits of English authors from Chaucer to
Dr. Johnson [H 14; P 13]

## 1892

JANUARY   Watercolor drawings by Eugène Grivaz illustrating *Peg Woffington*

> FEBRUARY MEETING   Address by William C. Prime, "Genealogy of
> a Book." [T, pt. 2]

MARCH   Posters by Chéret

APRIL   Etchings by Philip Zilcken [H 15]

MAY   Illuminated and painted manuscripts [P 15]

OCTOBER   Caricatures by Honoré Daumier

NOVEMBER   Portraits of French artists and authors in drypoint and etchings
by Desboutin

DECEMBER   Four centuries of line engraving [H 16]
Speaker: Frederick Keppel

## 1893

JANUARY   Engraved portraits by Robert Nanteuil

> JANUARY MEETING   Address by Clarence W. Bowen, "Historic
> Portraits of Benjamin Franklin."

FEBRUARY   Engraved portraits by William Faithorne [H 17]

APRIL   Recent and valuable additions to the library; bronze and silver medals
by J. C. Champlain, Louis O. Roty, and Désiré Ringel d'Illzach [H 18]

APRIL   Books printed by William Bradford and other printers in the Middle
Colonies prior to the Revolution [H 19]
Speaker: Charles R. Hildeburn

MAY   Original and early editions of the works of English writers from
Langland to Wither [H 20; P 16]

JUNE   Framed drawings and prints belonging to the Club

NOVEMBER   Bookbindings and artistic objects in leather, plus works in silver,
enamel, and ivory, and miniature painting

DECEMBER   Waltoniana: being commemorative of the 300th anniversary
of the birth of Izaak Walton [H 21]

## 1894

JANUARY   Portraits in pastel by J. Wells Champney [H 22]
Speaker: J. Wells Champney

FEBRUARY   The decennial of the Club's existence: publications, drawings,
manuscripts, and other material

APRIL   Commercial bookbindings [H 23]

OCTOBER   Early American bookplates [H 24; P 18]

NOVEMBER   Early printed books from the David Wolfe Bruce collection
presented to the Grolier Club [H 25; P 21]

DECEMBER   Etchings, drypoints, and some pencil drawings by James
McNeill Whistler

# 1895

JANUARY    Historic bookbindings [P 19]

MARCH    Engraved portraits of women writers from Sappho to George
Eliot [H 26]
Speaker: Elizabeth W. Champney [T, pt. 3]

APRIL    The engraved work of Asher Brown Durand [H 27; P 20]

OCTOBER    The centenary of the birth of John Keats

NOVEMBER    Books of *vers de société* and some engravings by Ferdinand Gaillard

DECEMBER    Engraved portraits of French writers prior to 1800 [H 28]

# 1896

JANUARY    Etchings by Charles Joshua Chaplin and some English artists

MARCH    A century of artistic lithography, 1796–1896 [H 29; P 23]

APRIL    Japanese color prints [H 30]
Speaker: Howard Mansfield [T, pt. 3]

MAY    Original drawings from Oriental art objects

OCTOBER    Engraved work by Charles W. Burt

NOVEMBER    Books, blocks, prints from the Chiswick Press

DECEMBER    Color lithographs by Louis Prang of Oriental porcelains in the
Walters collection
Speaker: Louis Prang (January 1897) [T, pt. 3]

# 1897

JANUARY    Etchings, drypoints, and engravings on copper by Albrecht
Dürer [P 25]

MARCH MEETING    Address by Frederick Keppel, "Seymour Haden,
Painter-Etcher." [T, pt. 3]

APRIL    Recent American bookbindings
Speaker: Evelyn Hunter Nordhoff

MAY    Plaques and medals by A. Scharff, S. Schwartz, J. Tautenhayn,
K. Radnitzky, F. Pawlik, H. Jauner, and other Austrian artists

NOVEMBER    The works of Alfred, Lord Tennyson [H 31]

DECEMBER   A collection of plans and views of New York City,
1651–1860 [H 32]

## 1898

JANUARY   Etchings and drawings by Charles Méryon [H 33]

APRIL   Early English engraved title pages and frontispieces [H 34]
Speaker: Clarence Cook [T, pt. 3]

MAY   Recent additions to the library, together with bindings and
typographical medals

NOVEMBER   English literary portraits [H 35]

DECEMBER   Portraits and views issued by the Society of Iconophiles

## 1899

JANUARY   Decorated early English bookbindings [H 36]

MARCH   Portraits by Charles Balthazar Julien Févret de Saint-Mémin,
1770–1852 [H 37]

APRIL   Engraved portraits of Abraham Lincoln [H 38]
Speaker: Charles Henry Hart [T, pt. 3]

MAY   The 300th anniversary of the death of Edmund Spenser [H 39]

NOVEMBER   Dramatic portraits

DECEMBER   Engraved portraits of George Washington—commemorative
of the 100th anniversary of his death [H 40]

## 1900

JANUARY   The 500th anniversary of the death of Geoffrey Chaucer [H 41]

MARCH   The 200th anniversary of the death of John Dryden [H 42; P 30]

APRIL   Lithographs by James McNeill Whistler

APRIL   Etchings by Rembrandt [P 31]
Speaker: Howard Mansfield [T, pt. 4]

NOVEMBER   Engravings by Ferdinand Gaillard [H 43]

DECEMBER   The 500th anniversary of the birth of Johann Gutenberg

# 1901

JANUARY   Selected works of the Poets Laureate of England [H 44; P 34]

MARCH   Etchings by Corot, Daubigny, and Legros

MARCH MEETING   Informal address by Howard Mansfield

APRIL   Engravings, etchings, and lithographs by women [H 45]
Speaker: Charles de Kay

MAY   Dramatic prints

OCTOBER   Bookbindings from the Club library and engravings after
Gilbert Stuart

DECEMBER   German woodcuts of the 15th and 16th centuries

DECEMBER MEETING   Address by Henry Watson Kent, "Library
Classification."

# 1902

JANUARY   Mosaic bindings [H 46]
Speaker: Henry Watson Kent (February)

MARCH   Etchings of ancient Rome by Giovanni Piranesi, 1720–1778

APRIL   Etchings, drypoints, and mezzotints by Sir Francis Seymour Haden
(Part 1) [H 47]
Speaker: Royal Cortissoz

NOVEMBER   Etchings, drypoints, and mezzotints by Sir Francis Seymour Haden
(Part 2)
Speaker: Royal Cortissoz

DECEMBER   Original and early editions of Italian books [H 48; P 40]
Speaker: F. Marion Crawford

# 1903

JANUARY   One hundred books famous in English literature [P 37; P 38]
Speaker: Hamilton Wright Mabie (February)

MARCH   Early Italian prints
Speaker: Royal Cortissoz

APRIL   Embroidered, silver, and curious bookbindings [H 49]

APRIL MEETING  Address by F. Hopkinson Smith, "The Quality of the Picturesque."

NOVEMBER  Portraits of men connected with the American Revolution

DECEMBER  Dramatic folios of the 17th century [H 50]

# 1904

JANUARY  Engraved portraits of George Washington [P 39]

MARCH  Prints by early English engravers

APRIL  Etchings and drypoints by Whistler (Part 1) [H 51]
Speaker: Royal Cortissoz

NOVEMBER  Etchings and drypoints by Whistler (Part 2)

DECEMBER  Hawthorne Centenary: first editions of the works of Nathaniel Hawthorne [H 52; P 43]

# 1905

JANUARY  The works of William Blake [H 53]

MARCH  American Revolutionary broadsides

APRIL  French engravings of the 18th century [H 54]
Speaker: Frederic R. Halsey

NOVEMBER  A collection of portraits of book collectors, printers, publishers, authors, engravers, and binders—the gift of William F. Havemeyer (Part 1)

DECEMBER  French almanacs, 1694–1883, in fine and contemporary bindings, with armorial bearings [H 55]

# 1906

JANUARY  The 200th anniversary of the birth of Benjamin Franklin [H 56]
Speaker: R. T. Haines Halsey (March)

APRIL  A collection of portraits of book collectors, etc. (Part 2)

APRIL  Artistic bindings done at The Club Bindery [H 57]
Speaker: Henry Watson Kent

NOVEMBER  A collection of portraits of book collectors, etc. (Part 3)

DECEMBER  A collection of portraits of book collectors, etc. (Part 4)

# 1907

JANUARY   Engraved portraits of famous actors of olden times [H 58]

MARCH   Medals and plaques by Victor D. Brenner [H 59]

APRIL   Lithographs by Whistler [H 60]
Speaker: Howard Mansfield

NOVEMBER   Ornamental leather bookbindings executed in America before
1850 [H 61]

DECEMBER   A collection of portraits of book collectors, etc. (Part 5)

# 1908

JANUARY   Early American engravers, 1727–1850 [H 62]

MARCH   Mezzotint portraits of ladies

APRIL   The complete etchings and drypoints of D. Y. Cameron [H 63]
Speaker: Arthur Hoeber [T, pt. 4]

NOVEMBER   Etchings by Joseph Pennell [H 64]

DECEMBER   The 300th anniversary of the birth of John Milton [H 65]

# 1909

JANUARY   Retrospective exhibition of the work of the Club since its
foundation; George H. Boughton's watercolors for *The Scarlet Letter* [P 48]

JANUARY MEETING   Performance by members of the Grolier Club
of a medieval printers' masque, *Depositio Cornuti Typographici*
[T, pt. 4; P 52]

MARCH   Bronzes and paintings by Antoine-Louis Barye [H 66]

APRIL   The engraved work of Edwin Davis French [H 67]
Speaker: Ira H. Brainerd

NOVEMBER   The bicentenary of the birth of Samuel Johnson [H 68]
Speakers: Johnsonian scholars in the membership of the Club

# 1910

JANUARY   Etchings and drypoints by Whistler [P 49]

JANUARY MEETING   Performance by members of the Grolier Club

of a sketch, *Reading a Poem*, by William Makepeace Thackeray
[T, pt. 4; P 53]

MARCH   Engraved work by J. Winfred Spenceley

APRIL   Thackeray's drawings

APRIL MEETING   Repeat performance of *Reading a Poem*

NOVEMBER   A collection of portraits of book collectors, etc. (Part 6)

NOVEMBER MEETING   Informal discussion of paper and printing ink
prior to 1500

DECEMBER   Selected prints from the Club's collection

DECEMBER MEETING   Address by Austin Baxter Keep, "Libraries of
Colonial New York: Their Founders and Patrons."

# 1911

JANUARY   First editions of the works of Alexander Pope, 1688–1744, with
engraved portraits of the poet and his friends [H 69; P 54]
Speakers: Members of the Club in informal discussion (March)

APRIL   Engravings printed in color
Speaker: Royal Cortissoz

NOVEMBER   Additions to the collection of portraits of book collectors,
printers, publishers, authors, engravers, and binders made during the past year

DECEMBER   Angling books, manuscripts, bookplates, prints, medals, etc.
[H 70]

# 1912

JANUARY   The 100th anniversary of the birth of William Makepeace
Thackeray, 1811–1863 [H 71; P 56]
Speakers: Members of the Club in informal discussion (March)

APRIL   Fashion books and fashion plates
Speaker: Frances Morris, "The History and Development of Costume."
Repeated in May.

APRIL MEETING   Informal discussion on three Dutch etchers of the 17th
century: Neyts, Waterloo, and DeGoudt

NOVEMBER   Prints, portraits, and books relating to the War of 1812 [H 72]
Speakers: James Barnes (November); members of the Club in informal
discussion (December)

# 1913

JANUARY   The works of Charles Dickens [H 73; P 59]
Speakers: Members of the Club in informal discussion (March)

APRIL   Early woodcuts
Speakers: Members of the Club in informal discussion (April and May)

NOVEMBER   Books and engravings presented to the Club library by the late
William F. Havemeyer
Speakers: Members of the Club in informal discussion (November and
December)

# 1914

JANUARY   The works of John Leech [P 61]
Speakers: Members of the Club in informal discussion (March)

APRIL   The revival of the woodcut
Speakers: Members of the Club in informal discussion

MAY   Books and broadsides printed by Giambattista Bodoni
Speaker: Thomas M. Cleland

NOVEMBER   The works of Robert Louis Stevenson [H 74; P 63]
Speakers: Members of the Club in informal discussion

DECEMBER   Trade cards and announcements of French and English
engravers, printers, and booksellers
Speakers: Members of the Club in informal discussion

# 1915

JANUARY   Engraved work by Jacques Callot
Speakers: George S. Hellman (January); members of the Club in informal
discussion (March)

APRIL   American books illustrated with woodcuts from 1850 [P 65]
Speakers: Samuel W. Marvin, W. F. Hopson, George Haven Putnam, William
M. Ivins, Jr., Thomas M. Cleland (April); Timothy Cole, Elbridge Kingsley,
Alexander W. Drake, Thomas M. Cleland (May)

NOVEMBER  Books and prints relating to pirates and highwaymen
Speaker: Don C. Seitz

DECEMBER  Maps, plans, and views of Old New York
Speakers: I. N. Phelps Stokes and R. T. Haines Halsey

## 1916

JANUARY  War posters, 1914–1915

MARCH  Etched work of Francesco Goya
Speakers: William E. V. Starkweather, Frank Weitenkampf

APRIL  Important edited editions of Shakespeare's plays, and engraved portraits
of the poet [H 75; P 66]
Speakers: Henrietta C. Bartlett, W. A. White, George Parker Winship (April);
Ashley H. Thorndike, John Corbin (May)

NOVEMBER  Book illustrations and drawings by Thomas Rowlandson
[H 76; P 67]
Speakers: Walter Jack Duncan, Royal Cortissoz, William M. Ivins, Jr.

DECEMBER  Facsimiles of early German engravings
Speaker: Address by Fitzroy Carrington (paper read by A. E. M. Paff)

## 1917

JANUARY  Japanese prints in black and white
Speaker: Howard Mansfield (March)

APRIL  Books illustrative of the history of English prose fiction [H 77; P 68]
Speakers: William P. Trent, Wilbur L. Cross

MAY MEETING  Farewell dinner in the old clubhouse [T, pt. 4]

DECEMBER  Formal opening of the new clubhouse: exhibition of books and
miniatures from Persia and the Levant
Speakers: Brander Matthews, Henry Golden Dearth, and Meyer Riefstahl

## 1918

JANUARY  Chronological exhibition of mezzotints (Part 1) from Von Siegen
to Barney [H 78]

APRIL  Artistic lithographs
Speaker: Joseph Pennell

MAY   Chronological exhibition of mezzotints (Part 2) from Dixon to Cousins
Speaker: Horace Townsend

JUNE   A collection of angling bookplates [H 79]

JUNE MEETING   Address in memory of Daniel B. Fearing

NOVEMBER   Books and engravings illustrative of the arts of the architect
and the interior decorator principally in the 18th century
Speakers: Lloyd Warren, William M. Ivins, Jr. (November); Charles R.
Richards (December)

## 1919

JANUARY   Early printed liturgical books

MARCH MEETING   Address by Seymour de Ricci [T, pt. 4]

APRIL   Prints by Edouard Manet

MAY   Historical exhibition of bookbindings, 1200–1800
Speakers: Cortlandt Field Bishop, Mortimer L. Schiff; Ruth Shepard Granniss
(Ladies' Day)

JULY   Publications of the Society of Iconophiles

OCTOBER   19th-century bookbindings
Speakers: Members of the Club in informal discussion

NOVEMBER MEETING   Joint meeting with the American Institute of
Graphic Arts; address by Samuel W. Marvin, "Fifty Years in the
Manufacture of Books."

DECEMBER   Works of William Blake [H 80]
Speakers: A. Edward Newton, Henry Watson Kent, S. Foster Damon

## 1920

JANUARY   Silver, ivory, and embroidered bindings

MARCH   Important English literary manuscripts and books

APRIL   The works of Randolph Caldecott and Kate Greenaway

APRIL MEETING   Joint meeting with the Society of Iconophiles to
honor the memory of William Loring Andrews

MAY MEETING   Loraine Wyman singing old English children's songs

NOVEMBER   Fine printing from Didot the Elder to the Ashendene Press
Speakers: Henry Watson Kent, George Parker Winship, and others (November);
Thomas M. Cleland (December)

### EXHIBITIONS HELD IN THE PRINT ROOM

FEBRUARY   Woodcuts and etchings by Rudolph Ruzicka

MAY   Etchings by Mahonri Young

NOVEMBER   Early American and other bookplates, donated to the Club by
Beverly Chew

## 1921

JANUARY   Etchings by Mary Cassatt
Speaker: Mrs. Henry O. Havemeyer (February)

MARCH   The 100th anniversary of the death of John Keats [G, v. 1, no. 1]
Speaker: John Erskine

APRIL   "The Penman's Paradise": Renaissance and later writing books and
examples of fine penmanship
Speaker: George A. Plimpton

JUNE   Early printed books from the Club library [G, v. 1, no. 3 & no. 4]

NOVEMBER   One hundred illustrated books, 1472–1896 [H 81]
Speakers: Mortimer L. Schiff, Mahonri Young, William M. Ivins, Jr.

### EXHIBITIONS HELD IN THE PRINT ROOM

JANUARY   Etchings by Charles H. Woodbury

JULY   Pictorial trade cards

## 1922

JANUARY   Prints, drawings, and bronzes by Degas [H 82]
Speaker: Royal Cortissoz (March)

APRIL   The 100th anniversary of the death of Percy Bysshe Shelley [P 76]
Speaker: John Erskine

JULY   Recent acquisitions of the library and the print collection

NOVEMBER   First and other important editions of the works of Molière
[G, v. 1, no. 4]
Speakers: Brander Matthews, Mortimer L. Schiff

EXHIBITIONS HELD IN THE PRINT ROOM

APRIL   Selections from the collection of engraved portraits donated by Edward G. Kennedy

JULY   Illustrations to *The Divine Comedy* of Dante by William Blake: reproductions donated by Frank Altschul

## 1923

JANUARY   Japanese figure prints from Moronobu to Toyokuni [H 83; P 82]
Speakers: Howard Mansfield, Don C. Seitz, William M. Ivins, Jr. (February)

MARCH   Books printed in England by William Bulmer and his contemporaries
Speakers: Henry Watson Kent (March); Douglas C. McMurtrie (April)

JULY   Recent acquisitions of the library and the print collection

NOVEMBER   First editions, manuscripts, and memorabilia of Charles Lamb
Speaker: Ernest Dressell North [G, v. 1, no. 6]

DECEMBER MEETING   Address by Frederic W. Goudy, "The Forms of Letters."

EXHIBITION HELD IN THE PRINT ROOM

JANUARY   Lithographs by Joseph Pennell, donated by Richard M. Hoe

## 1924

JANUARY   The development of typography as a fine art, 1884–1924
Speaker: Harry Lyman Koopman (February)

MARCH   Modern books illustrated in color
Speaker: Harry A. Groesbeck

APRIL   Japanese landscape, bird, and flower prints and Surimono [P 83]
Speakers: Howard Mansfield; Arthur Davison Ficke (Ladies' Day)

NOVEMBER   Silver bindings and portraits donated by the late Beverly Chew
Speakers: Memorial tributes by members [G, v. 1, no. 7]

DECEMBER   The 100th anniversary of the death of Lord Byron
Speaker: Leonard L. Mackall

## 1925

JANUARY   Etchings by Charles A. Platt [H 84]

FEBRUARY MEETING    Address by Howard Clayton, "Papermaking in Japan."

MARCH    Early anatomical books
Speaker: Fielding M. Garrison

APRIL    Early garden books
Speaker: Alvin C. Beal

MAY    The Fifty Books of the Year [New York: American Institute of Graphic Arts, 1925]; and contemporary French illustrated books

NOVEMBER    English colored sporting books and prints [G, v. 1, no. 8]
Speaker: Harry T. Peters

DECEMBER    The works of Thomas Gosden [G, v. 1, no. 8]
Speaker: David Wagstaff

## 1926

JANUARY    Books printed by Walter Gilliss
Speakers: William M. Ivins, Jr., Howard Mansfield, Robert Jaffray, Henry Watson Kent, Douglas C. McMurtrie, George F. Kunz, Seymour de Ricci

FEBRUARY MEETING    Auction of Grolier Club publications

MARCH    Lithographs by Paul Gavarni [G, v. 1, no. 9]
Speakers: Frank Altschul, Frank Weitenkampf

APRIL    Books and broadsides of the Middle West [G, v. 1, no. 9]
Speaker: Philip Ashton Rollins

MAY    The Fifty Books of the Year [New York: American Institute of Graphic Arts, 1926]
Speaker: David T. Pottinger

JULY    Type specimen books and broadsides printed before 1900 [H 85]
Speaker: Carl Purington Rollins (November)

DECEMBER    Books illustrated by George Cruikshank
Speaker: George Parker Winship [G, "Extra number," i.e., v. 1, no. 10]

## 1927

JANUARY MEETING    Address by Don C. Seitz, "American Humor."

FEBRUARY    Etchings by Jacques Beurdeley
Speaker: Frank Weitenkampf

MARCH   Books on magic
Speaker: Address and magic act by John Mulholland

APRIL MEETING   Address by Henry Watson Kent, "The Montgomery Monument."

MAY   The Fifty Books of the Year [New York: American Institute of Graphic Arts, 1927]
Speaker: David Silve (paper read by Edward F. Stevens)

JUNE   Chiaroscuro prints from Anton Reichel's *Die Clair-Obscur Schnitte*

NOVEMBER   Books on jewels and precious stones
Speaker: George F. Kunz

DECEMBER   Books relating to Geoffroy Tory and his times
Speakers: Theodore Sizer, William M. Ivins, Jr., Henry Watson Kent

# 1928

FEBRUARY   Publications of book clubs

MARCH   The work of J.-E. Laboureur
Speaker: Harold W. Bell

APRIL   The Kelmscott Press
Speaker: Frederic W. Goudy

MAY   The Fifty Books of the Year [New York: American Institute of Graphic Arts, 1928]
Speaker: Carl Purington Rollins

JULY   Books donated to the Club library by Leonard L. Mackall

NOVEMBER   The work of Theodore Low De Vinne [P 92]
Speakers: John Clyde Oswald, Ira H. Brainerd

NOVEMBER MEETINGS   Dinner in honor of Howard Mansfield; address by Ernest Dimnet, "The Art of Thinking."

DECEMBER   Children's books
Speaker: A. S. W. Rosenbach

# 1929

FEBRUARY   The works of Rudyard Kipling [P 93; P 94]
Speaker: Ellis Ames Ballard

APRIL   Books issued by contemporary German presses
Speaker: Willy Wiegand [*Imprimatur: Ein Jahrbuch für Bücherfreunde*, Jg. I
Hamburg: Gesellschaft der Bücherfreunde, 1930]

MAY   The Fifty Books of the Year [New York: American Institute of Graphic
Arts, 1929]
Speakers: George Parker Winship, William A. Kittredge

NOVEMBER   Currier and Ives prints
Speakers: Harry T. Peters (November); informal remarks by Harry T. Peters
and Frank Weitenkampf (December)

# 1930

JANUARY   18th-century French illustrated books
Speakers: William M. Ivins, Jr. (January); Seymour de Ricci (February)

MARCH   Books and manuscripts illustrating the formation of the English
language
Speakers: George A. Plimpton (March); John Erskine (April)

MAY   Early American books and broadsides
Speaker: Lawrence C. Wroth

AUGUST   Special copies of Grolier Club publications; bookplates by
Edwin Davis French

NOVEMBER   15th-century woodcuts
Speaker: James Clark McGuire

DECEMBER   The private papers of James Boswell from Malahide Castle [P 95]
Speakers: Ralph Heyward Isham (December); Frederick A. Pottle (January
1931); A. Edward Newton, "An Imaginary Conversation between
Benjamin Franklin and Samuel Johnson." (February 1931)

# 1931

FEBRUARY   Modern French prints
Speaker: William M. Ivins, Jr.

APRIL   German illustrated books of the last 150 years
Speakers: Richard von Kühlmann, Willy Wiegand

AUGUST   Publications of Grolier Club members of the past two years;
bookplates designed by C. W. Sherborn; selections from the bequests of
James Clark McGuire and Mrs. William Loring Andrews

NOVEMBER   The 200th anniversary of the birth of George Washington
Speakers: Dixon Ryan Fox (November); John Hill Morgan, Harry MacNeill
Bland (December)

## 1932

JANUARY   Literature in English on polar exploration
Speakers: Isaiah Bowman, Vilhjalmur Stefansson

FEBRUARY   The literature of Charles Dickens's *The Mystery of Edwin Drood*
Speaker: Howard Duffield

MARCH   American silhouettes
Speaker: Glenn Tilley Morse

JUNE   The work of Bruce Rogers from the Club library and the collections
of members

NOVEMBER   Spanish books
Speakers: Roger Bigelow Merriman (November); Philip Hofer (December)

## 1933

JANUARY   Writing and lettering books
Speaker: Stanley Morison

FEBRUARY   The work of Honoré Daumier
Speaker: William M. Ivins, Jr.

MARCH   Books, pamphlets, and broadsides representing popular and literary
interest in crime during the last 150 years
Speaker: Edmund Lester Pearson

APRIL   Books and prints from the Club library
Speakers: Ruth Shepard Granniss (paper read by Lucius Wilmerding),
William A. Jackson

NOVEMBER   The 300th anniversary of the birth of Samuel Pepys
Speaker: Chauncey Brewster Tinker

DECEMBER   The prints of Winslow Homer
Speaker: Frank Jewett Mather, Jr.

## 1934

JANUARY   The 50th anniversary of the Grolier Club

MARCH   Books and prints related to the China trade
Speakers: Karl C. Cutler, Samuel W. Woodhouse, Jr.

APRIL   Books of imaginative literature by medical men
Speaker: Dudley Roberts

JUNE   Recent acquisitions of the Club library, including 18th-century French illustrated books

NOVEMBER   Lithographs celebrating the 100th anniversary of the death of Alois Senefelder
Speaker: Frank Weitenkampf

DECEMBER   Nine tastes in prints
Speakers: Allen Evarts Foster and members of the Club in informal discussion

# 1935

JANUARY   Renaissance illustrated books
Speaker: William M. Ivins, Jr.

FEBRUARY   Certain 19th-century pamphlets
Speaker: John Carter

MARCH   Chinese illustrated books
Speaker: Chi-Chen Wang

APRIL   Graphic and literary work of Joseph and Elizabeth Robins Pennell
Speaker: Edward Larocque Tinker

JULY   Bibliographical books of the 16th to 18th century, association copies, and recently acquired prints—all from the Club library

NOVEMBER   17th-century line-engraved portraits [H 86]

DECEMBER   Books, prints, and manuscripts by and about the Rev. Thomas Frognall Dibdin
Speaker: William A. Jackson

> DECEMBER MEETING   Reception to honor Ruth Shepard Granniss's 30 years as Club librarian

# 1936

JANUARY   Works of Horace Walpole
Speaker: Wilmarth Sheldon Lewis

FEBRUARY   Books on travel of the Tudor and Stuart periods
Speaker: Boies Penrose

MARCH   Engravings by Paul Revere
Speaker: Clarence Saunders Brigham

APRIL MEETING   Address by Ruth Shepard Granniss, "Book Collecting in America before 1884"; address by George L. McKay, "Early American Book Auctions."

MAY   Prints from the Club library

NOVEMBER   Book collectors of the past
Speaker: Seymour de Ricci

DECEMBER   Renaissance bookbindings [P 103]
Speaker: Lucius Wilmerding

# 1937

JANUARY   Early American sporting books [P 104]
Speaker: David Wagstaff

FEBRUARY   Book illustrations by Geoffroy Tory and Oronce Finé
Speaker: Ernst Philip Goldschmidt

MARCH   Italian drawings of the 16th to the 18th century
Speaker: Dan Fellows Platt

APRIL   Books, prints, and manuscripts by and about Sir Kenelm Digby
Speaker: John F. Fulton [New York: Peter & Katharine Oliver, 1937]

JUNE   Books and prints relating to libraries

NOVEMBER   Prints and drawings by Hans Holbein
Speaker: Paul Ganz

DECEMBER   Printed music with some manuscript examples
Speaker: Otto Kinkeldey, and a performance of music on old instruments

# 1938

JANUARY   Great trails of the Far West
Speaker: Philip Ashton Rollins

FEBRUARY   The literature of radical movements in America since the Revolution [Stamford, Conn.: The Overbrook Press, 1939]
Speaker: Frederick B. Adams, Jr.

MARCH   The history of navigation
Speaker: George E. Roosevelt

APRIL   Books, prints, and posters illustrating the development of the circus from Noah's Ark to New York (a joint exhibition with the Museum of the City of New York, held at the Museum)
Speaker: Harry T. Peters

JUNE   The Doves Press and other English presses of the 19th century

NOVEMBER   The work of Bruce Rogers (a joint exhibition with the American Institute of Graphic Arts) [New York: Oxford University Press, 1939]
Speakers: Carl Purington Rollins, John T. McCutcheon (paper read by Melbert B. Cary, Jr.), Rudolph Ruzicka (paper read by Henry Watson Kent), Daniel Berkeley Updike, Frederic Warde, and Bruce Rogers

DECEMBER MEETING   Address by Elmer Adler, "The History of the Recorded Word."

# 1939

JANUARY   The poetry and polemics of Alexander Pope
Speaker: George Sherburn

FEBRUARY MEETING   Address by Harry T. Peters, "California, Here I Come."

MARCH   Frankliniana
Speaker: George Simpson Eddy

APRIL   American life as portrayed by American illustrators
Speakers: Frederic Dorr Steele, Charles Dana Gibson, Albert Sterner, Gelett Burgess

OCTOBER   Contemporary American prints: living artists and self-portraits
Speaker: John Taylor Arms

NOVEMBER   Four American poets—Edwin Arlington Robinson, Robert Frost, Edna St. Vincent Millay, Stephen Vincent Benét
Speaker: Robert Frost reading poetry

DECEMBER MEETING   Address by Hellmut Lehmann-Haupt, "The Terrible Gustave Doré."

# 1940

JANUARY   The development of aeronautics
Speaker: Jerome C. Hunsaker

FEBRUARY MEETING   Address by Dixon Ryan Fox, "The Turnpike
Era."

MARCH   The work of Daniel Berkeley Updike and the Merrymount Press
(a joint exhibition with the American Institute of Graphic Arts) [P 105]
Speakers: Royal Cortissoz, David T. Pottinger, Lawrence C. Wroth, and
Daniel Berkeley Updike

APRIL   The centenary of the birth of Thomas Hardy [Waterville, Maine:
Colby College Library, 1940]
Speaker: Richard L. Purdy

JULY   The bibliography and iconography of printing (a smaller version of
this exhibition had been on view in the library from January to June)

OCTOBER   Selected books, manuscripts, and prints from the Club library
Speakers: Ruth Shepard Granniss (October); Francis Henry Taylor (December)

DECEMBER   Six hundred years of sport [P 106]
Speakers: David Wagstaff (December); Harry T. Peters (January 1941)

# 1941

JANUARY MEETING   Address by Henry Watson Kent

FEBRUARY   The history of plant illustration to 1850 (a joint exhibition with
the Garden Club of America) [P 107]
Speaker: Mrs. Allen Marquand

MARCH MEETINGS   Address and demonstration of the making of an
etching of the Grolier Club library by John Taylor Arms [P 108];
address by Peter Oliver, "A Few By-Products of Researches Concerning
Events in the Year 1800."

APRIL   Engravings and etchings by Jacques Callot
Speaker: Edwin De T. Bechtel

JULY   The history of the Grolier Club

OCTOBER   Research material on the life and writings of Robert Louis Stevenson
Speaker: Edwin J. Beinecke

NOVEMBER   Books relating to tobacco
Speaker: George Arents

DECEMBER MEETING   Address by Richardson Little Wright, "Diaries:
Why People Keep Them, Why Others Collect Them."

## 1942

JANUARY   The accomplishments and history of the Grolier Club

JANUARY MEETING   Address by Royal Cortissoz

FEBRUARY   Color and the printed book of today
Speakers: Thomas M. Cleland, Harry A. Groesbeck, Hellmut Lehmann-Haupt
(February); Alexander W. Weddell (March)

FEBRUARY MEETING   Address by Alexander J. Wall, "New York
City Then and Now, 1626–1942."

APRIL   Books and prints on healing by faith, fraud, and superstition during
the 17th and 18th centuries
Speaker: Edward L. Keyes

JULY   Books from the collection of Waters S. Davis given to the Club by his
children

OCTOBER MEETING   Address by Charles R. Henschel, "Sidelights on
Collecting."

NOVEMBER   Prints of American naval engagements and of American naval
commanders, 1776–1815 [P 109]
Speakers: Irving S. Olds (November); Griffith Baily Coale (December)

## 1943

JANUARY   Posters of World War I
Speaker: Charles Dana Gibson

FEBRUARY MEETING   Address by Terry Ramsaye, "People,
Propaganda, and Motion Pictures."

MARCH   Books printed by Aldus Manutius and his successors
Speaker: Arthur Edwin Neergaard

APRIL   The work of Frederic W. Goudy from the Melbert B. Cary, Jr.,
collection of Goudyana
Speaker: Frederic W. Goudy (April); a reception for Mrs. Melbert B. Cary, Jr.,
and Frederic W. Goudy (June)

OCTOBER   Publications and memorabilia relating to exhibitions held by the
Grolier Club, 1884–1943
Speaker: Ruth Shepard Granniss [P 110]

NOVEMBER   Items from the Club's iconographic collections
Speaker: Henry Watson Kent [P 111]

DECEMBER   Portraits, books, and letters of botanists and horticulturalists
with prints of plants and flowers discovered by and named after them
Speakers: William J. Robbins (December); Mrs. Roy Arthur Hunt, Richardson
Little Wright (January 1944)

DECEMBER   Editions of Dickens's *A Christmas Carol* on the 100th anniversary
of its publication
Speaker: Philo C. Calhoun

# 1944

JANUARY MEETING   Address by Archibald MacLeish

FEBRUARY   American calligraphy (a joint exhibition with the American
Institute of Graphic Arts) [G, v. 2, no. 3]
Speaker: Ray Nash

MARCH   Books, letters, manuscripts, and caricatures by Sir Max Beerbohm
[G, v. 2, no. 3]
Speakers: Harley Granville-Barker, Albert E. Gallatin

APRIL   Unique books, pamphlets, and broadsides [G, v. 2, no. 3]
Speaker: James T. Babb

OCTOBER   Modern French prints
Speakers: T. Catesby Jones [G, v. 2, no. 4] and a demonstration of the
making of a burin engraving by Stanley William Hayter

NOVEMBER   Venetian books before 1800 [G, v. 2, no. 4]
Speaker: A. Hyatt Mayor

DECEMBER   Prints of the Flight into Egypt [G, v. 2, no. 4]
Speaker: Allen Evarts Foster

# 1945

JANUARY   Early views of American colleges [G, v. 2, no. 4]
Speakers: Herbert Davis, "The Future of the Liberal Arts" (January); James P.
Baxter III, "The War and the Liberal Arts" (February)

MARCH   Drawings and books illustrated by Aubrey Beardsley [H 87]
Speaker: J. Harlin O'Connell

APRIL   Contemporary Latin American prints (a joint exhibition with the
American Institute of Graphic Arts) [New York: Hastings House, 1946]
Speaker: Jean Charlot

OCTOBER   Books, manuscripts, and memorabilia by and about Emily
Dickinson [G, v. 2, no. 6]
Speaker: Millicent Todd Bingham

NOVEMBER   The 200th anniversary of the death of Jonathan Swift
[G, v. 2, no. 6]
Speaker: Herbert Davis

DECEMBER   Seven centuries of music [G, v. 2, no. 6]
Speaker: A. Tillman Merritt, with a program of 18th-century French, German,
and Italian music by Janos Scholz, 'cello, and Robert C. Hufstader, piano

# 1946

JANUARY   Prints, drawings, and etched plates by John Taylor Arms
[G, v. 2, no. 5]
Speaker: John Taylor Arms

> FEBRUARY MEETING   Address by Carl Zigrosser, "Architectural
> Prints." [G, v. 2, no. 6]

> MARCH MEETING   Address by A. Hyatt Mayor, "Méryon and the
> Enigma of Paris."

APRIL   One hundred influential American books, 1640–1900 [P 114]
Speakers: Frederick B. Adams, Jr., John T. Winterich (April); Thomas H.
Johnson (May)

OCTOBER   First editions, manuscripts, and memorabilia by and about Henry
James [G, v. 2, no. 7]
Speakers: W. H. Auden (October) [G, v. 2, no. 7]; Clifton Fadiman
(November) [G, v. 2, no. 7]

DECEMBER   Caricatures relating to America, 1760–1815
Speaker: Robert W. G. Vail

# 1947

JANUARY MEETING   Address by William Ernest Hocking, "The Freedom of the Press."

JANUARY   Association books
Speaker: Sherman P. Haight (February)

MARCH   The Fifty Books of the Year (a joint exhibition with the American Institute of Graphic Arts) [New York: American Institute of Graphic Arts, 1947]
Speakers: Karl Küp, Philip Hofer

APRIL   Iconography of American industry
Speaker: Richardson Little Wright

OCTOBER   Contemporary American hand bookbindings
Speakers: Edward Larocque Tinker (October); Gerhard Gerlach, Roland Baughman (November)

OCTOBER MEETING   Address by Edward Alexander Parsons, "The Alexandrian Library: The Glory of the Hellenic World."

DECEMBER   Romances of chivalry
Speakers: Jean Seznec (December); C. Otto von Kienbusch (January 1948)

# 1948

FEBRUARY   The Little Magazine
Speakers: Donald Goddard Wing (February) [G, v. 2, no. 8]; Allen Tate (March)

APRIL   The Work of Rudolph Ruzicka [P 115]
Speaker: Walter Muir Whitehill

SEPTEMBER   The work of American type designers (a joint exhibition with the American Institute of Graphic Arts)
Speakers: Members of the Club and members of AIGA in informal discussion (September); Alfred A. Knopf (October)

NOVEMBER   First editions, letters, and memorabilia of famous American women writers
Speakers: Donald C. Gallup (November); Marianne Moore (December)
[G, v. 2, no. 8]

## 1949

JANUARY MEETING   Address by Robert K. Root

FEBRUARY   The writings of Edgar Allan Poe
Speakers: Malcolm Cowley (February); William K. Wimsatt (March)

APRIL   The work of Carl Purington Rollins
Speakers: Carl Purington Rollins [New York: New York Public Library, 1949], Ray Nash

JUNE   Woodcuts and drawings by Eric Gill

OCTOBER   The writings of Anthony Trollope
Speakers: Willard Thorp (October); Henry S. Drinker (November) [P 119]

DECEMBER   French political cartoons of the reign of Louis-Philippe [P 120]
Speakers: Sherman Kent (December); Edwin De T. Bechtel (January 1950)

## 1950

FEBRUARY   The 50th anniversary of the publication of *The Oxford Book of English Verse*
Speakers: Chauncey Brewster Tinker (February); John D. Gordan (March)

APRIL   First and early editions of great books in *belles-lettres* of countries belonging to the United Nations
Speaker: Luther H. Evans

OCTOBER   Great autobiographies
Speakers: J. Donald Adams (October); Henry C. Hutchins, "Daniel Defoe: A Crusoe in Scotland." (November)

DECEMBER   Chinese printing and writing
Speaker: Aschwin Lippe

## 1951

JANUARY MEETING   Address by Frederick A. Pottle, "The Boswell Papers: Their Nature and the Plans for Their Publication."

FEBRUARY   Books, manuscripts, and letters of James Fenimore Cooper
Speakers: James M. Grossman (February); James Franklin Beard, Jr. (March)

APRIL   Treaties, and maps reflecting their effects
Speaker: Lloyd A. Brown

OCTOBER   Important books in English, 1901–1950
Speakers: Harry Hansen (October); George F. Whicher (November)

DECEMBER   Old American music
Speaker: Frank M. Warner

# 1952

JANUARY MEETING   Address by John Cranford Adams

FEBRUARY   Writings by and memorabilia of Antoine-Laurent Lavoisier [P 121]
Speakers: Denis I. Duveen (February); John F. Fulton (March)

APRIL   Books of the first half century of printing, 1450–1500 [P 122]
Speaker: Curt F. Bühler

JUNE   Prints published by the Society of Iconophiles

OCTOBER   Printed and manuscript material produced in America during the
year 1777 to illustrate events of the year
Speakers: Colton Storm (October); Alfred Hoyt Bill (November)

DECEMBER   First editions, manuscripts, and letters of George Bernard Shaw
Speaker: John Mason Brown

# 1953

JANUARY MEETING   Address by Ralph A. Beals

FEBRUARY   The sea in literature
Speakers: Edward Ellsberg (February); Samuel Eliot Morison (March)

APRIL   The work of English book illustrators, mostly of the 1860's
Speakers: Edward Fenton, Hellmut Lehmann-Haupt, David A. Randall,
Robert H. Taylor

OCTOBER   English books issued during the reign of Queen Elizabeth I
Speakers: Charles Tyler Prouty (October); Oscar J. Campbell (November)

DECEMBER   Famous children's books—American, British, Continental
Speakers: Louise Seaman Bechtel, Edward Naumburg, Jr.

# 1954

JANUARY MEETING   Address by Wilmarth Sheldon Lewis

FEBRUARY  First editions, manuscripts, and memorabilia of Henry David
Thoreau and other American nature writers on the 100th anniversary of the
publication of *Walden*
Speakers: Walter Harding (February); Raymond Adams (March)

APRIL  "Collectors' Choice": books, manuscripts, prints, and other material
from the collections of Grolier members
Speaker: John T. Winterich [New York: Privately printed by the Peter Pauper
Press for C. Otto von Kienbusch, 1954]

*June 1954 – January 1955  Rehabilitation of the exhibition hall*

> NOVEMBER MEETING (held at the New-York Historical Society)
> Address by LeRoy E. Kimball

> DECEMBER MEETING (held at the Pierpont Morgan Library)
> Addresses by Frederick B. Adams, Jr., and Herbert T. F. Cahoon

# 1955

FEBRUARY  Retrospective view of notable Grolier Club exhibitions
Speaker: Lawrance R. Thompson

MARCH  First editions, manuscripts, and memorabilia of Walt Whitman on
the 100th anniversary of the publication of *Leaves of Grass*
Speakers: Gay Wilson Allen (March); Malcolm Cowley (April)

OCTOBER  "Authors at Work": manuscripts and other material illustrating the
evolution of great literary works [P 124]
Speakers: Robert H. Taylor (October); Charles D. Abbott (November)

DECEMBER  "Odd Volumes": books of interest for the unusual nature of their
format, bindings, or materials
Speaker: Walter Hart Blumenthal

# 1956

JANUARY MEETING  Address by August Heckscher

FEBRUARY  The 100th anniversary of the birth of Sigmund Freud
Speakers: Gregory Zilboorg (February) [New York: Privately printed by the
Peter Pauper Press for C. Otto von Kienbusch, 1956]; Goddard Lieberson
(March)

APRIL  Modern prints
Speaker: A. Hyatt Mayor

MAY   Contemporary American bookbindings, on the 50th anniversary of the Guild of Book Workers

OCTOBER   Second editions
Speakers: Herman W. Liebert (October); John Cook Wyllie (November)

DECEMBER   Pulitzer Prize winners: novels, plays, and verse
Speaker: Carlos Baker [*Princeton University Library Chronicle*, v. 16, no. 2, 1956]

# 1957

JANUARY MEETING   Address by Arthur Mizener

FEBRUARY   Japanese book illustration from the 9th to the 19th century
Speakers: Karl Küp, and a performance of a Nō play by Beate Gordon and Tatsuo Minagawa (February); Donald L. Keene (March)

APRIL   The 200th anniversary of the birth of William Blake
Speaker: Edwin Wolf 2nd

OCTOBER   American literature of the South
Speakers: Willard Thorp (October); Louis B. Wright (November)

DECEMBER   Illustrated natural history books
Speaker: Albert E. Lownes

# 1958

JANUARY MEETING   Address by Fairfield Osborn

FEBRUARY   One hundred books famous in science [P 131]
Speakers: I. Bernard Cohen (February); I. I. Rabi (March)

APRIL   Vellum—books, manuscripts, documents, and bindings
Speaker: Laurence C. Witten II

OCTOBER   "Astronautica Incunabula, or Zoom to the Moon": the history—in books, prints, manuscripts—of man's efforts to fly
Speakers: Richard Gimbel (October); Thomas D. Nicholson (November)

DECEMBER   Calligraphy
Speakers: Philip Hofer, Arnold Bank

# 1959

JANUARY   "From Poet to Premier"—an exhibition of the year 1809
Speakers: Gordon S. Haight (January); Howard Mumford Jones (February)

MARCH   75 years of the Grolier Club [P 125]
Speakers: C. Waller Barrett, Alexander Davidson, Jr.

SEPTEMBER   Historical and literary Americana mainly from the collections of
Thomas W. Streeter and C. Waller Barrett in honor of the visit of the
International League of Antiquarian Booksellers [P 127]

OCTOBER   "Esto Perpetua": The Club of Dr. Johnson and his friends
Speakers: Lewis P. Curtis (October) [Hamden, Conn.: Archon Books, 1963];
Herman W. Liebert (November) [Hamden, Conn.: Archon Books, 1963]

DECEMBER   American literature of the 1920's
Speaker: Maxwell Geismar

# 1960

JANUARY MEETING   Address by Glenway Wescott

FEBRUARY   Masters of Italian drawing, 1400–1800, from the collection of
Janos Scholz
Speaker: Janos Scholz

MARCH   Modern fine printing
Speakers: Alvin Eisenman (March); Norman H. Strouse (April) [New York:
Philip C. Duschnes, 1960]

SEPTEMBER   Spies and intelligence
Speaker: Walter L. Pforzheimer

OCTOBER   The Restoration, 1660–1960
Speakers: Donald Goddard Wing (October); George deF. Lord (November)

DECEMBER   Gastronomy
Speakers: Ted Patrick (December); James Beard (January 1961)

# 1961

FEBRUARY   Lewis and Clark
Speakers: Archibald Hanna (February); John Bakeless (March)

APRIL   "Imagerie Populaire": an exhibition of prints
Speakers: Karl Küp, A. Hyatt Mayor

JUNE   Contemporary British bookbindings

SEPTEMBER   The dramatic works of W. S. Gilbert [Charlottesville: The Bibliographical Society of the University of Virginia, 1963]
Speaker: Reginald Allen

OCTOBER   Italian influence on American literature [P 128]
Speakers: C. Waller Barrett (October); a panel discussion on "Dante in America" with Robert J. Clements, Thomas G. Bergin, Joseph A. Mazzeo, Howard H. Schless, Thomas C. Chubb (November)

DECEMBER   The work of Edward Lear
Speaker: Philip Hofer [New York: Oxford University Press (distributed by the Typophiles), 1962]

# 1962

JANUARY MEETING   Address by Walter Muir Whitehill

FEBRUARY   The book of India and Persia
Speakers: Karl Küp, with an entertainment (February); Charles K. Wilkinson (March)

APRIL   Demonology and witchcraft
Speaker: Lewis Leary

OCTOBER   "The Indomitable Irishry": Irish literature from Yeats to Beckett [G, n.s. 2]
Speakers: William York Tindall, and a reading by Padraic Colum (October); Denis Johnston (November)

DECEMBER   Additions to de Ricci: a quarter century of American collecting of medieval and renaissance manuscripts
Speaker: William H. Bond

# 1963

JANUARY MEETING   Address by Brendan Gill

FEBRUARY   "Other People's Mail": literary and historical letters
Speaker: Robert H. Taylor

MARCH   The work of Elmer Adler
Speakers: John T. Winterich, Frederick B. Adams, Jr. [P 130]

*April–November   Renovation of exhibition cases*

DECEMBER   The centenary of the death of William Makepeace Thackeray
Speaker: Gordon N. Ray

# 1964

JANUARY MEETING  Address by Lawrence Clark Powell, "The Three L's: Life, Landscape, and Literature." [Los Angeles: The Press in the Gate House, 1964]

FEBRUARY  "Since *The Waste Land*": modern poetry in English
Speakers: John L. Sweeney, Stephen Fassett (February); Cleanth Brooks (March)

APRIL  "Splendid Occasions": festival books of three centuries
Speaker: A. Hyatt Mayor

JUNE  Bibliography and book collecting from the Club library, on the occasion of the New York World's Fair

OCTOBER  The centenary of the death of Nathaniel Hawthorne [H 88; G, n.s. 5]
Speakers: Norman Holmes Pearson (October); Matthew J. Bruccoli (November)

DECEMBER  Shakespeare's Rivals
Speaker: Daniel Seltzer

# 1965

FEBRUARY  Illustrated books of the 1860's
Speakers: Robert H. Rosenblum (February); A. Hyatt Mayor (March)

APRIL  Jean Grolier and his times: the 400th anniversary of his death
Speaker: Colin Eisler

OCTOBER  "Dusty Diamonds": English boys' books
Speakers: Norman Holmes Pearson (October); James K. Folsom (November)

DECEMBER  American illustrated books since 1945 [H 89]
Speaker: Thomas Cornell

# 1966

FEBRUARY  "Upon Subtler Wings": French Parnassian and Symbolist poetry [G, n.s. 1]
Speakers: Henri Peyre (February); William Jay Smith (March)

APRIL  Dedication Copies [G, n.s. 1]
Speaker: Robert H. Taylor

JULY  A retrospective of Small Exhibitions

OCTOBER  Exiles and expatriates
Speakers: Alan Pryce-Jones (October) [G, n.s. 3]; Robert Halsband (November)

DECEMBER   The book of eastern Christendom
Speaker: Dorothy Miner [G, n.s. 3]

# 1967

FEBRUARY   Classics in translation
Speakers: Gilbert Highet (February) [G, n.s. 4]; Lewis Galantière (March)
[G, n.s. 4]

APRIL   Travelers in the desert
Speaker: Richard N. Frye [G, n.s. 4]

OCTOBER   "Second Thoughts": authors' corrected proofs [G, n.s. 6]
Speakers: Herman W. Liebert (October); Evan Thomas (November)

DECEMBER   The art nouveau book [G, n.s. 6]
Speaker: Alan Fern

# 1968

FEBRUARY   The 500th anniversary of the death of Johann Gutenberg
[G, n.s. 7]
Speakers: Frederick R. Goff (February); Hellmut Lehmann-Haupt (March)

APRIL   Treasures from the John Carter Brown Library [Providence, R.I.:
Associates of John Carter Brown Library, 1968]
Speaker: Thomas R. Adams [G, n.s. 8]

OCTOBER   Architects in the theatre, 1500–1800 [G, n.s. 9]
Speakers: Alois M. Nagler (October); A. Hyatt Mayor (November)

DECEMBER   Art Déco: French illustrated books, drawings, bindings, and
objets d'art of the 1920's [G, n.s. 10]
Speaker: A. Hyatt Mayor

# 1969

FEBRUARY   The 150th anniversary of the birth of Herman Melville [G, n.s. 11]
Speakers: Norman Holmes Pearson (February); Hennig Cohen (March)

APRIL   "A Society's Chief Joys": Americana from the American Antiquarian
Society [Worcester, Mass.: The American Antiquarian Society, 1969]
Speaker: Henry Steele Commager [G, n.s. 10]

OCTOBER   Queen Victoria's lady novelists
Speakers: David A. Robertson, Jr. (October) [G, n.s. 12]; Robert H. Taylor
(November)

DECEMBER   The Bodleian Library and its Friends [G, n.s. 12; Oxford: The Bodleian Library, 1969]
Speakers: Alfred H. Howell, John Freeman, Lord Caradon, Robert Shackleton

## 1970

FEBRUARY   Modern German fine printing
Speakers: Ernst Hauswedell (February) [G, n.s. 13]; Fritz Kredel (March)

APRIL   Bruce Rogers: sixty years of book design (to celebrate the centenary of his birth)
Speaker: Joseph Blumenthal [G, n.s. 14]

OCTOBER   The French book, 1510–1970 [G, n.s. 15]
Speakers: Arthur Vershbow (October) [G, n.s. 15]; Philip Hofer (November)

DECEMBER   Artists and architects in the theatre, 1800–1970
Speaker: Joseph Verner Reed (December)

## 1971

JANUARY MEETING   Address by Arnold Whitridge

FEBRUARY   Great American book collectors to 1800 [G, n.s. 16]
Speakers: Edwin Wolf 2nd (February) [G, n.s. 16]; Frederick R. Goff (March)

APRIL   The Maya scribe and his world [P 139]
Speaker: Michael D. Coe

JUNE   Bookbindings by Gerhard Gerlach (an exhibition by the Guild of Book Workers)

OCTOBER   Americana from members' collections on the occasion of the visit of L'Association Internationale de Bibliophilie to New York
Speaker: Ben Grauer (November)

DECEMBER   The works of Sir Max Beerbohm
Speaker: Robert H. Taylor [G, n.s. 17]

## 1972

FEBRUARY   The 400th anniversary of the birth of John Donne [P 137]
Speakers: John Sparrow (February); Louis L. Martz (March)

APRIL   Proust and his friends: the 50th anniversary of the death of Marcel Proust [G, n.s. 18]
Speaker: Roger Shattuck

OCTOBER   Picasso and his poets
Speakers: Douglas Cooper (October); Roland Penrose (November)

DECEMBER   Sir Thomas Phillipps: portrait of a collector, on the 100th
anniversary of his death
Speaker: Herman W. Liebert [G, n.s. 18]

# 1973

JANUARY MEETING   Address by Norman H. Strouse, "John Henry
Nash: A Collector's Reappraisal." [G, n.s. 19]

FEBRUARY   "A Selection from Our Shelves": books, manuscripts, and drawings
from the Philip H. and A. S. W. Rosenbach Foundation Museum and Library
[Philadelphia: Philip H. & A. S. W. Rosenbach Foundation, 1973]
Speakers: Lessing J. Rosenwald (February); Clive E. Driver (March) [G, n.s. 19]

APRIL   Fritz Kredel: fifty years of book illustration
Speaker: Warren Chappell [G, n.s. 19]

OCTOBER   "Murder by the Book"
Speakers: Carolyn G. Heilbrun, alias Amanda Cross (October) [G, n.s.
20/21]; Aaron Marc Stein, alias George Bagby, alias Hampton Stone
(November) [G, n.s. 20/21]

DECEMBER   John Milton: the poet illustrated, 1688–1973 [G, n.s. 20/21]
Speaker: Roland Mushat Frye

# 1974

FEBRUARY   "And Now a Bow": a centennial tribute to Gertrude Stein
[G, n.s. 20/21]
Speakers: James Mellow (February); a presentation of "When This You See
Remember Me," a documentary film produced by WNET-TV (March)

APRIL   The 90th anniversary of the Grolier Club: a retrospective from the
library [G, n.s. 20/21]

OCTOBER   "Prelude to Independence": the printed word and the American
Revolution [G, n.s. 22/23]
Speakers: Charles J. Tanenbaum (October) [G, n.s. 22/23]; Thomas R.
Adams (November)

DECEMBER   "The Truthful Lens": a survey of books illustrated with original
photographs, 1844–1914 [P 141]
Speaker: Beaumont Newhall

# 1975

FEBRUARY  "The World and *The New Yorker*": a 50th anniversary tribute
Speakers: Brendan Gill (February); Charles Addams, Geoffrey T. Hellman, Philip Hamburger, and Brendan Gill (March)

APRIL  "Nature's Handmaid Art": landscape architecture from the Garden of Eden to Central Park
Speaker: William F. Shellman

OCTOBER  Chess: the bibliophile's view [G, n.s. 22/23]
Speakers: Arthur Bisguier (October); Walter Goldwater (November)

DECEMBER  The 200th anniversary of the birth of the Rev. Thomas Frognall Dibdin
Speaker: Theodore Yonge

# 1976

FEBRUARY  The Gothic novel and the literature of ghosts and horror
Speakers: Robert H. Taylor (February); John C. Riely (March)

APRIL  "To Delight, Surprise, and Inform": literary sources of opera libretti [G, n.s. 24/25]
Speaker: Sarah Caldwell

OCTOBER  Europe in 1776 [H 90]
Program: A performance of music published in 1776 followed by a panel discussion with Charles J. Tanenbaum, Frederick R. Selch, and Marshall B. Davidson (October); William Howard Adams (November)

DECEMBER  Books as troublemakers
Speaker: Mortimer J. Adler

# 1977

FEBRUARY  The 20th anniversary of the Harper Bequest: acquisitions of the Grolier Club library, the New York Public Library, the Pierpont Morgan Library, the John Carter Brown Library, the William L. Clements Library, and the New-York Historical Society, and publications of the Bibliographical Society of America—all derived from the bequest of Mabel Herbert Harper, widow of Lathrop Colgate Harper
Speakers: Thomas R. Adams (February) [G, n.s. 26/27]; Thomas V. Lange, Gordon N. Ray, Joseph T. Rankin, Stuart B. Schimmel, and Frank S. Streeter (March)

APRIL  "Rare and Endangered": book illustrations depicting endangered plants and animals
Speaker: Howard S. Irwin, Jr.

OCTOBER  Literary and historical forgeries
Speakers: P. William Filby [G, n.s. 26/27], Stuart B. Schimmel (October);
Samuel Schoenbaum (November)

DECEMBER  "Splendor in Books": treasures from the Walters Art Gallery
of Baltimore
Speaker: Lilian M. C. Randall [G, n.s. 26/27]

# 1978

FEBRUARY  Printing in France, 1850–1900: the artist and new technologies
[G, n.s. 28/29]
Speakers: Peter A. Wick (February) [G, n.s. 28/29]; P. Dennis Cate (March)

APRIL  "O Magic City": New York in literature
Speaker: R. W. B. Lewis [G, n.s. 28/29]

JUNE  The Grolier Club: treasures from the library and archives

OCTOBER  Noah Webster and his dictionary
Speakers: Crawford Lincoln (October); Herman W. Liebert, David Guralnik,
Laurance Urdang (November)

DECEMBER  "Printer's Choice": American press books, 1968–1978 [Austin,
Texas: W. Thomas Taylor, 1983]
Speaker: Alan Fern

# 1979

FEBRUARY  "Prized Prints": selected from members' collections
Speakers: Arthur Vershbow (February); Riva Castleman, Colta Feller Ives
(March)

APRIL  "The Flower of Kings": an exhibition on King Arthur
Speaker: Robert A. Ackerman

JUNE  "In the Shadow of Duchamp": the photomechanical revolution and the
artist's book, 1968–1978, a loan exhibition from the Franklin Furnace Archive

OCTOBER  Jean Grolier: the man in his time
Speakers: Eugene Rice, Jr. (October) [G, n.s. 30/31]; John H. M. Salmon
(November) [G, n.s. 30/31]

DECEMBER   "Trade Roots": fine trade books, 1920–1950
Speaker: Donald S. Klopfer

# 1980

FEBRUARY   The Brinley centenary: the anniversary of the auction of the
George Brinley Americana collection
Speakers: Marcus A. McCorison (February) [G, n.s. 32]; William S. Reese
(March) [G, n.s. 32]

APRIL   Books and prints on musical instruments
Speaker: Howard Mayer Brown

OCTOBER   The centenary of the birth of H. L. Mencken
Speakers: Performance of a one-man show by John Rothman (October);
Carl Bode (November)

DECEMBER   Treasures from the Lilly Library, Indiana University
Speaker: William R. Cagle

# 1981

FEBRUARY   Color in books
Speakers: Leonard B. Schlosser (February); Thomas V. Lange (March)

APRIL   Bibliography: milestones in its history and development [P 144]
Speaker: Bernard H. Breslauer

JUNE   The 75th anniversary of the Guild of Book Workers [New York:
The Guild of Book Workers, 1981]

OCTOBER   18th-century Venetian illustrated books
Speakers: Eleanor M. Garvey (October); Andrew Robison (November)

DECEMBER   Ballet before 1800
Speaker: Parmenia Migel Ekstrom

# 1982

FEBRUARY   The 100th anniversary of the birth of James Joyce [G, n.s. 33/34]
Speakers: Hugh Kenner (February); John J. Slocum, Herbert T. F. Cahoon
(March) [G, n.s. 33/34]

APRIL   "Quarter of a Millennium": the 250th anniversary of the founding of
the Library Company of Philadelphia [Philadelphia: The Library Company
of Philadelphia, 1981]
Speaker: Edwin Wolf 2nd

OCTOBER  "Printmakers Observe Their Own World"
Speakers: Sinclair H. Hitchings (October); Suzanne Boorsch, P. Dennis Cate
(November)

DECEMBER  The Houghton Library—40th anniversary [Cambridge, Mass.:
The Houghton Library, 1982]
Speaker: Roger E. Stoddard

# 1983

FEBRUARY  "Honour'd Relics": objects having once belonged to eminent
writers
Speaker: Robert Nikirk (March)

APRIL  The 200th anniversary of the birth of Washington Irving
Speaker: Andrew Breen Myers

SEPTEMBER  The 100th anniversary of the Metropolitan Opera: a selection of
original stage and costume designs and early books on opera from the
collection of Robert L. B. Tobin

OCTOBER  "The Taste of 1884": a centennial exhibition on collectors and
collecting in the early years of the Grolier Club
Speaker: Terry Belanger (November)

DECEMBER  Publications of the Grolier Club: second exhibition marking the
centennial of the Grolier Club
Speaker: Roderick D. Stinehour

## SMALL EXHIBITIONS

# 1959

NOVEMBER  H. Bacon Collamore: First editions of American poets; books and
sketches by Beatrix Potter

# 1960

JANUARY  Paul Mellon: Costume books

APRIL  Norman H. Strouse: Books printed by Victor Hammer

NOVEMBER   Donald S. Stralem: Rarities of 19th-century American literature

## 1961

OCTOBER   Stuart B. Schimmel: Literary forgers and forgeries

DECEMBER   David McCandless McKell: Children in Books

## 1962

JANUARY   Selections from 1961 acquisitions of the Grolier Club library

FEBRUARY   Albert E. Lownes: Natural history books

APRIL   W. Hugh Peal: Charles Lamb and his circle

JULY   H. Bradley Martin: 19th-century French literature

OCTOBER   Michael Papantonio: Early American bindings

DECEMBER   Giorgio Uzielli: Aldine imprints and Renaissance bindings [A handlist was privately printed]

## 1963

FEBRUARY   Robert S. Pirie: Early English literature [A handlist was privately printed]

MARCH   Jack H. Samuels: 19th-century fiction [A handlist was privately printed]

DECEMBER   Morris H. Saffron: Drawings, prints, and books of Thomas Rowlandson [A handlist was privately printed]

## 1964

FEBRUARY   Charles E. Feinberg: Walt Whitman

APRIL   Norman H. Strouse: Bindings by T. J. Cobden-Sanderson, mainly for the Doves Bindery

JUNE   Bindings, manuscripts, and early printed books from the Club library

SEPTEMBER   John M. Crawford, Jr.: William Morris and the Kelmscott Press

## 1965

JANUARY   Gordon N. Ray: French lithographs, 1820–1860 [A handlist was privately printed]

FEBRUARY   H. Dunscomb Colt, Jr.: Rudyard Kipling centenary

APRIL   Frederic W. Goudy centenary from the Melbert B. Cary, Jr., collection of Goudyana

SEPTEMBER   Frederick W. Hilles: Sir Joshua Reynolds

NOVEMBER   Donald F. Hyde: Oscar Wilde

DECEMBER   Alfred H. Perrin: Sir Max Beerbohm

## 1966

JANUARY   Frank Altschul: French 18th-century illustrated books [G, n.s. 1]

MARCH   Lessing J. Rosenwald: Illustrated incunabula [G, n.s. 1]

APRIL   Jerome P. Webster: "Embassies to the Far East" [G, n.s. 1]

SEPTEMBER   Robert Dechert: Americana [G, n.s. 3]

NOVEMBER   Raphael Esmerian: 16th-century French bindings [G, n.s. 3]

DECEMBER   William E. Stockhausen: English literature, 18th–20th century, and American literature, 19th–20th century [G, n.s. 3]

## 1967

JANUARY   Herbert D. Schimmel: Henri de Toulouse-Lautrec [G, n.s. 4]

MARCH   William H. Scheide: Music [G, n.s. 4]

APRIL   Arthur A. Houghton, Jr.: Literary and historical manuscripts [G, n.s. 4]

SEPTEMBER   Books purchased by members during the Iter Septentrionale

OCTOBER   Charles Beecher Hogan: Jane Austen [G, n.s. 6]

DECEMBER   Grolier Club publications and bindings from The Club Bindery, plus prints from the Society of Iconophiles (in celebration of the 50th anniversary of the clubhouse)

## 1968

JANUARY   Paul Mellon: Fifty-five books printed in England before 1525 [P 134]

MARCH   Walter L. Pforzheimer: Molière [G, n.s. 8]

APRIL   Harrison D. Horblit: Sir Thomas Phillipps

SEPTEMBER   Herman W. Liebert: Samuel Johnson [G, n.s. 9]

October   Francis A. Kettaneh: Manuscripts, illuminated books, and bindings [G, n.s. 9]

December   Alfred C. Berol: English literature and Americana [G, n.s. 9]

## 1969

January   Arthur Vershbow: Etchings, engravings, and illustrated books, 15th–17th century [G, n.s. 10]

March   Robert H. Taylor: Association copies [G, n.s. 10]

April   Carl H. Pforzheimer Library: Shelley as a young radical [G, n.s. 11]

September   Leonard B. Schlosser: Books on papermaking [G, n.s. 12]

December   James Gilvarry: Modern literature and drawings [G, n.s. 12]

## 1970

January   James Osborn: 17th-century English manuscripts [G, n.s. 13]

February   Henry C. Taylor: Early books and manuscripts on navigation [G, n.s. 13]

September   John R. B. Brett-Smith: Later 17th-century English literature [G, n.s. 15]

October   Andrew Oliver, Jr.: Travellers in Greece and the Levant [G, n.s. 15]

December   Robert F. Metzdorf: Queen Victoria and her circle [G, n.s. 17]

## 1971

January   Bern Dibner: Heralds of Science

March   Edward S. Litchfield: Sporting books

April   Norman Holmes Pearson: Elizabethan to 20th-century literature

September   H. Bradley Martin: Americana and American literature [G, n.s. 17]

November   Kenneth A. Lohf: Sir Edward Burne-Jones [G, n.s. 17]

December   Paul Gourary: Festival books

## 1972

January   C. Waller Barrett: Twenty-five important works of American literature [A handlist was privately printed]

APRIL   Nathan Comfort Starr: Arthuriana [G, n.s. 18]

SEPTEMBER   James Laughlin: Giovanni Mardersteig and the Officina Bodoni

OCTOBER   Daniel Maggin: English and American literature

DECEMBER   Franklin H. Kissner: The rediscovery of classical Rome in
the 16th century [A handlist was privately printed]

## 1973

JANUARY   Norman H. Strouse: John Henry Nash [G, n.s. 19]

APRIL   David P. Wheatland: Scientific books and instruments

SEPTEMBER   Gordon W. Jones: Medical practice in 18th-century Virginia—
two Virginia doctor-collectors

OCTOBER   C. E. Frazer Clark, Jr.: Nathaniel Hawthorne

DECEMBER   E. Clark Stillman: Illuminated manuscripts and 16th-century
illustrated books

## 1974

JANUARY   Edward Naumburg, Jr.: Ford Madox Ford [G, n.s. 20/21]

MARCH   Charles A. Ryskamp: William Blake and his followers [G, n.s. 20/21]

SEPTEMBER   Alan Fern: The Eragny Press and drawings by Lucien Pissarro

DECEMBER   Stephen R. Parks: The Gothic Revival

## 1975

JANUARY   Abel E. Berland: Fifty books famous in English literature [A
handlist was privately printed]

APRIL   Matthew J. Bruccoli: *The Great Gatsby*, on the 50th anniversary of
its publication

SEPTEMBER   Arthur G. Rippey: Samuel Johnson

OCTOBER   Alexandre Rosenberg: Incunabula

DECEMBER   Duncan Andrews: "Tally Ho! 400 Years of Foxhunting" [A
handlist was privately printed]

## 1976

JANUARY   Donald C. Gallup: T. S. Eliot and Ezra Pound

MARCH   William Salloch: Illustrations of books and people

OCTOBER   The 300th anniversary of the first English book auction, from the collections of William P. Barlow, Jr., Harrison D. Horblit, and the Grolier Club

DECEMBER   Charles W. Mann: The Crystal Palace

## 1977

JANUARY   Louis Szathmary: Cookery books

APRIL   Walter Pond: 19th-century New York theatre illustrated by handbills, programs, and ephemera [G, n.s. 26/27]

SEPTEMBER   John Davis Hatch: John Vander Lyn and "Panoramania"

OCTOBER   Robert A. Wilson: W. H. Auden

## 1978

JANUARY   R. Dyke Benjamin: John Ruskin [G, n.s. 28/29]

APRIL   Julia Parker Wightman: Bookbindings from the 16th to the 19th century

SEPTEMBER   Frank S. Streeter: "A French Captain Cook—Jean de La Pérouse and French Exploration in the South Pacific"

NOVEMBER   Charles Zitner: *Livres de peintres*

## 1979

JANUARY   J. M. Edelstein: The Black Sun Press

APRIL   Mrs. Ewing P. Reilley: The literature of the English landscape park

SEPTEMBER   John S. Kebabian: The history of crafts, tools, and technology

DECEMBER   Hope Weil: Contemporary fine bindings

## 1980

JANUARY   Mrs. Linton R. Massey: Five centuries of herbals and medical botany books

APRIL   Robert D. Graff: The 100th anniversary of the birth of Sean O'Casey

SEPTEMBER   Henry H. Clifford: California pictorial letter sheets

## 1981

JANUARY   Peter A. Wick: Books and journals illustrated by J. J. Grandville [A handlist was privately printed]

JUNE   Bookplates from the Club library; lithographs and book illustrations by Joseph Pennell

SEPTEMBER   Mrs. John D. Gordan: Giovanni Francesco Poggio Bracciolini and other 15th-century Italian humanists

NOVEMBER   William P. Barlow, Jr.: John Baskerville

## 1982

JANUARY   Kenneth E. Hill: American ornithology books

MARCH   Robert N. Essick: William Blake's commercial book illustrations

MAY   Selections from the collections of new members

SEPTEMBER   Carl Woodring: Charles Ricketts

NOVEMBER   Jack W. C. Hagstrom: Richard Wilbur

DECEMBER   BR Today: the 25th anniversary of the death of Bruce Rogers (organized by the Committee on Modern Fine Printing) [P 143]

## 1983

JANUARY   Recent acquisitions of the Grolier Club library

MARCH   Samuel J. Wagstaff, Jr.: Photographic reproduction processes

APRIL   Charles Liebman, Jr.: Books, maps, and views of Paris

JUNE   Selections from the collections of new members

SEPTEMBER   "The Vintage of 1884": books published in the year of the Grolier Club's founding

NOVEMBER   Works written or produced by Grolier Club members in the Club library

EXHIBITIONS ORGANIZED BY THE
COMMITTEE ON MODERN FINE PRINTING
(HELD IN THE LOBBY OF THE CLUBHOUSE)

## 1971

JULY   Will and Sebastian Carter and the Rampant Lions Press

SEPTEMBER   Saul and Lillian Marks and the Plantin Press [Los Angeles:
The Plantin Press, 1971]

## 1972

JANUARY   Henry Morris and the Bird & Bull Press; and Leonard F. Bahr and
the Adagio Press

MARCH   Lewis Allen and the Allen Press

JUNE   David R. Godine

OCTOBER   Walter Hamady and the Perishable Press

## 1973

FEBRUARY   Adrian Wilson

APRIL   A retrospective of Typophiles Chapbooks

NOVEMBER   Cambridge University Press Christmas books

## 1974

FEBRUARY   Printing by students of Philip M. Hamilton of the University of
Wisconsin at Madison, Department of Art

JUNE   Printing by students of Philip M. Hamilton of the University of
Wisconsin at Madison, Department of Art (a second, all different, exhibition)

SEPTEMBER   The 100th anniversary of the Stanbrook Abbey Press

## 1975

FEBRUARY   Private presses in Lexington, Kentucky: Victor Hammer
(Stamperia del Santuccio and The Anvil Press), The Bur Press, The Gravesend
Press, and The King Library Press of the University of Kentucky

OCTOBER   Harry Duncan—the Cummington Press and Abattoir Editions of the University of Nebraska at Omaha (from the collection of Jack W. C. Hagstrom)

## 1976

JANUARY   Carroll Coleman and the Prairie Press

SEPTEMBER   Personal printing by P. J. Conkwright

NOVEMBER   Bookplates of Grolier Club members

## 1977

MAY   A 90th birthday tribute to Frank Altschul

## 1978

JANUARY   Modern fine printing purchased for the Club library since 1970

# Index

Abattior Editions, 1975 Committee on Modern Fine Printing exhibition on, 224

Abbey, Edwin Austin, 1886 exhibition of his drawings for Goldsmith's *She Stoops to Conquer*, 167, 176; publication on, 155 (H2)

Abbey, John Roland, his copy of the MacCarthy Reagh sale, 65; Grolier Club purchases at auction sale of, 41, 69

Abbott, Charles D., 1955 Club speaker on Authors at Work, 205

Ackerman, Robert A., 1979 Club speaker on King Arthur, 214

"Acte concernyng printers and bynders of bokes," 55

Actors, 1907 exhibition of engraved portraits of, 184; publication on, 159 (H58)

*Ad censuras theologorum parisiensium, quibus Biblia a R. Stephano . . . responsio*, 55

Adagio Press, 1972 Committee on Modern Fine Printing exhibition on, 223

Adam, Robert Borthwick, catalogue of his library, 71

Adams, Frederick B., Jr., 52; on Committee on Publications, 114; his talk on 100 Influential American Books published, 146–147 (P114); his talk on Elmer Adler published, 150–151 (P130)

—Club speaker: in 1938 on literature of radical movements in America, 171, 196; in 1946 on 100 influential American books, 201; in 1954, 205; in 1963 on Elmer Adler, 208

Adams, J. Donald, 1950 Club speaker on great autobiographies, 203

Adams, John Cranford, 1952 Club speaker, 204

Adams, Katherine, bookbinding by, 42

Adams, Raymond, 1954 Club speaker on Thoreau and *Walden*, 205

Adams, Thomas R., Club speaker: in 1968 on the John Carter Brown Library, 210; in 1974 on printing and the American Revolution, 212; in 1977 on Harper Bequest, 213

Adams, William Howard, 1976 Club speaker on Europe in 1776, 213

Addams, Charles, 1975 Club speaker on *The New Yorker*, 213

"Additions to de Ricci," 1962 exhibition of medieval and Renaissance manuscripts in American collections, 208

Adler, Elmer, 113; autograph letters of, 79; 1938 Club speaker on the history of the recorded word, 197; 1963 exhibition on, 208; publication designed and printed by, 144–145 (P105); publication designed by, 146–147 (P114); publication on, 150–151 (P130)

Adler, Mortimer J., 1976 Club speaker on books as troublemakers, 213

Aeronautics, 1940 exhibition on development of, 198

Alchemy, 1891 exhibition on, 168, 178; publication on, 155 (H12)

Aldine Club, 88

Aldine Homer (1504), owned by Grolier, 43

*Aldus in his Printing Establishment*, bookbinding, 42–43; etching, 121; painting, 107

Alexander, John W., portrait of Robert Hoe III by, 108

Alexandrian Library, 1947 Club speaker on, 202

Allen Press, 1972 Committee on Modern Fine Printing exhibition on, 223

Allen, Charles Dexter, *A Classified List of Early American Book-plates*, 123

Allen, Gay Wilson, 1955 Club speaker on Whitman and *Leaves of Grass*, 205

Allen, Lewis, 1972 Committee on Modern Fine Printing exhibition on, 223

Allen, Reginald, 1961 Club speaker on W. S. Gilbert, 208

Almanacs, French, 1905 exhibition of, 183; publication on, 159 (H55)

*Alphabeticum chaldaicum*, copy owned by John Evelyn, 58

Altschul, Frank, 141 (P89); gifts of prints, 82; on Committee on Publications, 114; 1922 exhibition of his gift of reproductions of Blake's illustrations for *The Divine Comedy*, 190; 1926 Club speaker on Gavarni, 191; 1966 small exhibition from the collection of, 218; 1977 Committee on Modern Fine Printing exhibition on, 224

Americana

—exhibitions: in 1888, 167, 177; in 1926, 191; in 1930, 193; in 1938, Western, 196; in 1959 from the collections of Thomas W. Streeter and C. Waller Barrett, 207; in 1969 from the American Antiquarian Society, 210; in 1971 to mark the visit of L'Association Internationale de Bibliophilie, 211; in 1980, 215

—publications: 149–150 (P127); 155 (H5)

—small exhibitions: in 1966, 218; in 1968, 219; in 1971, 219

American Antiquarian Society, 1969 exhibition from, 210; American auction catalogue collection of, 63; 149–150 (P127)

American books, 100 influential, 1946 exhibition of, 201

American book auctions, George L. McKay's 1936 talk on, 196

*American Book Auction Catalogues, 1713–1934*, 63

*American Engravers upon Copper and Steel*, 130

Index

American history, publications on: 122 (P14), 129 (P41), 140 (P87)

American humor, 1927 Club speaker on, 191

American industry, 1947 exhibition on iconography of, 202

American Institute of Graphic Arts, 144–145 (P105)
—joint exhibitions with: in 1938, 197; in 1940, 198; in 1944, 200; in 1945, 201; in 1947, in 1948, 202
—joint meeting with: in 1919, 188

American life, portrayed by American illustrators, 1939 exhibition on, 197

American literature
—exhibitions: 168–169; 170; in 1957, Southern, 206; in 1959, 207; in 1961 on Italian influence on, 208
—publications: 146–147 (P114), 150 (P128)
—small exhibitions: 172; in 1960, 217; in 1966, 218; in 1971, 219; in 1972, 219, 220

American poetry, 1939 exhibition of, 197; 1959 small exhibition of, 172, 216

American press books, 1978 exhibition of, 214

American Revolution, 1903 exhibition of portraits of men connected with, 183; 1952 exhibition on, 204; 1974 exhibition on, 212

American Revolutionary broadsides, 1904 exhibition of, 183

American Society of Wood Engravers, gift of woodcuts, 81

American women writers, 1948 exhibition on, 202

Analectic Magazine (Phila., 1819), first American lithograph in, 55

Anatomical books, 1925 exhibition of, 191

"And Now a Bow," 1974 exhibition on Gertrude Stein, 212

Anderson, John, Jr., 79

Andreini, Joseph M., gift of Daniel Press collection, 39

Andrews, Duncan, 1975 small exhibition from the collection of, 220

Andrews, Mrs. William Loring, gifts to library, 38–39; 1931 exhibition of bequest of, 193

Andrews, William Loring, manuscript library catalogue of, 71; autograph letters from Fitz-Greene Halleck, 78; establishes Society of Iconophiles, 82; his scrapbooks, 87; on first Committee on Publications, 112; 1920 memorial meeting for, 188
—gifts: of prints, 81; of private library catalogues, 69

Angers, Pierre Jean David d', bronze statue of Gutenberg by, 109–110

Angling bookplates. See Bookplates, angling

Angling books, 1911 exhibition of, 185; publications on: 156 (H21), 160 (H70)

Animals, endangered, 1977 exhibition of book illustrations of, 214

Anthoensen Press, 113; publication designed and printed by, 152 (P134); publication printed by, 147 (P116)

Anthony, A. V. S., Wood-Engraving: Three Essays, 135–136

Anvil Press, 1975 Committee on Modern Fine Printing exhibition on, 223

Architects and artists in the theatre, 1970 exhibition on, 211

Architects in the theatre, 1968 exhibition on, 210

Architectural prints, 1946 Club speaker on, 201

Architecture, 1918 exhibition on, 188

Arents, George, 1941 Club speaker on books relating to tobacco, 199; catalogue of his library, 71

Areopagitica, 121

Ariosto, marble bust of, 109

Aristarchus; or Principles of Composition, 56

Aristotle, De arte poetica, copy owned by W. W. Greg, 58

Arms, John Taylor, 1941 demonstration of making an etching of the Grolier Club Library, 198; 1946 exhibition of prints, drawings, and etched plates by, 201
—Club speaker: in 1939 on contemporary American prints, 197; in 1946 on his own work, 201

Art, exhibitions of: 167, 168, 170; in 1893, 179

Art Age, The, report of first meeting of Grolier Club in, 165

Art déco, 1968 exhibition of French books and objects of the 1920s, 210

Art nouveau books, 1967 exhibition of, 210

Arte de escribir, 54

Arthur, King, 1972 small exhibition on, 220; 1979 exhibition on, 214

Artists and architects in the theatre, 1970 exhibition on, 211

Artist's books, 1979 Franklin Furnace Archive exhibition of, 214

Asaf, Allen, 117, 175

Ascensius, Joducus Badius, device of, 54

Ashburnham, 4th Earl of, manuscript library catalogue of, 70

Ashendene Press, 1920 exhibition of fine printing from Didot the Elder to the, 189

Association copies, 1935 exhibition of, 195; 1947 exhibition of, 202; 1969 small exhibition of, 219; in Grolier Club Library, 57–58

Association Internationale de Bibliophilie, 1971 exhibition to mark visit of, 211

"Astronautica Incunabula," 1958 exhibition of books, prints, manuscripts on man's efforts to fly, 206

Aubrey Beardsley: Catalogue of Drawings and Bibliography, 146

Auction catalogues, 59–67, 95; ephemeral nature of, 59; significance and value of Grolier Club collection, 59–60; earliest English, 60; American, 63; French, 64–65; from other countries, 66–67

Auctions, first English, 1976 small exhibition on, 221

Auden, W. H., 1946 Club speaker on Henry James, 171, 201; 1977 small exhibition on, 221

Audsley, William James and George Ashdown, Outlines of Ornament, 119 (P2)

Augustine, Saint, De Civitate Dei, first printing, 50–51

Austen, Jane, 1967 small exhibition on, 218

Austin, Gabriel, and growth of auction catalogue collection, 40–41; Club Librarian, 46; The Grolier

*Club Iter Italicum*, 150; *The Library of Jean Grolier*, 46, 115, 152

Authors, exhibitions of portraits of, 168; in 1905, in 1906, in 1907, in 1910, in 1911, 183–185

*Authors at Work*, 1955 exhibition on, 205; 149

Authors' corrected proofs, 1967 exhibition of, 210

Autobiographies, 1950 exhibition of, 203

Avery, Samuel Putnam, 122 (P11); his bookbinding collection, 42; commissions Meunier bookbinding, 42–43; dedicates catalogue of his bookbinding collection to Grolier Club, 173; letters to Beverly Chew, 79; on Committee on Publications, 114; portrait of, 21

—gifts: of incunabula, 50–51; of prints, 81; of private library catalogues, 69; to library, 38; of *Catalogus Bibliothecae Thuanae*, 65; of French auction catalogues, 40; of painting of *Aldus in his Printing Establishment*, 107

Avery, Samuel Putnam, Jr., gift of his father's collection of Grolier Club printing, 84

A. W. Stevens Printing Co., publication printed by, 142 (P92)

Babb, James T., 1944 Club speaker on unique books, prints, and broadsides, 200

Babcock, Betty, 144 (P104)

Bagby, George. *See* Stein, Aaron Marc

Bahr, Leonard F., 1972 Committee on Modern Fine Printing exhibition on, 223

Bakeless, John, 1961 Club speaker on Lewis and Clark, 207

Baker, Carlos, 1956 Club speaker on Pulitzer Prize winners, 206

Bale, John, *Illustrium Maioris Britanniae scriptorum*, 42

Ballard, Ellis Ames, 1929 Club speaker on Kipling, 192

"Ballet before 1800," 1981 exhibition on, 215

Bangs, John Kendrick, letters to Beverly Chew, 79

Bank, Arnold, 1958 Club speaker on calligraphy, 206

Barbedienne, Ferdinand, 108

Barker, Robert, 113; 117 (P1)

Barletius, Marinus, 43

Barlow, William P., Jr., 68; 1976 small exhibition from the collection of, 221; 1981 small exhibition from the collection of, 222

Barnes, James, 1912 Club speaker on the War of 1812, 186

Barney, William Whiston, 1918 exhibition of mezzotints by, 187; publication on, 160 (H78)

Barnheim, Hofrat, late 19th-century Berlin book collector, 50

*Barons of the Potomack and the Rappahannock*, 122

Barrett, C. Waller, 112; 1959 Club speaker on Grolier Club's 75th anniversary, 207; his 75th anniversary address published, 149 (P125); 1959 exhibition of Americana from his collection, 207; catalogue of 1959 exhibition, 149–150 (P127); 1961 Club speaker on Italian influence on American literature, 208; his *Italian Influence on American Literature* ad-

dress published, 150; 1972 small exhibition from the collection of, 219

Bartlett, Henrietta C., 1916 Club speaker on William Shakespeare, 187

Barye, Antoine-Louis, 1909 exhibition of bronzes and paintings by, 184; publication on, 159 (H66)

Baskerville, John, 1981 small exhibition on, 222

Baskin, Leonard, his Johann Gutenberg–Jean Grolier Medal, 153 (P140), 164

Bauer, Douglas F., 41, 90

Baughman, Roland, 1947 Club speaker on contemporary American hand bookbindings, 202

Bavarian Royal Library, 50

Baxter, James P., III, 1944 Club speaker on "The War and the Liberal Arts," 200

Baynes, William and Richard, catalogues of in Grolier Club Library, 62

*Baziliωlogia*, 134

Beal, Alvin C., 1925 Club speaker on early garden books, 191

Beale, Charles, his portrait, originally thought to be of Dryden, 127 (P30)

Beale, Mary, portrait thought to be of Dryden attributed to, 110, 127 (P30)

Beals, Ralph A., 1953 Club speaker, 204

Beard, James, 1960 Club speaker on gastronomy, 207

Beard, James Franklin, Jr., 1951 Club speaker on James Fenimore Cooper, 203

Beardsley, Aubrey, 1945 exhibition of drawings and book illustrations by, 201; publications on: 146 (P112); 161 (H87)

Bechtel, Edwin De T., 1941 Club speaker on Jacques Callot, 198; 1950 Club speaker on political cartoons of the reign of Louis-Philippe, 203; *Freedom of the Press and L'Association Mensuelle*, 148

Bechtel, Louise Seaman, 1953 Club speaker on children's books, 204

Beckett, Samuel, 1962 exhibition on, 208

Beerbohm, Max, 1944 exhibition on, 200; 1971 exhibition on, 211; 1965 small exhibition on, 218

Beilenson, Peter, 113; publications designed and printed by: 148 (P122); 149 (P124–P125)

Beinecke, Edwin J., 1941 Club speaker on Stevenson, 198; his Stevenson collection, 45

Belanger, Terry, 102; 1983 Club speaker on "The Taste of 1884," 216

Bell, Harold W., 1928 Club speaker on J.-E. Laboureur, 192

*Belles-lettres*. *See* Literature

*Belles-Lettres Repository*, 141

Bement, Edward, gift of *Horae*, 40

Bender, J. Terry, Club Librarian, 45–46

Benét, Stephen Vincent, 1939 exhibition on, 197

Benjamin, R. Dyke, 1978 small exhibition from the collection of, 221

Bennett, Paul A., editor of *Elmer Adler in the World of Books*, 150–151 (P130); notes on uncompleted biography of Frederic Warde, 87

Benson, John Howard, book decorations by, 144–145 (P105)

Bergin, Thomas G., 1961 Club speaker on Dante in America, 208

Berland, Abel E., 1975 small exhibition from the collection of, 220

Berol, Alfred C., 1968 small exhibition from the collection of, 219

Berry, Agnes, bookplate of Anna Damer designed by, 58

Berthelet, Thomas, printer, 55

Beurdeley, Jacques, 1927 exhibition of etchings by, 191

Bible, first printed in vernacular language, 49; fragments of 36-line, 49; photograph of, 22; 42-line: in Grolier Club exhibition, 170; leaves from, 49

*Bibliographical Notes on One Hundred Books Famous in English Literature*, 115

Bibliographical Society, 89

Bibliographical Society of America, 1977 exhibition of its publications made possible by the Harper Bequest, 213

Bibliography, 1935 exhibition, 195; 1964 exhibition to mark the 1964 New York World's Fair, 209; collecting of, 95

*Bibliography, its History and Development*, 115, 154; 1981 exhibition on, 215

*Bibliography of William Blake*, 137

*Bibliomania*, 111

Bibliophile Society, The, 1903 edition of Dibdin's *Bibliomania*, 111

*Bibliotheca Heberiana*, 61

*Bibliotheca Heinsiana*, 69

Bibliotheca Lindesiana, 60

*Bibliothecae Cordesianae catalogus*, 65, 69

Bierstadt process, reproductions by, 120 (P4); 122–123 (P15)

Bierstadt, Edward, reproductions by, 122 (P13)

Bill, Alfred Hoyt, 1952 Club speaker on the American Revolution, 204

Bingham, Millicent Todd, 1945 Club speaker on Emily Dickinson, 171, 201

Bird & Bull Press, 1972 Committee on Modern Fine Printing exhibition on, 223

Birell, Augustine, *Three Essays: I. Book-Buying, II. Book-Binding, III. The Office of Literature*, 139

Bisguier, Arthur, 1975 Club speaker on chess books, 213

Bishop, Cortlandt Field, 79; 1919 Club speaker on historical bookbindings, 188

Black Sun Press, 1979 small exhibition on, 221

Blake, William
—exhibitions: in 1904, 169, 183; in 1919, 188; in 1922 of reproductions of his illustrations for *The Divine Comedy*, 190; in 1957, 206
—publications: 137 (P73); 148–149 (P123); 158 (H53); 160 (H80)
—small exhibitions: in 1974, 220; in 1982 of his commercial book illustrations, 222

Bland, Harry MacNeill, 1931 Club speaker on George Washington, 194

Bluet, catalogue of his library, 71

Blumenthal, Joseph, 113, 115; 1970 Club speaker on Bruce Rogers, 211; *Typographic Years*, 154
—publications designed by: 147 (P117); 149 (P126); 150 (P128); 151–152 (P133); 152 (P135); 154 (P142)

Blumenthal, Walter Hart, 1955 Club speaker on "Odd volumes," 205

Blyenberch, Abraham, Ben Jonson portrait now attributed to, 110

Boccaccio, Giovanni, *Genealogie Deorum*, 51; *Life of Dante*, 126

Bode, Carl, 1980 Club speaker on Mencken, 215

Bodleian Library, 1969 exhibition of items from, 211; Bowyer-Nichols Ledgers deposited at, 89

Bodoni, Giambattista, 1914 exhibition of books and broadsides printed by, 186

*Bohemian Girl* (painting), 1891 exhibition of, 178

Bolton, H. Carrington, 1891 Club speaker on books on alchemy and chemistry, 178

Bond, W. H., editor of *Eighteenth-Century Studies*, 152

Bonet, Paul, bookbinding by, 42

Book Arts Press, 104

*Book Catalogues: Their Varieties and Uses*, 72

Book clubs, 1928 exhibition of publications of, 192

Book collecting, 1942 Club speaker on, 199; 1964 exhibition to mark the 1964 New York World's Fair, 209; resources for study of, in Grolier Club Library, 73, 95; its relationship to scholarship, 90–91

Book collecting in America before 1884, Granniss's 1936 talk on, 196

Book collectors, American, 1971 exhibition on, 211; exhibitions of portraits of: 168; in 1905, in 1906, in 1907, in 1910, in 1911, 183–185

Book collectors and collecting, 1983 exhibition on, 216

Book collectors of the past, 1936 exhibition on, 196

*Book Decorations*, 115, 143

Book Fellows' Club, 78

Book illustration, exhibitions on, 168, 172; 1885 exhibition on, 176; resources for study of, in Grolier Club Library, 55–56

Book illustrators, English, 1953 exhibition on, 204

Book of eastern Christendom, 1966 exhibition on, 210

Book of India and Persia, 1962 exhibition on, 208

Bookbinders, autograph letters and manuscripts of, 75–76; English, trade cards of, 81; exhibitions of portraits of: 168; in 1905, in 1906, in 1907, in 1910, in 1911, 183–185

Bookbindings, bibliography of books on, 131 (P47); collecting of, 41
—exhibitions: by place: American, in 1897, 180; in 1907, 168, 184; in 1947, 202; in 1956, 206; British, in 1961, 207; English, in 1899, 181; French, in 1905, 183; in 1968, 210
—by period: Renaissance, in 1936, 196; historic, in 1886, 176; in 1895, 180; in 1919, 188; 19th-century, in 1919, 188; modern, in 1886, 176; in 1890, 178; in 1906, 183

—general and miscellaneous subjects: 168, 172; in 1893, 167, 179; in 1894, commercial, 168, 197; in 1898, 181; in 1901, 182; in 1902, mosaic, 162, 182; in 1903, silver, embroidered, curious, 182; in 1905, armorial, 183; in 1920, ivory, embroidered, silver, 188; in 1924 from the bequest of Beverly Chew, 190; from the Guild of Book Workers: in 1971, by Gerhard Gerlach, 211; in 1981, 215

—publications: 120 (P4); American, 159 (H61); armorial, 124 (P19); commercial, 156 (H23); curious, 158 (H49); embroidered, 158 (H49); English, 157 (H36); French, 159 (H55); modern, 121 (P9), 155 (H1, H11), 159 (H57); mosaic, 158 (H46); Renaissance, 144 (P103); silver, 158 (H49)

—small exhibitions: in 1962, Renaissance, 217; in 1962, American, 217; in 1966, French, 16th-century, 218; in 1968, 219; in 1978, 16th–19th-century, 221; in 1979, contemporary, 221

—Club speakers: in 1885 on artistic history of, 176; in 1885 on modern, 176

Bookplates

—exhibitions: in 1930, designed by Edwin Davis French, 193; in 1931, designed by C. W. Sherborn, 193; in 1981 small exhibition from the Grolier Club Library, 222

—Angling: 1911 exhibition of, 185; 1918 exhibition of, 188; publication on, 160 (H70); publication on, 160 (H79). *See also* Angling books

—early American: 1894 exhibition of, 179; 1920 exhibition of, 189; publication on, 156 (H24)

—of Grolier Club members, 1976 Committee on Modern Fine Printing exhibition on, 224

Books, exhibitions of, in 1870s, 166

Books about books, research value of, 91

Books and people, 1976 small exhibition on, 221

Books as troublemakers, 1976 exhibition on, 213

Booksellers, autograph letters and manuscripts of, 75–77; 1914 exhibition of English and French trade cards of, 186; English, trade cards of, in Grolier Club Print Collection, 81

Booksellers' catalogues, 59–67, 95; ephemeral nature of, 59; significance and value of Grolier Club collection, 59–60; earliest English, 61–62; American, 63–64; French, 65; of other countries, 66–67

Boorsch, Suzanne, 1982 Club speaker on "Printmakers Observe Their Own World," 216

Borde, Philip, catalogue of, 65–66

*Boston Port Bill, The*, 129

Boswell, James, papers of, 1930 exhibition of, 171, 193; publication on, 142 (P95); Pottle's 1951 talk on, 203

Botanical books, 1943 exhibition on, 200; publication on, 145 (P107); medical, 1980 small exhibition of, 221

Bothwell, J. W., publication printed by, 142 (P92)

Boughton, George H., 119 (P3); his illustrations to the Grolier Club's edition of *The Scarlet Letter*, 115, 131; 1909 exhibition of his watercolors for *The Scarlet Letter*, 184

Bowen, Clarence W., 1893 Club speaker on portraits of Benjamin Franklin, 179

Bowman, Isaiah, 1932 Club speaker on polar exploration, 194

Bowyer-Nichols Ledgers, 88–89

Boys' books, English, 1965 exhibition of, 209

Boze, Claude Gros de, catalogue of his library, 72

Bracquemond, Jules, 1891 exhibition on, 178

Bradford, William, 123 (P17); 1893 exhibition on, 179; publication on, 156 (H19)

Brainerd, Ira Hutchinson, 142 (P92); 1909 Club speaker on Edwin Davis French, 184; 1928 Club speaker on De Vinne, 192

Brenner, Victor David, medallion portrait of Emerson modeled by, 164; 1907 exhibition of medals and plaques by, 184; publication on, 159 (H59)

Breslauer, Bernard H., 1981 Club speaker on bibliography, 215; and Folter, Roland, *Bibliography, its History and Development*, 154

Brett-Smith, John R. B., 1970 small exhibition from the collection of, 219

Bridges, Robert, bibliography of, by George L. McKay, 45

Brigham, Clarence Saunders, 1936 Club speaker on Paul Revere, 196

Brinley, George, 1980 exhibition on the auction of his Americana collection, 215

British Library, auction catalogue collection, 60

British Museum Catalogue, 104

Britwell Court, 61

Broadsides, 1926 exhibition of, 191; publications on, 161 (H85); American Revolutionary, 1904 exhibition of, 183; early American, 1930 exhibition of, 193

Brooks, Cleanth, 1964 Club speaker on modern English poetry, 209

Broval, Dr., autograph letters to Count Libri, 77

Brown, Howard Mayer, 1980 Club speaker on books and prints on musical instruments, 215

Brown, John Carter, catalogue of his library, 71

Brown, John Mason, 1952 Club speaker on George Bernard Shaw, 204

Brown, Lloyd A., 1951 Club speaker on treaties and maps reflecting their effects, 203

Browne, Irving, 1891 Club speaker on the pursuits of the bookworm, 178

Bruccoli, Matthew J., 1964 Club speaker on Hawthorne, 209; 1975 small exhibition from the collection of, 220

Bruce collection, 1894 exhibition of, 179

Bruce family, gift of early printed books, 38, 49–50; gift of *Horae*, 40

Bruce, David Wolfe, 48–49; manuscript library catalogue of, 71; purchases books at Barnheim auction sale, 50

Bruce, George, typefounder, 48

Bryan, Mina R., 48

*BR Today: A Selection of His Books with Comments*, 154; 1982 small exhibition, 222

Bühler, Curt F., 148 (P122); 1952 Club speaker on

Index incunabula, 204; *Early Books and Manuscripts: Forty Years of Research*, 153

Buhot, Félix Hilaire, 1891 exhibition on, 178

Bulmer, William, 1923 exhibition on, 190

Bur Press, 1975 Committee on Modern Fine Printing exhibition on, 223

*Bureau typographique, Le*, 54

Burgess, Gelett, 1939 Club speaker on American life as portrayed by American illustrators, 197

Burlen, Robert, & Son, publication bound by, 152 (P134)

Burne-Jones, Edward, 1971 small exhibition on, 219

Burroughs, Edith Woodman, medallion portrait of Poe modeled by, 164

Burt, Charles W., 1896 exhibition of engraved work by, 180

Byron, George Gordon, Lord, 1924 exhibition on, 170, 190

Cagle, William R., 1980 Club speaker on the Lilly Library, 215

Cahoon, Hebert T. F., 74; Club speaker: in 1954, 205; in 1982 on James Joyce, 215

Caldecott, Randolph, 78; 1920 exhibition on, 188

Caldwell, Sarah, 1976 Club speaker on literary sources of opera libretti, 213

Calhoun, Philo C., 1943 Club speaker on Dickens's *A Christmas Carol*, 200

"California, Here I Come," 1939 talk by Harry T. Peters, 197

California pictorial letter sheets, 1980 small exhibition of, 221

Calligraphy, 1958 exhibition of, 206; American, 1944 exhibition of, 200

Callot, Jacques, exhibitions of engravings and etchings by: in 1915, 186; in 1941, 198

Calverley, Charles, medallion portrait of Lowell modeled by, 164

Cambridge University Press, publications printed by: 143 (P99); 144 (P102); publication designed and printed by, 148–149 (P123); 1973 Committee on Modern Fine Printing exhibition of Christmas books from, 223; 113

Cameron, D.Y., 1908 exhibition of etchings and drypoints by, 184; publication on, 159 (H63)

Campbell, Oscar J., 1953 Club speaker on Elizabethan books, 204

Campbell, Samuel, *Sale Catalogue of Books for 1789*, 63

Camus de Limare, Le, catalogue of his library, 72

Canevarius, Demetrius, 1891 Club speaker on library of, 178

Canonici, Mateo, 40

Capel, Arthur, Earl of Essex, manuscript library catalogue of, 70

Caraccioli, Louis Antoine de, *Le livre de quatre couleurs*, 56

Caradon, Lord, 1969 Club speaker on the Bodleian Library, 211

Caricatures, 1892 exhibition on, 178

—relating to America, 1946 exhibition of, 201

Carlyle, Thomas, 125 (P26)

Carpenter, G. R., 126 (P29)

Carpi, Ugo da, *Thesauro de scritto*, 54

Carrière-Belleuse, Albert Ernest, bust of Dürer by, 109

Carrington, Fitzroy, 1916 Club speaker on early German engravings, 187

Carter, John, 1935 Club speaker on certain 19th-century pamphlets, 171, 195; on *One Hundred Books Famous in English Literature*, 169

Carter, Will and Sebastian, 1971 Committee on Modern Fine Printing exhibition on, 223

Carteret, Léopold, 131 (P46, P48)

Carteret Book Club, archives of, in Grolier Club, 87

Cary, Melbert B., Jr., 194; gift of Goudyana collection, 39

—Collection of Goudyana, 57; 1943 exhibition from, 199; 1965 small exhibition from, 218

Cary, Mrs. Melbert B., Jr., 1943 reception for Frederic W. Goudy and, 199

Casa del Libro (San Juan), joint publication with, 150–151 (P130); letters about, 79

Cassatt, Mary, 1921 exhibition of etchings by, 189

Castle, Frederick A., on House Committee, 106

Castleman, Riva, 1979 Club speaker on prints from members' collections, 214

*Catalogue of an Exhibition Commemorating the Hundredth Anniversary of the Birth of William Makepeace Thackeray*, 133

*Catalogue of an Exhibition Illustrative of a Centenary of Artistic Lithography*, 125

*Catalogue of an Exhibition Illustrative of the Text of Shakespeare's Plays*, 136

*Catalogue of an Exhibition of First and Other Editions of the Works of John Dryden*, 126

*Catalogue of an Exhibition of Historical and Literary Americana*, 149–150

*Catalogue of an Exhibition of Illuminated and Painted Manuscripts*, 122–123

*Catalogue of an Exhibition of Original and Early Editions of Italian Books*, 129

*Catalogue of an Exhibition of Renaissance Bookbindings*, 144

*Catalogue of an Exhibition of Selected Works of the Poets Laureate of England*, 127

*Catalogue of an Exhibition of the Private Papers of James Boswell from Malahide Castle*, 142

*Catalogue of an Exhibition of the Works of Charles Dickens*, 134

*Catalogue of an Exhibition of Works by John Leech*, 134

*Catalogue of Books Illustrated by Thomas Rowlandson*, 136

*Catalogue of Books in First Editions Selected to Illustrate the History of English Prose Fiction*, 136

*Catalogue of Books . . . with Arms or Devices upon the Bindings*, 124

*Catalogue of Etchings and Dry Points by Rembrandt*, 127

*Catalogue of Original and Early Editions of Some of the*

*Poetical and Prose Works of English Writers from Langland to Wither*, 123

*Catalogue of Original and Early Editions of Some of the Poetical and Prose Works of English Writers from Wither to Prior*, 129

*Catalogue of Printed Works by and Memorabilia of Antoine Laurent Lavoisier*, 148

*Catalogue of the Engraved Portraits of Washington*, 129

*Catalogue of the Engraved Work of Asher B. Durand*, 124

*Catalogue of the First Editions of the Works of Alexander Pope*, 133

*Catalogue of the Most Vendible Books in England*, 61–62

*Catalogue of the Works of Rudyard Kipling*, 142

*Catalogue of Work of the De Vinne Press*, 142

*Catalogus Bibliothecae Thuanae*, 65, 69

*Catalogus illustrium virorum*, 52

Cate, Phillip D., 80; 1978 Club speaker on French printing, 214; 1982 Club speaker on "Printmakers Observe Their Own World," 216

Cauliflower Club, master's chair, 109

Caxton, William, 50; device of, 128 (P35)

Caxton Celebration in 1877, exhibition of books at, 166

Centennial Exhibition of 1876, exhibition of books at, 166

Central Park, 1975 exhibition on, 213

*Century Magazine*, 83; redesigned by De Vinne, 112

"Certain 19th-century pamphlets," 1935 exhibition on, 171, 195

Chamberlain, J. C., his Hawthorne catalogue, 130 (P43)

*Champ Fleury*, 53–54, 115, 141

Champlain, J. C., 1893 exhibition of medals by, 179

Champney, Elizabeth W., 1895 Club speaker on engraved portraits of women writers, 180

Champney, J. Wells, publication on, 156 (H22); 1894 exhibition of pastel portraits by, 179

Chandler, Charles F., 1885 Club speaker on photomechanical processes, 176

Chandler, Lloyd H., *A Summary of the Work of Rudyard Kipling*, 142

Chapin, Howard M., his introduction to *Gazette Française*, 140

Chaplin, Charles Joshua, 1896 exhibition of etchings by, 180

Chappell, Warren, 1973 Club speaker on Fritz Kredel, 212

Charavay, J., E., & N., catalogues of, 66

Charlot, Jean, 1945 Club speaker on contemporary Latin American prints, 201

Chaucer, Geoffrey, 1900 exhibition on, 169, 181; publications on: 122 (P13); 156 (H14); 158 (H41)

Chaumont, Jean de, librarian to Louis XIII, signed document of, 75

Cheltenham Press, publication designed at, 143 (P97)

Chemistry, 1891 exhibition on, 168, 178; publication on, 155 (H12)

Chéret, Jules, 1892 exhibition of posters by, 178

Chess books, 1975 exhibition of, 213

Chew, Beverly, bookbindings bequeathed by, 42; collection of letters to, 79; library supervisor, 36; 1924 memorial meeting for, 190; on first Committee on Publications, 113; *Longfellow Collectors' Handbook*, 166

—gifts: to library, 38; of *Horae*, 40; of prints, 81; of portrait thought to be of Dryden, 127 (P30)

—exhibitions: in 1920 of his gift of bookplates, 189; in 1924 of silver bindings and portraits bequeathed by, 190

Chiaroscuro prints from Reichel's *Die Clair-Obscur Schnitte*, 1927 exhibition of, 192

Chichester, Charles F., on Committee on Publications, 114

Children in books, 1961 small exhibition on, 217

Children's books, exhibitions of: in 1928, 192; in 1953, 204

Children's songs, 1920 performance of, 188

China trade, 1934 exhibition of books and prints on, 195

Chinese books, 1887 exhibition on, 177

Chinese illustrated books, 1935 exhibition of, 195

Chinese printing. *See* Printing, Chinese

Chinese writing. *See* Writing, Chinese

Chiswick Press, 113; 1896 Grolier Club exhibition on, 180; publications printed by, 134 (P60), 137 (P73); illustrations printed by, 148–149 (P123)

Chivalry, romances of, 1947 exhibition of, 202

Christie-Miller copy, 61

*Christopher Plantin and the Plantin-Moretus Museum*, 120

*Chronological Catalogue of the Engravings, Dry-points and Etchings of Albert Dürer*, 125

Chubb, Thomas C., 1961 Club speaker on Dante in America, 208

Church, E. D., catalogue of his library, 71

Cicero, printed by Robert Estienne (1543), copy owned by Anna Damer, 58

Circuses, 1938 exhibition on, 197

*City Hall, New York*, 110

*City Hall Park, New York*, 110

Clark, C. E. Frazer, Jr., 1973 small exhibition from the collection of, 220

Clarke and Way, Inc., publications printed by, 162–163 (G1–G13)

Clarke, Bert, publication designed by, 154 (P143)

Classics in translation, 1967 exhibition of, 210

*Classification Used in the Library of the Grolier Club*, 132

*Classified List of Early American Book-plates*, 123

Clayton, Howard, 1925 Club speaker on papermaking in Japan, 191

Cleland, Thomas Maitland, 113; publication designed and printed by, 139 (P80); book decorations by, 144–145 (P105)

—Club speaker: in 1914 on Bodoni, in 1915 on American illustrated books, 186; in 1920 on fine printing from Didot the Elder to the Ashendene Press, 189; in 1942 on color printing, 199

Clements, Robert J., 1961 Club speaker on Dante in America, 208

Clifford, Henry H., 1980 small exhibition from the collection of, 221

Clowes, William, & Son, publication typeset by, 152 (P136)

Club Bindery, The, de Bury's *Philobiblon* bound by, 114; publication on, 159 (H57); 1967 small exhibition of bookbindings by, 218; 1906 exhibition of bookbindings by, 183

Coale, Griffith Baily, 1942 Club speaker on naval prints, 199

Cobden-Sanderson, T. J., 1964 small exhibition of bookbindings by, 217

Coe, Michael D., 1971 Club speaker on the Maya scribe, 211; *The Maya Scribe and His World*, 153

Cohen, Hennig, 1969 Club speaker on Melville, 210

Cohen, I. Bernard, 1958 Club speaker on 100 books famous in science, 206

Colbert, Jean-Baptiste, 72

Cole, Timothy, 1915 Club speaker on American illustrated books, 186; *Wood-Engraving: Three Essays*, 135–136

Coleman, Carroll, 1976 Committee on Modern Fine Printing exhibition on, 224

Colines, Simon de, printer, 57

Colish, A., Press of. See Press of A. Colish

Collamore, H. Bacon, asked to present first small exhibition, 172; 1959 small exhibition from the collection of, 216

"Collectors' Choice," 1954 exhibition of items from the collections of Grolier members, 205

Colleges, American, 1944 exhibition of early views of, 200

Collier, John Payne, 78

*Colonial Printer, The*, 143

Color in books, 1981 exhibition of, 215; resources for study of, in Grolier Club Library, 56

Color Printing, 1942 exhibition on, 199; publication on, 135 (P64)

*Coloritto or the Harmony of Colouring in Painting*, 56

Colt, H. Dunscomb, Jr., 1965 small exhibition from the collection of, 218

Colum, Padraic, 1962 Club speaker reading Irish literature, 208

Columbia University, Butler Library, 99; library school, 36; School of Library Service: 45, 46; and the Grolier Club Cataloguing Project, 103

Comings, Lois Leighton, editor of Kent's *What I Am Pleased to Call My Education*, 147

Commager, Henry Steele, 1969 Club speaker on the American Antiquarian Society, 210

*Complete Angler, The*, publication on, 156 (H21)

*Compromise of the King of the Golden Isles, The*, 139

Conkwright, P. J., 113; publications designed by, 150–151 (P130), 153 (P138); on Elmer Adler, 150–151 (P130); 1976 Committee on Modern Fine Printing exhibition of his personal printing, 224

Conway, Moncure Daniel, *Barons of the Potomack and the Rappahannock*, 122

Cook, Clarence, 1898 Club speaker on early English engraved title-pages and frontispieces, 181

Cookery books. See Gastronomy

Cooper, Douglas, 1972 Club speaker on Picasso and his poets, 212

Cooper, James Fenimore, 1951 exhibition on, 203

Cooper, William, auction catalogues of, in Grolier Club Library, 60

Copland, Robert, his translation of *The History of Helyas*, 128 (P35)

Coral, Lenore, and Munby, A. N. L., *English Book Sale Catalogues*, 60

Corbin, John, 1916 Club speaker on William Shakespeare, 187

Cornell, Thomas, 1965 Club speaker on American illustrated books since 1945, 209

Corning Museum of Glass, 46

Corot, Jean-Baptiste-Camille, 1901 exhibition of etchings by, 182

Cortissoz, Royal, his introduction to *The Etched Work of Whistler*, 131; his introduction to Dickens catalogue, 134 (P59); his Updike talk published, 144–145 (P105)

—Club speaker: in 1902 on Francis Seymour Haden, 182; in 1903 on early Italian prints, 182; in 1904 on etchings and drypoints by Whistler, 183; in 1911 on color engravings, 185; in 1916 on Thomas Rowlandson, 187; in 1922 on Edgar Degas, 189; in 1940 on D. B. Updike and Merrymount Press, 198; in 1942, 199

*Cosmographia*, 49

Costume, history and development of, 1912 Club speaker on, 185

Costume books, 1960 small exhibition of, 172, 216

Country Life Press, 113; publication printed by, 140 (P86)

Cousins, Samuel, 1918 exhibition of mezzotints by, 188

Cowley, Malcolm, 1949 Club speaker on Poe, 171, 203; 1955 Club speaker on Whitman and *Leaves of Grass*, 205

Crafts, tools, and technology, history of, 1979 small exhibition on, 221

Crane, Walter, 39, 78

Crane, Warren C., 82

Crawford, F. Marion, 1902 Club speaker on original and early editions of Italian books, 182; his talk published, 129 (P40)

Crawford, John M., Jr., 1964 small exhibition from the collection of, 217

Crime and mystery books, exhibitions of: in 1933, 194; in 1973, 212

Cross, Amanda. See Heilbrun, Carolyn G.

Cross, Wilbur L., 1917 Club speaker on history of English prose fiction, 187

Cruikshank, George, exhibitions on: in 1887, 177; in 1926, 191

Crutchley, Brooke, publication designed and printed by, 148–149 (P123)

Crystal Palace, 1976 small exhibition on, 221

*Culprit Fay and Other Poems*, 138

Cummington Press, 1975 Committee on Modern Fine Printing exhibition on, 224

Cupid's Bow Binder, Grolier binding by, 43

Currier and Ives prints, 1929 exhibition of, 193

Curtis, George William, *Washington Irving: A Sketch*, 122

Curtis, Lewis P., 1959 Club speaker on Samuel Johnson, 207

Cutler, Karl C., 1934 Club speaker on the China trade, 195

*C. D. Correctorvm in typographiis ervditorvm centvria*, 54

Damer, Anna, 58

Damon, S. Foster, 1919 Club speaker on William Blake, 188

Dampier, William, 65

*Daniel Berkeley Updike and the Merrymount Press*, 144–145

Daniel Press, 57; works of, in library, 39

Dante, 1922 exhibition of reproductions of Blake's illustrations for *The Divine Comedy*, 190; *A Translation of Giovanni Boccaccio's Life of*, 126 (P29)

"Dante in America," 1961 panel discussion on, 208

Darley, F. O. C., drawings by, 83

Daubigny, Charles-François, 1901 exhibition of etchings by, 182

Daumier, Honoré, 1892 exhibition on, 168, 178; 1933 exhibition on, 194

Davidson, Alexander, Jr., Club Librarian, 45; institutes small exhibitions series, 172; his address at Club's 75th anniversary published, 149 (P125); 1959 Club speaker on Grolier Club's 75th anniversary, 207

Davidson, Marshall B., 1976 Club speaker on Europe in 1776, 213

Davies, Arthur B., 122 (P12)

Davis, Alexander Jackson, watercolors by, 110

Davis, Herbert, 1944 Club speaker on "The Future of the Liberal Arts," 200; 1945 Club speaker on Jonathan Swift, 201

Davis, Waters S.
—gifts: of auction catalogues, 40, 64; private library catalogues, 69
—1942 exhibition of books from his collection given to the Grolier Club by his children, 199

*De arte poetica*, 58

de Bury, Richard, *Philobiblon*, 114, 120–121

*De Civitate Dei*, first printing, 50–51

de Kay, Charles, 1901 Club speaker on engravings, etchings, and lithographs by women, 182

de Picques, Claude, Grolier binding by, 43

de Ricci, Seymour
—*Census of Medieval and Renaissance Manuscripts in the United States and Canada*: Grolier Club included in, 39; 1962 exhibition of additions to, 208
—Club speaker: in 1919 on early printed liturgical books, 188; in 1926 on Walter Gilliss, 191; in 1930

on 18th-century French illustrated books, 193; in 1936 on book collectors of the past, 196

De Vinne Press, publication on, 142 (P92); publications printed by, 53, 119–136, 155–160

De Vinne, Theodore Low, 54; letter accepting Turnure's invitation to meeting founding the Grolier Club, 20; dedicates *The Invention of Printing* to David Wolfe Bruce, 48; letters to Beverly Chew, 79; gift of marble busts, 109; on first Committee on Publications, 112; 1885 Club speaker on historic printing types, 176; bust of, 108; publication on, 142 (P92); 1928 exhibition on, 192
—works: *The Invention of Printing*, 112; *Historic Printing Types*, 120; *Christopher Plantin and the Plantin-Moretus Museum*, 120; *Title-Pages as Seen by a Printer*, 127; *Notable Printers of Italy During the Fifteenth Century*, 132

de Worde, Wynkyn, 50, 128 (P35)

Dearth, Henry Golden, 1917 Club speaker on books and miniatures from Persia and the Levant, 187

Dechert, Robert, 1966 small exhibition from the collection of, 218

*Decree of Star Chamber Concerning Printing*, 113, 119

*Decree of Starre-Chamber*, title-page of 1637 edition, 25

Dedication copies, 1966 exhibition of, 209

Defoe, Daniel, 1950 Club speaker on, 203

Degas, Edgar, archival material for 1922 exhibition on, 86; 1922 exhibition of prints, drawings and bronzes by, 189; publication on, 160 (H82)

DeGoudt, Hendrick, 1912 informal discussion on, 185

Delandine, Antoine François, *Histoire abrégée de l'imprimerie*, 54–55

Demonology, 1962 exhibition on, 208

*Depositio Cornuti Typographici*, 132; 1909 performance of, 184

Des Cordes, Jean, catalogue of his library, 64–65

Desaunays, Abbé, 72

Desboutin, Marcelin-Gilbert, 1892 exhibition on, 178

*Description of the Early Printed Books Owned by the Grolier Club*, 53, 124

*Descriptive Catalogue of an Exhibition of Japanese Figure Prints*, 139

*Descriptive Catalogue of an Exhibition of Japanese Landscape, Bird and Flower Prints*, 140

*Descriptive Catalogue of the First Editions in Book Form of the Writings of Percy Bysshe Shelley*, 138

Dewey, Melvil, 36, 102

Diaries, 1941 Club speaker on, 199

Dibdin, Thomas Frognall, autograph letters of, 77; extra-illustrated copy of *The Bibliographical Decameron*, 77; *Bibliomania*, 111; Spencer Library catalogues, 70
—exhibitions: in 1935, 171, 195; in 1975, 213

Dibner, Bern, 1971 small exhibition from the collection of, 219

Dickens, Charles
—exhibitions: in 1913, 169, 186; in 1932 on *The Mystery of Edwin Drood*, 194; in 1943 on *A Christmas Carol*, 200

—publications: 134 (P59); 160 (H73)

Dickinson, Emily, 1945 exhibition on, 171, 201

Dictionary, Webster's, 1978 exhibition on, 214

Didot, the Elder, 1920 exhibition on, 189

Digby, Kenelm, 1937 exhibition on, 196

Dikhoff, Frans, tall-case clock by, 110

Dimnet, Ernest, 1928 Club speaker on the art of thinking, 192

*Disputationes Questiones et Concilia*, 50

*Dissertation Upon English Typographical Founders and Founderies*, 54, 140

*Distribution of Books by Catalogue to A.D. 1800*, 66

*Divine Comedy, The*, 1922 exhibition of reproductions of Blake's illustrations for, 190

Dixon, Robert, 1918 exhibition of mezzotints by, 188

Doctors as authors, 1934 exhibition on, 195

Dodd, James William, 75–76

Dodd, Mead & Co., Rare Book Dept., catalogues of, 64

Dodsley, Robert, 77

Donne, John, *Poems* of, 124; 1972 exhibition on, 211; publication on, 152–153 (P137)

Doré, Gustave, 1939 Club speaker on, 197

Doves Bindery, 1964 small exhibition of Cobden-Sanderson bindings for, 217

Doves Press, 1938 exhibition on, 197; works of, in library, 39

Dowson, Ernest, *The Pierrot of the Minute*, 138–139

Doyle, Richard, 39, 78

Drake, Alexander W., 36; on House Committee, 106; on first Committee on Publications, 112; 1915 Club speaker on American illustrated books, 186; portrait of, 108

Drake, James F., catalogues of, 64

Drake, Joseph Rodman, *The Culprit Fay and Other Poems*, 138

Drake, Will H., 119 (P3)

Dramatic folios, 1903 exhibition of, 169, 183; publication on, 158 (H50)

Dramatic portraits, 1899 exhibition of, 181

Dramatic prints, 1901 exhibition of, 182

Drawings, 1969 small exhibition of, 219

Drinker, Henry S., 1949 Club speaker on Trollope, 203; "The Lawyers of Anthony Trollope," 148 (P119)

Driver, Clive E., 1973 Club speaker on Rosenbach Foundation Museum and Library, 212

Dryden, John, 1900 exhibition on, 169, 181; publications on, 126 (P30), 158 (H42); portrait incorrectly thought to be of, 110

Du Maurier, George, autograph letter to Locker-Lampson, 79

Duchamp, Marcel, 1979 Franklin Furnace Archive exhibition on, 214

*Duchess of Portland's Museum*, 143–144

Duffield, Howard, 1932 Club speaker on Dickens's *The Mystery of Edwin Drood*, 194

Duncan, Harry, 1975 Committee on Modern Fine Printing exhibition on, 224

Duncan, Walter Jack, 1916 Club speaker on Thomas Rowlandson, 187

Dunsany, Edward John Moreton Drax Plunkett, Lord, *The Compromise of the King of the Golden Isles*, 139

Duplessis, J. S., 126 (P27)

Durand, Asher Brown, 1895 exhibition of engraved work of, 180; publications on, 124 (P20), 157 (H27)

Dürer, Albrecht, 1897 exhibition of etchings, drypoints, and engravings by, 168, 180; publications on, 125 (P25); *Of the Just Shaping of Letters*, 137; terra cotta bust of, 109

Duschnes, Philip C., on Elmer Adler, 150–151 (P130)

"Dusty Diamonds," English boys' books, 1965 exhibition of, 209

Dutch kitchen, gift of Edwin B. Holden, 107

Dutch tall-case clock, gift of Mrs. William Loring Andrews, 39

Duveen, Denis I., 1952 Club speaker on Lavoisier, 204; his Lavoisier catalogue, 148 (P121)

Dwiggins, W. A., book decorations by, 133 (P53), 144–145 (P105)

Dyson, Humphrey, 60

*Early American Sport*, 144

*Early Books and Manuscripts: Forty Years of Research*, 153

Early printed books

—exhibitions: in 1887, 177; in 1921, 189

—publications: 124 (P21); 152 (P134); 153 (P138); 155 (H3); 156 (H25)

—English, 1968 small exhibition of, 218

—from the Bruce collection, 1894 exhibition of, 179

—illustrated, publications on, 122–123 (P15)

—liturgical, 1919 exhibition of, 188

*See also* Incunabula

Eastern Christendom, book of, 1966 exhibition on, 210

Eaton, Walter Prichard, his text to Ruzicka's *New York*, 135

Eddy, George Simpson, 1939 Club speaker on Franklin, 197

Edelstein, J. M., 1979 small exhibition from the collection of, 221

*Edit du roy pour la réglement des imprimeurs*, 55

Edward VI, King, dedication copy to, 42

Edwards, A. Arlent, 127 (P34)

Edwards, E. B., binding designed by, 126 (P29)

Edwards, Francis, catalogues of in Grolier Club Library, 62

*Effigies of the Most Famous English Writers from Chaucer to Johnson*, 122

Ehrman, Albert, and Pollard, Graham, *The Distribution of Books by Catalogue to A.D. 1800*, 66

1809, 1959 exhibition on, 206

*Eighteenth-Century Studies in Honor of Donald F. Hyde*, 152

Eisenman, Alvin, 1960 Club speaker on modern fine printing, 207

Eisler, Colin, 1965 Club speaker on Jean Grolier and

his times, 209; "Jean Grolier and the Renaissance," 152 (P136)

Ekstrom, Parmenia Migel, 1981 Club speaker on ballet books and prints, 215

*Elegiac Sonnets,* 58

Eliot, George, 1895 exhibition of engraved portraits of women writers from Sappho to, 180; publication on, 157 (H26)

Eliot, T. S., 1975 small exhibition on, 220

Elizabeth I, Queen, 1953 exhibition of books issued during her reign, 204

Elkins, W. M., seconds nomination of T. J. Wise for membership, 85

Ellsberg, Edward, 1953 Club speaker on the sea in literature, 204

*Elmer Adler in the World of Books,* 150–151

Elzevir, Daniel, 1681 list of books available from his shop, 66

*El plus ultra,* 56

"Embassies to the Far East," 1966 small exhibition on, 218

Emerson, Ralph Waldo, medallion portrait of, 164

Enfield, William, *Observations on Literary Property,* 55

Engelmann, Godefroy, 56

England, Stuart and Tudor, travel in, 1936 exhibition on, 196

English authors, exhibitions on, 168; exhibitions of portraits of: in 1891, 178; in 1898, 181; publication on, 157 (H35)

*English Book Sale Catalogues,* 60

English books, issued during the reign of Elizabeth I, 1953 exhibition of, 204

English drama, 1903 exhibition of, 183; publication on, 158 (H50)

English language, 1930 exhibition on the formation of, 193

English literary portraits, publications on, 157 (H35)

English literature
—exhibitions: 168–169, in 1893, 179; in 1901, in 1903, 182; in 1917, 187; in 1920, 188; in 1951, 204; in 1960, 207
—publications: 123 (P16); 127 (P34); 128 (P37–P38); 129 (P42); 136 (P68); 156 (H20); 158 (H44); 160 (H77)
—small exhibitions: in 1963, 217; in 1968, 219; in 1971, 219; in 1972, 220; in 1975, 220
—Victorian: 1969 exhibition of, 210
—17th-century: 1970 small exhibition of, 219
—18th–20th-century: 1966 small exhibition of, 218
—19th-century: 1963 small exhibition of, 217

English poetry, modern, 1964 exhibition of, 209

English prose fiction, 1917 exhibition of, 187; publication on, 160 (H77)

*Engraved and Typographic Work of Rudolph Ruzicka,* 147

Engraved portraits, 1935 exhibition of, 195; Grolier Club publications on, 161 (H86); 1922 exhibition of Edward G. Kennedy's gift of, 190

Engraved portraits of actors, 1907 exhibition of, 184; publication on, 159 (H58)

Engraved portraits of English authors from Chaucer to Johnson, 1891 exhibition of, 178

Engraved portraits of French authors, 1895 exhibition of, 180

Engraved portraits of women writers from Sappho to George Eliot, 1895 exhibition of, 180

Engraved title-pages and frontispieces, early English, 1898 exhibition of, 181; publication on, 157 (H34)

Engravers
—American: 1908 exhibition on, 184; publication on, 130 (P45)
—English: 1914 exhibition of trade cards of, 186
—French: 1914 exhibition of trade cards of, 186
—exhibitions of portraits of: in 1905, in 1906, in 1907, in 1910, in 1911, 183–185; 168

Engravings, 1892 exhibition of, 179; publication on, 156 (H16)
—American: publication on, 159 (H62)
—color: 1911 exhibition of, 185
—English: 1887 exhibition of, 177; 1904 exhibition of, 183
—French: 1904 exhibition of, 183; publication on, 158 (H54)
—German: 1916 exhibition of facsimiles of, 187
—15th–17th-century: 1969 small exhibition of, 219

Engravings, etchings, and lithographs by women, 1901 exhibition of, 182; publication on, 158 (H45)

Engravings of women writers, publication on, 157 (H26)

Eno, Henry C., 119 (P3)

Enschedé, Joh., en Zonen, publication printed by, 148 (P119)

*Epreuves des caracteres de la fonderie du Sr. Marquet,* 54

Eragny Press, 1974 small exhibition on, 220

Erskine, John, Club speaker: in 1921 on John Keats, 189; in 1922 on Percy Bysshe Shelley, 189; in 1930 on the formation of the English language, 193

Esmerian, Raphael, 1966 small exhibition from the collection of, 218

Espionage, 1960 exhibition on, 207

Essick, Robert N., 1982 small exhibition from the collection of, 222

Estienne, Robert, printer, 58

"Esto Perpetua," 1959 exhibition on The Club of Dr. Johnson and his friends, 207

*Etched Work of Whistler,* 115, 131, 137, 138

Etchings, 1884 exhibition on, 176; 1969 small exhibition of, 219

Etchings, engravings, and lithographs by women, 1901 exhibition of, 182

"Europe in 1776," 1976 exhibition on, 213; publication on, 161 (H90)

European Americana, 1888 exhibition of, 167, 177

Evans, Luther H., 1950 Club speaker on *belles-lettres* from countries in the United Nations, 203

Evelyn, John, his copy of *Alphabeticum chaldaicum,* 58; publications on, 144 (P102)

*Exhibition Celebrating the Seventy-fifth Anniversary of the Grolier Club,* 149

Exhibitions of books in 1870s, 166

Index Exiles and expatriates, 1966 exhibition on, 209

Exploration, French, in the South Pacific, 1978 small exhibition on, 221

Eyton, W. K., 61

*Facsimile of the Laws and Acts of the General Assembly for their Majesties Province of New-York*, 123

Fadiman, Clifton, 1946 Club speaker on Henry James, 201

Faithorne, William, publications on, 121 (P10), 156 (H17); 1893 exhibition of engraved portraits by, 179

Fans, 1891 exhibition on, 168, 178; publication on, 155 (H13)

Far West, Great trails of, 1938 exhibition on, 196

Fashion books, 1912 exhibition of, 185

Fass, John, publication designed by, 144 (P104)

Fassett, Stephen, 1964 Club speaker on modern English poetry, 209

Faÿ, Bernard, *Notes on the American Press*, 141

Fearing, Daniel B., gifts to library, 39; gift of *Horae*, 40; 1918 memorial meeting for, 188

Feinberg, Charles E., 1964 small exhibition from the collection of, 217

Fenton, Edward, 1953 Club speaker on English book illustrators of the 1860s, 204

Fequet, Emile, illustrations for Ruzicka's *New York* printed by, 135 (P64)

Fern, Alan, 1974 small exhibition from the collection of, 220

—Club speaker: in 1967 on art nouveau books, 210; in 1978 on American press books, 214

Festival books, 1964 exhibition of, 209; 1971 small exhibition of, 219

Ficke, Arthur Davison, 1924 Club speaker on Japanese prints, 190

Field & Beattie Division of Chas. P. Young Co., publication printed by, 161 (H88)

Field, W. B. Osgood, gift of *Bibliotheca Heberiana*, 61

*Fifteenth Century Books and the Twentieth Century*, 148

Fifty Books of the Year, AIGA exhibition of: in 1925, in 1926, 191; in 1927, in 1928, 192; in 1929, 193; in 1947, 202

*Fifty-five Books Printed Before 1525 Representing the Works of England's First Printers*, 152; 1968 small exhibition of, 218

Filby, P. William, 84; 1977 Club speaker on literary and historical forgeries, 214

Finé, Oronce, 1937 exhibition of book illustrations by, 196

Fine printing from Didot the Elder to the Ashendene Press, 1920 exhibition of, 189

Firmin-Didot, Ambroise, auction sale of his library, 51; auction catalogue of, 65; statue of, 110

First editions, collecting of, 166

*First Editions of the Works of Nathaniel Hawthorne*, 130

*First Editions of the Works of Robert Louis Stevenson*, 135

FitzGerald, Edward, 119 (P2)

Flameng, François, *Aldus in his Printing Establishment*: his painting of, 107, 108; Meunier's bookbinding of, 42–43; Léopold Flameng's etching of; 122 (P11)

Flameng, Léopold, his etching of *Aldus in his Printing Establishment*, 121; 1891 exhibitions on, 178

Flanagan, John, medallion portrait of Longfellow modeled by, 164

Flight, 1959 exhibition on, 206

Flight into Egypt, 1944 exhibition of prints of, 200

"Flower of Kings," 1979 exhibition on King Arthur, 214

Folger, Henry Clay, 88

Folsom, James K., 1965 Club speaker on English boys' books, 209

Folter, Roland, and Breslauer, Bernard H., *Bibliography, its History and Development*, 154

Ford, Ford Madox, 1974 small exhibition on, 220

Forgeries, 1935 exhibition of, 195; 1977 exhibition of, 214; 1961 small exhibition of, 217

Forman, Buxton, *A Shelley Library*, 166

Foster, Allen Evarts, Club speaker: in 1934 on prints, 195; in 1944 on the Flight into Egypt, 200

Fowler, Frank, portrait of William Dean Howells by, 108

Fowler, Robert Ludlow, 123 (P17)

Fox, Dixon Ryan, Club speaker: in 1931 on George Washington, 194; in 1940 on the Turnpike Era, 198

Foxhunting, 1975 small exhibition of books on, 220

*Fra Luca de Pacioli*, 115, 143; photograph of title-page, 32

*Framed Paintings, Water-colors, and Prints*, 127

Francis, David G., catalogues of, 64

Franklin, Benjamin, bust of, 107–108; portrait of, 126 (P27); imaginary conversation between Johnson and (1931), 193; 1893 Club speaker on portraits of, 179

—exhibitions: in 1906, 183; in 1939, 197; 169

—publications: 135 (P62); 159 (H56)

*Franklin and his Press at Passy*, 135

Franklin Furnace Archive, 1979 exhibition from, 214

Franzen, Greta, publication designed by, 152 (P136)

Fraser, W. Lewis, 1888 Club speaker on American wood engravers, 177

Freedom of the press, publication on, 117 (P1); 1947 Club speaker on, 202; resources for study of, in Grolier Club Library, 55

*Freedom of the Press and L'Association Mensuelle*, 148

Freeling, George Henry, 77

Freeman, John, 1969 Club speaker on the Bodleian Library, 211

Freer, Charles Lang, gifts of prints, 81

French, Edwin Davis

—exhibitions: in 1909, of engraved work, 184; in 1930, of bookplates, 193

—publication: 159 (H67)

French artists, 1892 exhibition of portraits of, 178

French authors, portraits of

—exhibitions: in 1892, 178; in 1895, 180; publication on, 157 (H28)

French books, 1970 exhibition of, 211

French literature, 1962 small exhibition of, 217

French Parnassian and Symbolist poetry, 1966 exhibition of, 209

Freud, Sigmund, 1956 exhibition on, 205

*Friar Roger Bacon in his Cell*, 111

Friedburg, Peter von, printer, 52

"From Poet to Premier," 1959 exhibition on the year 1809, 206

Frontispieces, and title-pages, engraved, 1898 exhibition of, 181

Frost, Robert, publication on, 151 (P132); 1939 exhibition on, 197; 1939 Club speaker, 171, 197

Froullé, French bookseller, 76

Frye, Richard N., 1967 Club speaker on travelers in the desert, 210

Frye, Roland Mushat, 1973 Club speaker on John Milton, 212

Fugger, Ulrich, 50

Fulton, John F., Club speaker: in 1937 on Kenelm Digby, 196; in 1952 on Lavoisier, 204

Gaillard, Ferdinand, 1895 exhibition of engravings by, 180; 1900 exhibition of engravings by, 181; publication on, 158 (H43)

Gaine, Hugh, 77

Galantière, Lewis, 1967 Club speaker on classics in translation, 210

Gallatin, Albert E., 1944 Club speaker on Max Beerbohm, 200; *Aubrey Beardsley*, 146

Gallup, Albert, on first Committee on Publications, 112

Gallup, Donald C., 1948 Club speaker on famous American women writers, 202; 1976 small exhibition from the collection of, 220

Gamut, David, "The Grolier Club's Work," 1887 New York *Times* article, 167

Ganz, Paul, 1937 Club speaker on Holbein, 196

Garden books, 1925 exhibition of, 191

Garden Club of America, 1941 joint exhibition with, 145 (P107); 198

Garden of Eden, 1975 exhibition on, 213

Garrett, Wendell, 106

Garrison, Fielding M., 1925 Club speaker on early anatomical books, 191

Garvey, Eleanor M., 1981 Club speaker on 18th-century Venetian illustrated books, 215

Gastronomy, 1960 exhibition on, 207; 1977 small exhibition on, 221

Gavarni, Paul, 1890 exhibition of lithographs by, 177; 1926 exhibition of lithographs by, 191

*Gazette Françoise*, 140

*Gazette of the Grolier Club*, 116, 162–163

Geismar, Maxwell, 1959 Club speaker on American literature of the 1920s, 207

*Genealogie Deorum*, 51

*General History of Printing*, 54

George Grady Press, 113; publications printed and bound by: 147 (P115); 148 (P120–P121); publications printed by, 146 (P110–P112)

Gerlach, Gerhard, 39; 1947 Club speaker on contemporary American hand bookbindings, 202; 1971 Guild of Book Workers exhibition of bookbindings by, 211

Ghost and horror books, 1976 exhibition of, 213

Gibson, Charles Dana, 1939 Club speaker on American life as portrayed by American illustrators, 197; 1943 Club speaker on posters of World War I, 199

Gilbert, W. S., 1961 exhibition of dramatic works of, 208

Gill, Brendan, 1963 Club speaker, 208; 1975 Club speaker on *The New Yorker*, 213

Gill, Eric, 1949 exhibition of woodcuts and drawings by, 203

Gilliss Brothers and Turnure, Art Age Press, publications printed by, 155 (H2); 162

Gilliss Press, 57, 113; publication on, 140 (P86); publications printed by: 124 (P20); 127 (P32); 128 (P36); 129 (P41); 131 (P47); 132 (P51); 133 (P55); 135–136 (P65); 137 (P69); 138 (P76); 139 (P82); 140 (P83); 157 (H26–H27); 160 (H80–H83); 162

Gilliss, Walter, 113; gift of his collection of Grolier Club printing, 84; publication printed by, 138; 1926 exhibition of books printed by, 191; *Recollections of the Gilliss Press*, 140

Gillot, Charles, *El plus ultra*, 56

Gilvarry, James, 1969 small exhibition from the collection of, 219

Gimbel, Richard, 1958 Club speaker on Astronautica Incunabula, 206

Godine, David R., 1972 Committee on Modern Fine Printing exhibition on, 223

Goff, Frederick R., 1968 Club speaker on Gutenberg, 210; 1971 Club speaker on great American book collectors, 211

Goldschmidt, E. P. (firm), purchase of auction catalogues from, 40

Goldschmidt, Ernst Philip, 1937 Club speaker on Geoffroy Tory and Oronce Finé, 196

Goldschmidt, Lucien, and Naef, Weston J., *The Truthful Lens*, 115, 153–154

Goldsmith, Oliver, *She Stoops to Conquer*, 1886 exhibition of Edwin A. Abbey's drawings for, 176; publication on, 155 (H2)

Goldwater, Walter, 1975 Club speaker on chess books, 213

Goodhue, Bertram Grosvenor, *Book Decorations*, 115, 143; designer of clubhouse at 47 East 60 St., 87, 108; on Committee on Publications, 114; typographic designs by, 83

Goodspeed's, catalogues of, 64

Gordan, John D., 1950 Club speaker on the *Oxford Book of English Verse*, 203

Gordan, Mrs. John D., 1981 small exhibition from the collection of, 222

Gordon, Beate, 1957 performance of a Nō play, 206

Gosden, Thomas, 1925 exhibition on, 191

Gothic novels, 1976 exhibition of, 213

Gothic Revival, 1974 small exhibition on, 220

Goudy, Frederic W.
—Club speaker: in 1923 on the forms of letters, 190; in 1928 on the Kelmscott Press, 192; in 1943 on his own work, 199
—exhibitions from the Melbert B. Cary, Jr., Collection of Goudyana: in 1943, 199; in 1965, small exhibition, 218
—and Goudy, Bertha, 57; publication designed and printed by, 139 (P81); 113

Gough, Richard, his memoir of Mores, 140 (P84)

Gourary, Paul, 1971 small exhibition from the collection of, 219

Gowans, William, catalogues of, 63–64

Goya, Francesco, 1916 exhibition of etched work of, 187

Grady, George, Press. See George Grady Press

Graff, Robert D., 11; 1980 small exhibition from the collection of, 221

Grandville, J. J., 1981 small exhibition of books and journals illustrated by, 222

Granniss, Ruth Shepard, 102; Club Librarian, 44; 1935 Club meeting to honor her 30th anniversary as Club Librarian, 195; complimented on her Shelley catalogue by T. J. Wise, 85; scrapbooks about Hoe sale kept by, 63
—Club speaker: in 1919 on historical bookbindings, 188; in 1933 on Grolier Club Library, 194; in 1936 on book collecting in America before 1884, 196; in 1940 on Grolier Club Library, 198; in 1943 on Grolier Club exhibitions, 200
—works: compiles list of American books illustrated with woodcuts, 136 (P65); *Descriptive Catalogue of the First Editions in Book Form of the Writings of Percy Bysshe Shelley*, 138; "The New York Printers and the Celebration of the French Revolution of 1830," 141 (P88); *Grolier Club and Its Exhibitions Held From Time to Time*, 146, 171

Granswinckel, Theodore, auction catalogue of his library, 66

Granville-Barker, Harley, 1944 Club speaker on Max Beerbohm, 200

Grauer, Ben, 1971 Club speaker on visit of L'Association Internationale de Bibliophilie, 211

Gravesend Press, 1975 Committee on Modern Fine Printing exhibition on, 223

"Great American Book Collectors to 1800," 1971 exhibition on, 76, 211

*Great Gatsby, The*, 1975 small exhibition on, 220

Greenaway, Kate, 39, 78–79; 1920 exhibition on, 188

Greg, W. W., his copy of *De arte poetica*, 58

Gregory the Great, *Moralia in Job*, 39–40

Griffoul, A., & Bros. Co., medallion portrait of Longfellow cast by, 164

Griset, Ernest, 39, 78

Grivaz, Eugène, 1892 exhibition of watercolors for *Peg Woffington* by, 178

Groesbeck, Harry A., 1924 Club speaker on modern illustrated books in color, 190; 1941 Club speaker on color printing, 199

Grolier binding, on *Epistolae* of Pope Nicholas II, photograph of, 24

*Grolier Club and Its Exhibitions Held From Time to Time*, 146, 171

*Grolier Club and Its Iconographic Collections*, 146

*Grolier Club, 1884–1950: An Informal History*, 147

*Grolier Club, 1884–1967: An Informal History*, 116

*Grolier Club: The Library*, 140

Grolier Club, activities of, 12–13; and the future, 13–14; centennial marked by other institutions, 13; centennial year activities of, 13; early activities of, 35; first meeting of, 165; founding of: 11–12, 35, 102, 1983 exhibition on, 216; in New York cultural life, 12; purpose of, 12; scope of members' interests, 166; silver punch bowl, photograph of, 20; social contributions of, 12–13; Winterich's history of, 147 (P118), 151–152 (P133)
—Anniversary exhibitions: 10th, 1894, 179; 25th, 1909, 184; 50th, 1934, 194; 60th, 1943, 200; 75th, 1959, 207, 149 (P125–P126); 90th, 1974, 212
—Archives, 79, 84–89, 98; availability for scholarly use, 89; organizing of, 84; 1978 exhibition of items from, 214
—Cataloguing Project, established with Columbia University School of Library Service, 103
—Clubhouse(s), 106–111; archives of, 87
  —64 Madison Ave., 106–107; exhibitions in, 167; 1893 exhibition of art works in, 179
  —29 East 32nd St., 107–108; photograph of, 18; catalogue of art works in, 127 (P32); 1917 farewell dinner, 187
  —47 East 60 St., 108–111; 1931 list of art works in, 143 (P98); Dutch kitchen, 108; fifth floor furnishings, 111; 50th anniversary of in 1967, 218; first exhibition in (1917), 187; furnishings of lobby, 108–109; photograph of, 18; silver ware, 110–111
  —Exhibition hall, 109; 1929 photograph of, 19; 1954 rehabilitation of, 205; 1963 renovation of cases in, 208
  —Library Room, 109–110; 1941 etching of, 198; 1984 photograph of, 17
  —Rare Book and Small Exhibition Room, 109; renovation of, 45, 171
—Committee on Modern Fine Printing, exhibitions by, 172; list of exhibitions organized by, 223–224
—Committee on Publications, early members of, 112
—Committee on Small Exhibitions, 172. See also Grolier Club, Small exhibitions
—Council, index to minutes of, 86
—Exhibitions, 165–174; archives of, 86; changes in subjects of, 169–170; early popularity of, 167; early reflection of contemporary taste, 166–167; influence and importance of, 173; invitation to, 31; list of, 79, 175–224; publication on, 146 (P110); purpose of, 165–166; speakers at, 171; trends in subjects of, 172; 1943 retrospective of, 171, 200; 1955 retrospective of, 171, 205; 25th anniversary, in 1909, 184. See also Grolier Club, Small exhibitions

—History of, 147 (P118); 151–152 (P133)
  —exhibitions on: in 1941, 198; in 1942, 199
—House Committee, 106; archives of, 87
—Librarians, 43–46
—Library, 35–48; 140 (P85); acquisitions of, 37–38; as resource for collector and scholar, 90–101; auction catalogues, 40–41; availability for public use, 97; bibliography of its books on bookbinding, 131 (P47); bookbindings in, 41–43, 98; Book Fund, 37; book restoration program, 45; catalogue of pre-1800 books, 105; cataloguing of early printed books, 103; classification scheme, 36, 128 (P36), 132 (P51); Kent's 1901 talk on, 182; ease of use, 91–92, 96, 102; educational uses of, 102–105; endowment fund proposed, 37; establishment of, 35–36; gifts to, 38–39; incunabula collection, 48–52, 98; incunabula, sale of, 38; new shelving on fourth floor, 41; papers in Archives, 85–86; periodicals in, 41; photograph of, 17; post-1500 printed books, 53–58; research value of the collection, 91–92
  —exhibitions: in 1893, recent acquisitions, 179; in 1898, recent acquisitions, 181; in 1901, bookbindings, 182; in 1921, early printed books, 189; in 1922, recent acquisitions, 189; in 1923, recent acquisitions, 190; in 1933, 194; in 1934, recent acquisitions, 195; in 1940, 198; in 1978, 214
  —small exhibitions: in 1962, recent acquisitions, 217; in 1964, 217; in 1976, 221; in 1983, recent acquisitions, 222
—Library Committee, 94; reports of, 47
—Meetings, list of, 175–224
—Members, biographies of, 149 (P126); letters of nomination, 86
  —exhibitions from collections of: in 1954, 205; in 1971, Americana, 211; in 1979, prints, 214; in 1982, in 1983, small exhibitions, 222
  —other exhibitions: in 1931, publications by, 193; in 1976, Committee on Modern Fine Printing exhibition of bookplates of, 224; in 1983 small exhibition of works by, 222
—News Sheet, 163
—Print Collection, 80–83; as a resource for study of graphic arts, 82; accession books of, 81; formation of, 80; monetary value of, 81; publication on, 146 (P111); scope of, 80
  —exhibitions from: 83, 172; in 1910, 185; in 1922, 189; in 1923, recent acquisitions, 190; in 1933, 194; in 1935, recent acquisitions, 195; in 1936, 196; in 1940, 198; in 1943, 200
—Publications, 112–116; and standards of taste, 114; archives of, 86; 1926 auction of, 191; designers and printers of, 113; diversity of, 115; earliest, 113; exhibition handlists, 116; 1930 exhibition of special copies of, 193; 1943 exhibition of, 200; 1983 exhibition of, 216; in the 20th century, 114–115; medallion portraits, 116; original art work for, in Grolier Club Print Collection, 83; Printer's Series, 138–139; 1967 small exhibition, 218
  —published lists of: 1906, 130 (P44); 1917, 136–

137 (P69); 1928, 141–142 (P91); 1948, 117, 147 (P116); 1984, 79, 117–164
—Small exhibitions, from members' collections, 172; list of, 216–222; 1966 retrospective exhibition of, 209. See also Grolier Club, Exhibitions; Grolier Club, committee on Small Exhibitions
—Transactions, 162
—Yearbook, 116, 161
Grolier 75, 116, 149
Grolier, Jean, 12; books owned by, in Grolier Club Library, 43; medallion portrait of, 164; signed documents of, 74
  —exhibitions: in 1965, 209; in 1979, 214
  —publications: 115, 131 (P46); 152 (P136)
Gros de Boze, Claude, catalogue of his library, 72
Grossman, James M., 1951 Club speaker on James Fenimore Cooper, 203
Grushkin, Philip, 149 (P126); Grolier Club publication designed by, 154 (P144)
Guild of Book Workers, 50th anniversary exhibition in 1956, 206; 1971 exhibition of bookbindings by Gerhard Gerlach, 211; 75th anniversary exhibition in 1981, 215
Guralnik, David, 1978 Club speaker on Webster's dictionary, 214
Gutenberg Bible. See Bible, 42-line
Gutenberg, Johann, bronze statue of, 109–110; medallion portrait of, 164; exhibitions on: in 1900, 168, 181; in 1968, 170, 210

Haddaway, Arthur, 89
Haden, Francis Seymour, 1891 exhibition on, 178; Keppel's 1897 talk on, 180
  —etchings, drypoints, and mezzotints by: 1902 exhibition of, 182; publication on, 158 (H47)
Haebler, Konrad, The Study of Incunabula, 143
Haggard, H. Rider, McKay's bibliography of, 45
Hagstrom, Jack W. C., 1975 Committee on Modern Fine Printing exhibition from the collection of, 224; 1982 small exhibition from the collection of, 222
Hagué, Louis, bookbinding by, 39, 51
Haight, Gordon S., 1959 Club speaker on an exhibition of the year 1809, 206
Haight, Sherman P., 1947 Club speaker on association books, 202
Hall, Virginius Cornick, Jr., on Elmer Adler, 150–151 (P130)
Halleck, Fitz-Greene, autograph letters to William Loring Andrews, 78
Hallée, Étienne, 72
Halliday Lithograph Corporation, publication printed by, 152 (P136)
Halsband, Robert, 1966 Club speaker on exiles and expatriates, 209
Halsey, Frederic R., 1904 Club speaker on 18th-century French engravings, 183
Halsey, R. T. Haines, The Boston Port Bill, 129; on

declining attendance at Grolier Club exhibitions, 173–174
—Club speaker: in 1906 on Benjamin Franklin, 183; in 1915 on iconography of Old New York, 187

Hamady, Walter, 1972 Committee on Modern Fine Printing exhibition on, 223

Hamburger, Philip, 1975 Club speaker on *The New Yorker*, 213

Hamilton, Archibald, 77

Hamilton, Philip M., 1974 Committee on Modern Fine Printing exhibitions of printing by students of, 223

Hammer, Victor, 1975 Committee on Modern Fine Printing exhibition on, 223; 1960 small exhibition of books printed by, 172, 216

Hanna, Archibald, 1961 Club speaker on Lewis and Clark, 207

Hannah, George, 1888 Club speaker on European Americana, 177

Hansen, Harry, 1951 Club speaker on important books in English, 1901–1950, 204

Harbor Press, publications printed by, 143 (P98, P99); 144 (P104); 113

Harding, Walter, 1954 Club speaker on Thoreau and *Walden*, 205

Hardy, Thomas, 1940 exhibition on, 198

Hare, Mrs. Meredith, gift of Grolier binding owned by Dean Sage, 43

Harper Bequest, 36–37; Alexander Davidson's help with, 45; 1977 exhibition on, 213; incunabula purchased with funds from, 51–52

Harper, Francis P., catalogues of, 64

Harper, Lathrop Colgate, 37; catalogues of, 64

Harper, L. C. (firm), Alexander Davidson's association with, 45

Harper, Mabel Herbert, bequest of, 1977 exhibition of acquisitions and publications made possible by, 213

Hart, Charles Henry, his introduction to Asher B. Durand catalogue, 124 (P20); *Catalogue of the Engraved Portraits of Washington*, 129; 1899 Club speaker on engraved portraits of Abraham Lincoln, 181

Hartmann, Christian, bookbinder, autograph invoice of, 76

Hatch, John Davis, 1977 small exhibition from the collection of, 221

Hauswedell, Ernst, 1970 Club speaker on German modern fine printing, 211

Havemeyer, Mrs. Henry O., 1921 Club speaker on Mary Cassatt, 189

Havemeyer, William F., gifts of prints, 81; on Committee on Publications, 114
—exhibitions of gifts from: in 1912 of books and engravings, 186; in 1905, in 1906, in 1907, in 1910 of portraits, 183–185; 168

Hawthorn House, publication printed by, 144 (P101)

Hawthorne, Nathaniel, *The Scarlet Letter*, 115, 131; portrait of, by Thompson, 30, 109; medallion portrait of, 164; 1973 small exhibition on, 220
—exhibitions: in 1904, 183; in 1964, 209; 169

—publications: 130 (P43); 158 (H52); 161 (H88)

Hayday, bookbinding by, 61

Hayter, Stanley William, 1944 demonstration of making a burin engraving, 200

Healing by faith, fraud, and superstition, 1942 exhibition of books and prints on, 199

Heber, Richard, auction catalogue of his library, 61

Heckscher, August, 1956 Club speaker, 205

Heilbrun, Carolyn G., 1973 Club speaker on "Murder by the Book," 212

Hellman, George S., 1915 Club speaker on Jacques Callot, 186

Hellmann, Geoffrey T., 1975 Club speaker on *The New Yorker*, 213

Henchman, Humphrey, auction catalogue of his library, 60

Henderson, Robert W., *Early American Sport*, 144

Henry VIII, King, "Acte concernyng printers and bynders of bokes," 55

Henschel, Charles R., 1942 Club speaker on sidelights on collecting, 199

Herbals, 1980 small exhibition of, 221

Hewlett, Maurice, *Quattrocentisteria*, 138

Highet, Gilbert, 1967 Club speaker on classics in translation, 210

Highwaymen, 1915 exhibition on, 187

Hildebrandt, Joachim, bookbinder, autograph invoice of, 76

Hildeburn, Charles R., 1893 Club speaker on Bradford and printing in the Middle Colonies, 168, 179; 123 (P17)

Hill, Kenneth E., 1982 small exhibition from the collection of, 222

Hilles, Frederick W., 1965 small exhibition from the collection of, 218

Hine, Al, on Elmer Adler, 150–151 (P130)

*Histoire abregée de l'imprimerie*, 54–55

*Histoire de l'imprimerie et de la librairie*, 58

*Historic Printing Types*, 120; De Vinne's 1885 talk on, 176

*History of Helyas, Knight of the Swan*, 128

*History of New-York*, 114, 119; art work for, 83

Hitchings, Sinclair H., 1982 Club speaker on "Printmakers Observe Their Own World," 216

Hoblyn, Robert, catalogue of his library, 70

Hocking, William Ernest, 1947 Club speaker on the freedom of the press, 202

Hodgson, William B., catalogue of his library, 71

Hoe, Richard M., 1923 exhibition of his gift of Pennell lithographs, 190

Hoe, Robert, III, his bookbinding collection, 41; his collection of books about books, 98; letters to Beverly Chew, 79; on first Committee on Publications, 113; remarks at first meeting of Grolier Club, 165; gift of Payne and Foss catalogues, 62; portrait of, 108; auction catalogue of his library, 63; catalogue of his library, 71; Grolier Club reprint of his unique copy of *The History of Helyas*, 128 (P35)
—Club speaker: in 1884 at first meeting of Grolier

Club, 176; in 1885 on artistic history of bookbinding, 176

—works: *A Short History of the Printing Press*, 57; *A Lecture on Bookbinding as a Fine Art*, 120

Hoeber, Arthur, 1908 Club speaker on D. Y. Cameron, 184

Hofer, Philip, gift of incunabula, 51; Club speaker: in 1932 on Spanish books, 194; in 1947 on the Fifty Books of the Year, 202; in 1958 on calligraphy, 206; in 1961 on Edward Lear, 208; in 1970 on French books, 211

Hofstra University, 46

Hogan, Charles Beecher, 1967 small exhibition from the collection of, 218

Holbein, Hans, 1937 exhibition of prints and drawings by, 196

Holden, Edwin Babcock, manuscript library catalogue of, 71; gifts: of incunabula, 51; of lithographs, 81; of Dutch kitchen, 107

Homer, 1504 Aldine edition, Grolier's copy of, 43

Homer, Winslow, 1933 exhibition of prints by, 194

"Honour'd Relics," 1983 exhibition of objects once belonging to eminent writers, 216

Honthorst, Gerrit van, Ben Jonson portrait misattributed to, 110; 127 (P34)

Hopson, W. F., 1915 Club speaker on American illustrated books, 186

*Horae*, 40

*Horae ad Usum Parisiensum*, 50

Horblit, Harrison D., *One Hundred Books Famous in Science*, 115, 151, 170

—small exhibitions from the collection of: in 1968, 218; in 1976, 221

Horowitz, A., & Son, publication bound by, 152 (P136)

Hotten, John Camden, signed lease for bookshop, 78

Houdon, Jean-Antoine, bust of Benjamin Franklin by, 107–108

Houghton, Arthur A., Jr., 1967 small exhibition from the collection of, 218

Houghton Library, 1982 exhibition of items from, 216

Housayes, Abbé des, quoted on librarians, 44

*House Beautiful*, report on the Dutch kitchen in, 107

Howell, Alfred H., 1969 Club speaker on the Bodleian Library, 211

Howells, William Dean, portrait of, 108

Hoym, Charles Henry, Count, publication on, 126 (P28)

Hufstader, Robert C., 1945 musical performance by, 201

Humanists, Italian, 15th-century, 1981 small exhibition on, 222

Hunsaker, Jerome C., 1940 Club speaker on development of aeronautics, 198

Hunt, Mrs. Roy Arthur, 1943 Club speaker on botanical books, 200

Huntington, Archer M., gift to library, 40

Huntington, Daniel, drawings by, 83

Hutchins, Henry C., 1950 Club speaker on "Daniel Defoe: A Crusoe in Scotland," 203

Hyde, Donald F., establishes Committee on Small Exhibitions, 172; Grolier Club publication in honor of, 152 (P135); 1965 small exhibition from the collection of, 218

Illuminated books, 1968 small exhibition of, 219

Illustrated books

—exhibitions of, by place: American, in 1888, 177; in 1915, 186; in 1965, 209; Chinese, in 1935, 195; French, in 1925, 191; in 1930, 193; in 1934, 195; in 1968, 210; in 1966 small exhibition, 218; German, in 1931, 193; Japanese, in 1889, 177; in 1957, 206; Venetian, 18th-century, in 1981, 215

——by period: the Renaissance, in 1935, 195; the 15th–17th centuries, in 1969, 219; the 16th century, in 1973, 220

——miscellaneous: in 1921, 170, 189; on color, in 1924, 190; on natural history, in 1957, 206; in 1977, 214; of the 1860s, in 1965, 209

—publications: 135–136 (P65); 160 (H81); 161 (H89)

*Illustrium maioris Britanniae scriptorum*, 42

"*Imagerie populaire*," 1961 exhibition of prints, 207

"In the Shadow of Duchamp," 1979 Franklin Furnace Archive exhibition on the photomechanical revolution and the artist's book, 214

Incunabula, 1952 exhibition of, 204; publication on, 148 (P122); 1975 small exhibition of, 220; illustrated, 1966 small exhibition of, 218. *See also* Early printed books, and under Grolier Club, Library

*Index librorum prohibitorum*, 55

Indiana University, 1980 exhibition from the Lilly Library, 215

"Indomitable Irishry," 1962 exhibition of Irish literature from Yeats to Beckett, 208

Industry, American, 1947 exhibition on iconography of, 202

Interior decoration, 1918 exhibition on, 188

International League of Antiquarian Booksellers, 1959 exhibition to mark the visit of, 207

*Invention of Printing*, 112

Irish literature, 1962 exhibition of, 208

Irving, Washington, 1983 exhibition on, 216; publications on, 122 (P12); *History of New-York*, 114, 119, art work for, 83; *Notes and Journal of Travel in Europe*, 137

Irwin, Howard S., Jr., 1977 Club speaker on endangered plants and animals, 214

Isham, Ralph Heyward, 1930 Club speaker on Boswell papers from Malahide Castle, 171, 193

Italian books, 1902 exhibition of, 182; publications on, 158 (H48)

Italian drawings, 1937 exhibition of, 196; 1960 exhibition of, from the collection of Janos Scholz, 207

Italian humanists, 15th-century, 1981 small exhibition on, 222

*Italian Influence on American Literature*, 150, 1961 exhibition on, 208

Italian literature, publication on, 129 (P40)

Italian prints, 1903 exhibition of, 182

*Iter Germanico-Helveticum*, 153 (P140); Johann Gutenberg–Jean Grolier Medal commissioned to commemorate, 164

*Iter Italicum*, 46, 150

Iter Septentrionale, 1967 exhibition of books purchased during, 218

Ives, Brayton, auction catalogue of his library, 63; 1887 Club speaker on early printed books, 177

Ives, Colta Feller, 1979 Club speaker on prints from members' collections, 214

Ives, George B., his translation of Tory's *Champ Fleury*, 115, 141

Ives, Norman, publication designed by, 153 (P139)

Ivins, William M., Jr., gifts to Library by, 40; on Committee on Publications, 114

—Club speaker: in 1915 on American illustrated books, 186; in 1916 on Thomas Rowlandson, 187; in 1918 on the art of the architect and interior decorator of the 18th century, 188; in 1921 on 100 illustrated books, 189; in 1923 on Japanese prints, 190; in 1926 on Walter Gilliss, 191; in 1927 on Geoffroy Tory and his times, 192; in 1930 on 18th-century French illustrated books, 193; in 1931 on modern French prints, 193; in 1933 on Daumier, 194; in 1935 on Renaissance illustrated books, 195

J. F. Tapley Co. *See* Tapley, J. F., Co.

Jackson, William A., his description of Club's copy of Dibdin's *Bibliographical Decameron*, 77

—Club speaker: in 1933 on Grolier Club Library, 194; in 1935 on Dibdin, 171, 195

Jacquemart, Jules, 43; 1888 exhibition of etchings by, 177

Jacques, André, 1891 exhibition on, 178

Jaffray, Robert, 37; gift of his collection of Grolier Club printing, 84; 1926 Club speaker on Walter Gilliss, 191

James, Henry, 1946 exhibition on, 171, 201

James, John, catalogue for auction of his type foundry, 54

Japanese books, exhibitions of: in 1887, in 1889, 177; in 1957, 206

Japanese papermaking, 1925 Club speaker on, 191

Japanese prints, invitation to 1896 exhibition of, 31

—exhibitions: in 1889, 177; in 1896, 180; in 1917, 187; in 1922, 190; in 1924, 190; in 168

—publications: 139 (P82); 140 (P83); 155 (H7); 157 (H30); 160 (H83)

Japanese woodcut books, 40

Jauner, H., 1897 exhibition of medals and plaques by, 180

Jefferson, Thomas, autograph letter to M. Froullé, 29, 76

Jenckes, Charles M., 120 (P6)

Jenson, Nicolaus, *Officium B. V. M.* of 1475, 38–39, 51

Jerome, Saint, *Vitae sanctorum patrum*, 49–50

Jewels and precious stones, 1927 exhibition of books on, 192

Johann Gutenberg–Jean Grolier Medal, 153 (P140), 164

*Johannes Graevius Catalogus Bibliotheca Luculentissimae*, 66

Johansen, J. C., portrait of Alexander W. Drake by, 108

John Carter Brown Library, exhibitions from: in 1968, 170–171, 210; in 1977 of its Harper Bequest acquisitions, 213

*John Donne, 1572–1631: A Catalogue of the Anniversary Exhibition*, 152–153

*John Evelyn: A Study in Bibliophily*, 144

Johnson, Samuel, imaginary conversation between Franklin and (1931), 193

—exhibitions: in 1909, 184; in 1959, 207; 169

—publications: 122 (P13); 156 (H14); 159 (H68)

—small exhibitions: in 1968, 218; in 1975, 220

Johnson, Thomas H., 1946 Club speaker on 100 influential American books, 201; his talk published, 146–147 (P114)

Johnston, Denis, 1962 Club speaker on Irish literature, 208

Jones, Gordon W., 1973 small exhibition from the collection of, 220

Jones, Howard Mumford, 1959 Club speaker on an exhibition of the year 1809, 206

Jones, Owen, *Grammar of Ornament*, 119 (P2)

Jones, T. Catesby, 1944 Club speaker on modern French prints, 200

Jonson, Ben, portrait of, 110, 122 (P13); engraving of, 127 (P34)

Jovius, Paulus, 43

Joyce, James, 1982 exhibition on, 170, 215

Keats, John, 1895 exhibition on, 168, 180; 1921 exhibition on, 170, 189

Kebabian, John S., papers of, in Grolier Club Archives, 88; 1979 small exhibition from the collection of, 221

Keene, Donald L., 1957 Club speaker on Japanese illustrated books, 206

Keep, Austin Baxter, 1910 Club speaker on libraries of colonial New York, 185

Kelmscott Press, 1928 exhibition on, 192; 1964 small exhibition on, 217

Kennedy, Edward G., gifts of prints, 81; 1922 exhibition of his gift of engraved portraits, 190; on New York cultural life, 174

—works: *A List of Paintings and Prints Now Displayed on the Walls of the Grolier Club*, 143; *The Etched Work of Whistler*, 115, 131, 133–134, 137, 138

Kenner, Hugh, 1982 Club speaker on James Joyce, 215

Kent, Henry Watson, 102, 194; Club Librarian, 44; develops library classification system, 36; classification scheme published, 128 (P36)

—Club speaker: in 1901 on the Library classification scheme, 182; in 1902 on mosaic bookbindings, 182; in 1906 on The Club Bindery, 183; in 1919 on William Blake, 188; in 1920 on fine printing from Didot the Elder to the Ashendene Press, 189; in 1923 on Bulmer and his contemporaries, 190; in 1926 on Walter Gilliss, 191; in 1927 on Geoffroy Tory and his times, in 1927 on the Montgomery monument, 192; in 1941, 198; in 1943 on Grolier Club print collection, 200

—works: *Bibliographical Notes on 100 Books Famous in English Literature*, 37, 115, 128; *The Grolier Club and Its Iconographic Collections*, 146; *What I Am Pleased to Call My Education*, 116, 147

Kent, Sherman, 1949 Club speaker on political cartoons of the reign of Louis-Philippe, 203

Keppel, Frederick, gifts of prints, 81

—Club speaker: in 1891 on etchings, 178; in 1892 on engravings, 179; in 1897 on Francis Seymour Haden, 180

Kettaneh, Francis A., 1968 small exhibition from the collection of, 219

Keyes, Edward L., 1942 Club speaker on healing by faith, fraud, and superstition, 199

Keynes, Geoffrey, *A Bibliography of William Blake*, 137; *John Evelyn: A Study in Bibliophily*, 144; and Wolf, Edwin, 2nd, *William Blake's Illuminated Books*, 148–149

Kidner, Thomas, auction catalogue of his library, 60

Kienbusch, C. Otto von, 1947 Club speaker on romances of chivalry, 202

Killigrew, Thomas, portrait of, 122 (P13)

Kimball, Ingalls, publication designed by, 143 (P97)

Kimball, LeRoy E., 1954 Club speaker, 205

King Library Press, 1975 Committee on Modern Fine Printing exhibition on, 223

Kingsley, Elbridge, 1886 Club speaker on wood engraving, 176; 1915 Club speaker on American illustrated books, 186; *Wood-Engraving: Three Essays*, 135–136

Kinkeldey, Otto, 1937 Club speaker on music, 196

Kipling, Rudyard, 1929 exhibition on, 192; publications on, 142 (P93–P94); 1965 small exhibition on, 218

Kissner, Franklin H., 1972 small exhibition from the collection of, 220

Kittredge, William A., 1929 Club speaker on Fifty Books of the Year, 193

Klickstein, Herbert S., his Lavoisier catalogue, 148 (P121)

Klopfer, Donald S., 1979 Club speaker on trade books, 215

Kloss, Georg, 50

Knapp, William I., 1886 Club speaker on Thierry Martens and the early Spanish press, 176

Kneller, Godfrey, portrait thought to be of Dryden misattributed to, 126 (P30); portrait of Pope attributed to studio of, 110

Knickerbocker, Diedrich. *See* Irving, Washington

*Knight Errant, The*, Goodhue's original drawing for cover of, 83

Knopf, Alfred A., 1948 Club speaker on American type designers, 171, 202

Knox, Henry, catalogue of, 63

Koehler, S. R., *Chronological Catalogue of the Engravings, Dry-points and Etchings of Albert Dürer*, 125

Koopman, Harry Lyman, 1924 Club speaker on typography as a fine art, 190

Kraus, H. P., gifts to Grolier Club Archives, 88

Kredel, Fritz, 1970 Club speaker on German modern fine printing, 211; map of the Iter Germanico-Helveticum drawn by, 153 (P140); 1973 exhibition of book illustrations by, 212

Krimpen, Jan van, publication designed by, 148 (P119)

Kühlmann, Richard von, 1931 Club speaker on German illustrated books, 193

Kuniyoshi, Utagawa, *Strife of Good and Evil*, 111

Kunz, George F., 1926 Club speaker on Walter Gilliss, 191; 1927 Club speaker on books on jewels and precious stones, 192

Küp, Karl, his bibliography of Updike, 144–145 (P105)

—Club speaker: in 1947 on the Fifty Books of the Year, 202; in 1957 on Japanese illustrated books, 206; in 1961 on prints, 207; in 1962 on oriental books, 208

La Caille, Jean de, *Histoire de l'imprimerie et de la librairie*, Georges Lepreux's copy, 58

La Pérouse, Jean de, 1978 small exhibition on, 221

La Vallière, Duc de, *Catalogue de livres de la bibliothèque . . .*, 65

La Vallière, Duchesse de, manuscript library catalogue of, 72

Laboureur, J.-E., 1928 exhibition on, 192

Lackington, James, autograph letter of, 76; catalogues of, 62

Lada-Mocarski, Mrs. Valerian, gift of Bonet bookbinding, 42

Lalanne, Maxime, 1891 exhibition on, 178

Lamb, Charles, 1923 exhibition on, 190; 1962 small exhibition on, 217

Landauer, Bella C., gifts of book trade ephemera, 82

Landor, Walter Savage, 51

Landscape architecture, 1975 exhibition on, 213

Landscape parks, English, 1979 small exhibition on, 221

Lange, Thomas V., 1977 Club speaker on Harper Bequest, 213; 1981 Club speaker on color in books, 215

Langland, William, 1893 exhibition on, 179; publications on, 123 (P16), 156 (H20)

Lathem, Edward Connery, and Thompson, Lawrance, *Robert Frost and the Lawrence, Massachusetts, "High School Bulletin,"* 151

Lathrop, Francis, portrait of Lowell by, 110

Laughlin, James, 1972 small exhibition from the collection of, 220

Lavoisier, Antoine-Laurent, publication on, 148 (P121); 1952 exhibition on, 204

Lawrence, Richard Hoe, develops library classification system, 36; classification scheme published, 128 (P36); on Committee on Publications, 114

Lawsher, F. C., *Die lithographische Hochatzkunst*, 55

"Lawyers of Anthony Trollope," 148 (P119)

Le Blon, Jakob Christoffel, *Coloritto or the Harmony of Colouring in Painting*, 56

Le Roux de Lincy, A.-J.-V., *Researches Concerning Jean Grolier, His Life and His Library*, 131

Le Tellier, Cardinal, catalogue of his library, 72

Lear, Edward, 1961 exhibition on, 208

Leary, Lewis, 1962 Club speaker on demonology and witchcraft, 208

*Leaves of Grass*, 1955 exhibition on, 205

*Lecture on Bookbinding as a Fine Art, A*, 120

Ledoux, Louis V., *A Descriptive Catalogue of an Exhibition of Japanese Figure Prints*, 139; *A Descriptive Catalogue of an Exhibition of Japanese Landscape, Bird, and Flower prints*, 140

Lee Priory Press, 57

Leech, John, 1914 exhibition on, 168, 186; publication on, 134 (P61)

Lefebure, Ernest, bookbinding by, 51

Lefferts, Marshall C., gift of incunabula, 51; gifts of prints, 81

Lefort, Henri, *Portrait of Benjamin Franklin*, 126

Legros, Alphonse, exhibitions on: in 1889, 177; in 1891, 178; in 1901, 182; publications on, 155 (H6)

Lehmann-Haupt, Hellmut, Club speaker: in 1939 on Gustave Doré, 197; in 1942 on color printing, 199; in 1953 on English book illustrators of the 1860s, 204; in 1968 on Gutenberg, 210

Lepreux, Georges, 58

*Letter-book of Mary Stead Pinckney*, 146

Letter forms, publication on, 137 (P70); resources for study of, in Grolier Club Library, 54

Letter sheets, California pictorial, 1980 small exhibition of, 221

Lettering books, 1933 exhibition of, 171, 194

Letters, literary and historical, 1963 exhibition of, 208

Levis, H. C., *Baziliωlogia*, 134

Lewis, R. W. B., 1978 Club speaker on New York in literature, 214

Lewis, Walter, publication printed by, 144 (P102)

Lewis, Wilmarth Sheldon, his introduction to Walpole's *Duchess of Portland's Museum*, 143–144; on Committee on Publications, 114

—Club speaker: in 1936 on Walpole, 171, 195; in 1954, 204

Lewis and Clark, 1961 exhibition on, 207

*Liber Studiorum*, 1888 exhibition on, 177

Liberal arts, 1944 Club speakers on, 200

Libraries, 1937 exhibition on, 196

Library Company of Philadelphia, 1982 exhibition from, 215

Library of Congress, 99; Classification System, 36; collection of private library catalogues, 73; John Boyd Thatcher Collection, 50

*Library of Jean Grolier*, 46, 115, 152

Libri, Guglielmo, Count, 77

Lieberson, Goddard, 1956 Club speaker on Freud, 205

Liebert, Herman W., his *Authors at Work* catalogue, 149 (P124); 1968 small exhibition from the collection of, 218

—Club speaker: in 1956 on second editions, 206; in 1959 on Samuel Johnson, 207; in 1967 on authors' corrected proofs, 210; in 1972 on Sir Thomas Phillipps, 212; in 1978 on Webster's dictionary, 214

Liebman, Charles, Jr., 1983 small exhibition from the collection of, 222

*Life of Charles Henry Count Hoym*, 126

Lilly Library, 1980 exhibition from, 215

Lincoln, Abraham, engraved portraits of, 1899 exhibition of, 181; publication on, 157 (H38)

Lincoln, Crawford, 1978 Club speaker on Webster's dictionary, 214

Linton, W. J., 1886 Club speaker on wood engraving of 15th–16th centuries, 176

Lippe, Aschwin, 1950 Club speaker on Chinese printing and writing, 203

*List of Paintings and Prints Now Displayed on the Walls of the Grolier Club*, 143

*List of Publications and Exhibition Catalogues, 1884–1916*, 136–137

*List of Publications and Exhibition Catalogues Issued by the Grolier Club, 1917–1927*, 141–142 (P91)

Litchfield, Edward S., 1971 small exhibition from the collection of, 219

Literature, exhibitions of: 170, 172; in 1950, 203; in 1969 small exhibition of modern, 219; in 1934, written by medical men, 195

*Lithographische Höchatzkunst, Die*, 55

Lithographs, 1918 exhibition of, 187; 1934 exhibition of, 195; French, 1965 small exhibition of, 217

Lithographs, etchings, and engravings by women, 1901 exhibition of, 182

Lithographs by Louis Prang of Oriental porcelains from the Walters collection, 1896 exhibition of, 180

Lithography, 1896 exhibition on, 56, 180; publications on, 125 (P23), 157 (H29)

Little magazines, 1948 exhibition on, 171, 202

Liturgical books, 1919 exhibition of, 188

Livingston, Luther S., *Franklin and his Press at Passy*, 135

Livingston, Robert R., catalogue of his library, 71

*Livre de quatre couleurs, Le*, 56

*Livres de peintres*, 1978 small exhibition of, 221

Locker-Lampson, Frederick, autograph letters of, 78; works of, in library, 39; *London Lyrics*, 78

*Lodging for the Night, A*, 139

Loemker, Elmer, publication designed by, 148 (P120)

Lohf, Kenneth A., 1971 small exhibition from the collection of, 219

London, William, *A Catalogue of the Most Vendible Books in England*, 61–62

*London Lyrics*, 78

Longfellow, Henry Wadsworth, portrait of, 110; medallion portrait of, 164

*Longfellow Collectors' Handbook*, 166

Lord, George deF., 1960 Club speaker on the Restoration, 207

Louis-Philippe, King of France, 1949 exhibition of political cartoons on, 203

Lowell, James Russell, his introduction to *Areopagitica*, 121 (P10); his edition of Donne's *Poems*, 124 (P22); portrait of, 110; medallion portrait of, 164

Lownes, Albert E., 1962 small exhibition from the collection of, 217

Lucas, George A., 107; bronze portrait medallion of, 111

Lyell, James P. R., 52

*Lyff of the Faders*, 50


Mabie, Hamilton Wright, 1903 Club speaker on 100 books famous in English literature, 182; *The Writers of Knickerbocker New York*, 134

Macauley, Catherine, *A Modest Plea for the Property of Copyright*, 55

Mackall, Leonard L., gifts to library, 39; gifts of private library catalogues, 69; 1924 Club speaker on Lord Byron, 190; 1928 exhibition of books donated by, 192

MacLeish, Archibald, 1944 Club speaker, 171, 200

Maggin, David, 1972 small exhibition from the collection of, 220

Maggs Bros., catalogues of, 62

Maghee, John Holme, on House Committee, 106

Magic books, 1927 exhibition of, 192

*Mail & Express*, on early Grolier Club exhibition, 167

Malahide Castle, 1930 exhibition of private papers of James Boswell from, 193

Mall Press, publication printed by, 137 (P70)

Manet, Edouard, 1919 exhibition of prints by, 188

Mann, Charles W., 1976 small exhibition from the collection of, 221

Mansfield, Howard, on 1902 exhibition of mosaic bookbindings, 168; on members' indifference toward some Grolier Club exhibitions, 169; 1928 Club dinner in honor of, 192

—Club speaker: in 1889 on Alphonse Legros, 177; in 1896 on Japanese prints, 180; in 1900 on etchings by Rembrandt, 181; in 1901 on Corot, Daubigny, and Legros, 182; in 1907 on lithographs by Whistler, 184; in 1917 on Japanese prints, 187; in 1923 on Japanese prints, 190; in 1924 on Japanese prints, 190; in 1926 on Walter Gilliss, 191

Manuscripts, publication on, 153 (P138); 1968 small exhibition of, 219

—autograph: 74–79; 1888 exhibition of, 177; 1920 exhibition of, 188; 1955 exhibition of, 205; publication on, 149 (P124); 1967 small exhibition of, 218; 1970 small exhibition of, 219

—English, 17th-century: 1970 small exhibition of 219

—illuminated: 1884 exhibition on, 176; 1892 exhibition on, 178; publication on, 122–123 (P15); 1973 small exhibition of, 220

—literary: 1888 exhibition of, 167, 177; 1920 exhibition of, 188; 1955 exhibition of, 205; publication on, 149 (P124); 1967 small exhibition of, 218

—medieval: 39–40; 1962 exhibition of, 208

—Oriental: 40

—Persian: exhibition on, 169; publication on, 122–123 (P15)

—Renaissance: 1962 exhibition of, 208

Manutius, Aldus, books printed by: 1943 exhibition of, 199; 1962 small exhibition of, 217

Maps, reflecting the effects of treaties, 1951 exhibition of, 203

Marchand, Prosper, his copy of the de Thou catalogue, 65, 71

Mardersteig, Giovanni, 1972 small exhibition on, 220

Marguerite, Countess of Blessington, manuscript library catalogue of, 70

Marks, Saul and Lillian, 1971 Committee on Modern Fine Printing exhibition on, 223

Marlborough, 5th Duke of, auction catalogue of his White Knights Library, 61

Marquand, Mrs. Allen, 1941 Club speaker on history of plant illustration, 198

Marsand, Antonio, autograph letter of, 77

Martens, Thierry, 1886 Club speaker on, 176

Martin, H. Bradley, first chairman of Committee on Small Exhibitions, 172; 1962 small exhibition from the collection of, 217; 1971 small exhibition from the collection of, 219

Martz, Louis L., 1972 Club speaker on John Donne, 211

Marvin, Samuel W., 1915 Club speaker on American illustrated books, 186; 1919 Club speaker on fifty years in the manufacture of books, 188

Masefield, John, McKay's bibliography of, 45

Massey, Mrs. Linton R., 1980 small exhibition from the collection of, 221

Mather, Frank Jewett, Jr., 1933 Club speaker on Winslow Homer, 194

Matthews, Brander, 1917 Club speaker on books and miniatures from Persia and the Levant, 187; 1922 Club speaker on Molière, 189

Matthews, William, bookbindings by, 40; 1885 Club speaker on modern bookbinding, 176; publications bound by, 121 (P8), 122 (P12); *Modern Bookbinding Practically Considered*, 121

*Maya Scribe and his World*, 153; 1971 exhibition on, 170, 211

Mayor, A. Hyatt, Club speaker: in 1944 on Venetian books, 200; in 1946 on "Méryon and the Enigma of Paris," 201; in 1956 on modern prints, 205; in 1961 on prints, 207; in 1964 on festival books, 209; in 1965 on illustrated books of the 1860s, 209; in 1968 on architects in the theatre, 210; in 1968 on art déco, 210

Mazarin, Cardinal, purchase of Jean des Cordes's library, 65; signature of, 75

Mazzeo, Joseph A., 1961 Club speaker on Dante in America, 208

McAlpin, Charles Williston, gifts to library, 39; gift of his collection of Grolier Club printing, 84

McCombs, Charles F., his edition of *Letter-book of Mary Stead Pinckney*, 146

McCorison, Marcus A., 1980 Club speaker on the Brinley centenary, 215

McCoy, J. C., gift of leaf from Gutenberg Bible, 49

McCrea, Nelson Glenn, 124 (P21)

McCutcheon, John T., 1938 Club speaker on Bruce Rogers, 197

McDougall, W. E., 122 (P12)

McGuire, James Clark, 1930 Club speaker on 15th-century woodcuts, 193; 1931 exhibition of items bequeathed by, 193

McKay, George Leslie, Club Librarian, 44–45; 1936 Club speaker on early American book auctions, 196; *American Book Auction Catalogues, 1713–1934*, 45, 63

McKell, David McCandless, 1961 small exhibition from the collection of, 217

McMurtrie, Douglas C., 1923 Club speaker on Bulmer and his contemporaries, 190; 1926 Club speaker on Walter Gilliss, 191; publication printed by, 140 (P87)

McNulty, Kneeland, on Elmer Adler, 150–151 (P130)

McWilliams, David Jackson, on Elmer Adler, 150–151 (P130)

Mead, Edward, on first Committee on Publications, 112

*Mechanick Exercises*, 54

Medallic Art Company, Johann Gutenberg–Jean Grolier Medal cast by, 163

Medals, 1893 exhibition of, 179; typographical, 1898 exhibition of, 181

Medals and plaques, 1897 exhibition of, 180; publication on, 156 (H18); by Victor D. Brenner, publication on, 159 (H59)

Medical books, 1973 small exhibition of, 220

Medical botany books, 1980 small exhibition of, 221

Meisner, Christopher, catalogue of, 66

Mela, Pomponius, *Cosmographia*, 49

Mellon, Paul, catalogue of exhibition from his collection, 152 (P134); small exhibitions from collection of, 172; in 1960, 216; in 1968, 218

Mellow, James, 1974 Club speaker on Gertrude Stein, 212

Melville, Herman, 1969 exhibition on, 210

Memorabilia, writers', 1983 exhibition of, 216

Ménars Library, 65

Mencken, H. L., 1980 exhibition on, 215

Mentelin German Bible, 49

Mercier, G., 121 (P10)

Meriden Gravure Company, facsimiles printed by, 151 (P132); illustrations for publications printed by, 148 (P122); 149 (P124); 150 (P128); 151–152 (P133); 152 (P134–P135); 152–153 (P137); 153 (P138); 153–154 (P141); 154 (P142); publica-

tions printed by, 150 (P129); 150–151 (P130); 151 (P131); 153 (P139)

Merriman, Roger Bigelow, 1932 Club speaker on Spanish books, 194

Merritt, A. Tillman, Club speaker on seven centuries of music, 201

Merrymount Press, 1940 exhibition on, 198; publication on, 144–145 (P105); publications printed by, 132 (P52); 133 (P53); 137 (P72); 140 (P84); 143 (P96); 145 (P106–P107); 113

Merton, Wilfred, publication printed by, 137 (P70)

Méryon, Charles, 1946 Club speaker on, 201; publication on, 157 (H33); 1898 exhibition of etchings and drawings by, 181

Metropolitan Museum of Art, 112; Henry Watson Kent leaves Grolier Club for, 37

Metropolitan Opera, 1983 exhibition to mark the centenary of, 216

Metzdorf, Robert F., 1970 small exhibition from the collection of, 219

Meunier, Charles, bookbinding after Flameng painting, 42–43

Mezzotint portraits of ladies, 1908 exhibition of, 184

Mezzotints from Dixon to Cousins, 1918 exhibition of, 188

Mezzotints from Von Siegen to Barney, 1918 exhibition of, 187; publication on, 160 (H78)

Microscopic books. *See* Miniature books

Middle colonies, 1893 exhibition of books printed in, 168, 179

Middle West, 1926 exhibition of books and broadsides of, 191

Millay, Edna St. Vincent, 1939 exhibition on, 197

Millington, Edward, auction catalogues of, 60

Milton, John, *Areopagitica*, 121; 1908 exhibition on, 169, 184; 1973 exhibition on, 212; publication on, 159 (H65)

Minagawa, Tatsuo, 1957 performance of a Nō play, 206

Miner, Dorothy, 1966 Club speaker on the book of eastern Christendom, 210

Miniature books, 38; publication on, 133 (P55)

Miniatures, exhibitions of: in 1893, painted, 179; in 1917, Near Eastern, 187

Minto, Earls of, manuscript library catalogue of, 70

Mizener, Arthur, 1957 Club speaker, 206

*Modern Bookbinding Practically Considered*, 121

Modern fine printing, exhibitions of: in 1960, 207; in 1970, German, 211; in 1978, American, 214; 1978 Committee on Modern Fine Printing exhibition of, 224

*Modern Thinker, The*, 56

*Modest Plea for the Property of Copyright, A*, 55

Molière, 1922 exhibition on, 189; 1968 small exhibition on, 218

Montgomery monument, 1927 Club speaker on, 192

Moore, Marianne, 1948 Club speaker on American women writers, 171, 202

*Moralia in Job*, 39–40

Mores, Edward Rowe, *A Dissertation Upon English Typographical Founders and Founderies*, 54, 140

Morgan, John Hill, 1931 Club speaker on George Washington, 194

Morgand and Fatout, stock and sale records of, in Grolier Club Archives, 88

Morgand, Damacène, stock and sale records of, in Grolier Club Archives, 88

Morison, Samuel Eliot, 1953 Club speaker on the sea in literature, 204

Morison, Stanley, 1933 Club speaker on lettering and writing books, 171, 194; *Fra Luca de Pacioli*, 115, 143; photograph of title-page, 32

Moronobu, 1922 exhibition on, 190; 139 (P82)

Morrill Press, publication printed by, 144 (P103)

Morris, Frances, 1912 Club speaker on the history and development of costume, 185

Morris, Henry, 1972 Committee on Modern Fine Printing exhibition on, 223

Morris, May, bookbinding by, 42

Morris, William, his Albion hand press, 139; 1964 small exhibition on, 217

Morse, Glenn Tilley, 1932 Club speaker on American silhouettes, 194

Mortimer, Ruth, 53

Motion pictures, 1943 Club speaker on, 199

Mott Memorial Library, 107

Moxon, Joseph, *Mechanick Exercises*, 54

Mugridge, Donald, his introduction to *Letter-book of Mary Stead Pinckney*, 146

Mulholland, John, 1927 performances of magic act by, 192

Munby, A. N. L., 60, 62; on Count Libri, 77; Grolier Club purchases at auction sale of, 41, 69; and Coral, Lenore, *English Book Sale Catalogues*, 60

"Murder by the Book," 1973 exhibition of crime and mystery books, 212

Museum of Modern Art, 114

Museum of the City of New York, 1938 joint exhibition with, 197

Music, 1945 exhibition of, 201; 1967 small exhibition of, 218; American, 1951 exhibition of, 204; printed and in manuscript, 1937 exhibition of, 196; published in 1776, 1976 performance of, 213

Musical instruments, 1980 exhibition of books and prints on, 215

Myers, Andrew Breen, 1983 Club speaker on Washington Irving, 216

*Mystery of Edwin Drood*, 1932 exhibition on, 194

Naef, Weston J., and Goldschmidt, Lucien, *The Truthful Lens*, 153–154

Nagler, Alois M., 1968 Club speaker on architects in the theatre, 210

Nanteuil, Robert, 1893 exhibition of engraved portraits by, 179

Nash, John Henry, 113; publication designed and printed by, 138 (P74); 1973 small exhibition on, 220; Strouse's 1973 talk on, 212

Nash, Ray, 1944 Club speaker on American calligraphy, 200; 1949 Club speaker on Carl Purington Rollins, 203

*National Union Catalog Pre-1956 Imprints*, 94, 154 (P144)

Natural history books, 1962 small exhibition of, 217; illustrated, 1957 exhibition of, 206

"Nature's Handmaid Art," 1975 exhibition on landscape architecture, 213

Naumburg, Edward, Jr., on Elmer Adler, 150–151 (P130); 1974 small exhibition from the collection of, 220; 1953 Club speaker on children's books, 204

Naval prints, American, publication on, 160 (H72); 1942 exhibition of, 199

Navigation, 1938 exhibition on history of, 197; 1970 small exhibition of books on, 219

Neergaard, Arthur Edwin, 1943 Club speaker on Aldus Manutius, 199

New York, 1910 Club speaker on colonial libraries of, 185; 1915 exhibition of maps, plans, and views of, 187; history: publication on, 123, 1942 Club speaker on, 199; in literature: 1978 exhibition on, 214; literary history, publication on, 134 (P58); printing in, publication on, 141 (P88); theatre in the 19th century, 1977 small exhibition on, 221

*New York: A Series of Wood Engravings in Colour*, 115, 135

New York City, cultural life, 11–12, 174; publication on iconography of, 157 (H32); 1897 exhibition of plans and views of, 181

New-York Historical Society, 1954 Grolier Club meeting held at, 205; 1977 exhibition of its Harper Bequest acquisitions, 213

New York Public Library, 99; print collection based on gift of Samuel Putnam Avery, 81; 1977 exhibition of its Harper Bequest acquisitions, 213

—Berg Collection, Harvey A. Simmonds leaves, to come to Grolier Club, 46

New York *Times*, article on early exhibitions of Grolier Club, 167

New York University, 46, 112

New York World's Fair, 1964 exhibition to mark the, 209

*New Yorker, The*, 1975 exhibition on, 213

Newberry Library, collection of private library catalogues, 73

Newell, Mary J., book decorations by, 144–145 (P105)

Newhall, Beaumont, 1974 Club speaker on photography in books, 212

*News Sheet of the Grolier Club*, 163

Newton, A. Edward, proposes T. J. Wise for membership, 85; 1919 Club speaker on William Blake, 188; 1931 Club speaker on an imaginary conversation between Franklin and Johnson, 193

Neyts, Gillis, 1912 informal discussion on, 185

Nichol, R. T., his translation of Dürer's *Of the Just Shaping of Letters*, 137

Nicholas I, Pope, *Epistolae*, Grolier binding on, 43

Nichols, George Livingston, 39

Nichols, John, 140 (P84)

Nichols, John Gough, Grolier Club purchases at auction sale of, 89

Nicholson, Thomas D., 1958 Club speaker on "Astronautica Incunabula," 206

Nikirk, Robert, 35; Club Librarian, 46; 1983 Club speaker on "Honour'd Relics," 216; *The Grolier Club Iter Germanico-Helveticum*, 153

Nō play, 1957 performance of, 206

Noah's Ark, 1938 exhibition on, 197

Nordhoff, Evelyn Hunter, 1897 Club speaker on recent American bookbindings, 180

North, Ernest Dressell, 1923 Club speaker on Charles Lamb, 190

Northwick, Lord, Grolier Club purchase at auction sale of, 61

Norton, Charles Eliot, letters to Beverly Chew, 79; 124 (P22); 125 (P26)

Norwich Free Academy, 36

*Notable Printers of Italy During the Fifteenth Century*, 132

*Notes and Journal of Travel in Europe*, 137

*Notes on the American Press*, 141

Nutter, Valentine, 77

"O Magic City," 1978 exhibition on New York in literature, 214

*Observations on Literary Property*, 55

O'Casey, Sean, 1980 small exhibition on, 221

O'Connell, J. Harlin, 1945 Club speaker on Beardsley, 201

"Odd volumes," 1955 exhibition of books with unusual formats, bindings, or materials, 205

*Of the Just Shaping of Letters*, 114, 137

Officina Bodoni, 1972 small exhibition on, 220

*Officium Beatae Virginis Mariae*, printed by Nicolaus Jenson, 38–39, 51; photograph of, 23

Oldenburg, Peter, publication designed by, 153–154, (P141)

Olds, Irving S., has exhibition hall renovated, 109; 1942 Club speaker on naval prints, 199

Oliver, Andrew, Jr., 1970 small exhibition from the collection of, 219

Oliver, Peter, 1941 Club speaker on researches concerning the year 1800, 198

Omar Khayyám, Rubáiyát of, 119 (P2)

*One Hundred Books Famous in English Literature*, 37, 115, 128, 169; 1903 exhibition of, 182

*One Hundred Books Famous in Science*, 115, 151, 170; Roger Powell binding on, 42; 1954 exhibition of, 206

"One Hundred Illustrated Books," 170; 1921 exhibition of, 189

*One Hundred Influential American Books Printed Before 1900*, 115, 146–147, 170; 1946 exhibition of, 201

Opera, 1976 exhibition of literary sources for libretti, 213; 1983 exhibition of stage and costume designs for, 216

Oporinus, Joannes, obituary of, in Grolier Club Library, 54

*Oratio de ortv, vita, et obitv, Ioannis Oporinus Basiliensis*, 54

Oriental art objects, 1896 exhibition of original drawings from, 180

Oriental books, 1962 exhibition of, 208

Oriental porcelains from the Walters collections, 1896 exhibition of lithographs of, 180

Ornithology books, American, 1982 small exhibition of, 222

Osborn, Fairfield, 1958 Club speaker, 206

Osborn, James, 1970 small exhibition from the collection of, 219

Osborne, Lucy Eugenia, her translation of Haebler's *Study of Incunabula*, 143

Oswald, John Clyde, 1928 Club speaker on De Vinne, 192; 142 (P92)

"Other People's Mail," 1963 exhibition of literary and historical letters, 208

Overbrook Press, 113; publication printed by, 146 (P113)

*Oxford Book of English Verse*, 1950 exhibition on, 203

Pacific, South, French exploration in, 1978 small exhibition on, 221

Paff, A. E. M., 187

Palmer, Samuel, *Proposals for Publishing a General History of Printing*, 54; *General History of Printing*, 54

Panoramas, 1977 small exhibition on, 221

Papantonio, Michael, 1962 small exhibition from the collection of, 217

Paper, 1910 informal meeting on, 185

Paper sample books, in Grolier Club, 80

Papermaking, 1969 small exhibition of books on, 219

Papermaking in Japan, 1925 Club speaker on, 191

Paris, 1983 small exhibition of books, maps, and views of, 222

Paris Exposition of 1900, ephemera from, in Grolier Club Print Collection, 81

Parks, Stephen R., 1974 small exhibition from the collection of, 220

Parsons, Edward Alexander, 1947 Club speaker on the Alexandrian Library, 202

*Parthenon, The* (lithographically printed magazine), 56

Patrick, Ted, 1960 Club speaker on gastronomy, 207

Pawlik, F., 1897 exhibition of medals and plaques by, 180

Payne, Roger, bookbinding by, 42; 117 (P1)

Payne and Foss, photograph of page from catalogue of, 28; shop copy of catalogues, in Grolier Club Library, 62

Peal, W. Hugh, 1962 small exhibition from the collection of, 217

Pearson, Edmund Lester, 1933 Club speaker on crime and mystery books, 194

Pearson, Norman Holmes, 1971 small exhibition from the collection of, 219

—Club speaker: in 1964 on Hawthorne, 209; in 1965 on English boys' books, 209; in 1969 on Melville, 210

*Peg Woffington*, 114, 120; 1892 exhibition of watercolors by Grivaz for, 178

"Penman's Paradise," 1921 exhibition of writing books, 189

Penmanship, 1921 exhibition of examples of, 189

Pennell, Elizabeth Robins, 1935 exhibition on, 195

Pennell, Joseph, 120 (P7); 159 (H64); 1918 Club speaker on artistic lithography, 187

—exhibitions: in 1908, of etchings, 184; in 1923, of lithographs, 190; in 1935, 195; in 1981 small exhibition of lithographs and book illustrations, 222; 168

Penrose, Boies, 1936 Club speaker on travel in Tudor and Stuart England, 196

Penrose, Roland, 1972 Club speaker on Picasso and his poets, 212

Penton, John A., gift of Locker-Lampson's works, 39

Pepys, Samuel, 1933 exhibition on, 194

Perishable Press, 1972 Committee on Modern Fine Printing exhibition on, 223

Perrin, Alfred H., 1965 small exhibition from the collection of, 218

Peters, Harry T., his introduction to *Early American Sport*, 144

—Club speaker: in 1925 on sporting books and prints, 191; in 1929 on Currier and Ives, 193; in 1938 on circuses, 197; in 1939 on "California, Here I Come," 197; in 1941 on sporting books, 198

Petrarch, marble bust of, 109

Petrucius, *Disputationes Questiones et Concilia*, provenance of, 50

Peyre, Henri, 1966 Club speaker on French Parnassian and Symbolist poetry, 209

Pforzheimer, Carl H., catalogue of his library, 71; 1969 small exhibition from the Library of, 219

Pforzheimer, Walter L., 1968 small exhibition from the collection of, 218; 1960 Club speaker on spies and intelligence, 207

Philadelphia, Centennial Exhibition (1876), exhibition of books at, 166

Phillipps, Thomas, 62; catalogue of his manuscript collection, 71; 1972 exhibition on, 212; 1968 small exhibition on, 218

*Philobiblon*, 114, 120–121

Photographic reproduction processes, 1983 small exhibition on, 222

Photography, in books, publication on, 153–154 (P141); 1974 exhibition on, 212

Photomechanical processes, 1885 exhibition on, 176

Picasso, Pablo, 1972 exhibition of poetry illustrated by, 212

Pichon, Jérôme, *The Life of Charles Henry Count Hoym*, 126

Pickering, William, letters from Dibdin to, 77

*Pieces of Ancient Poetry from Unpublished Manuscripts...*, 56

Pierpont Morgan Library: Grolier Club purchases Tritheim's *Catalogus* from, 52; 1977 exhibition of its Harper Bequest acquisitions, 213; 1954 Club meeting held at, 205; joint publication with, 153 (P138)

*Pierrot of the Minute*, 138–139

Pigouchet, Phillippe, printer, 50

Pinckney, Mary Stead, letter-book of, 146 (P113)

Pinelli, Maffeo, catalogue of his library, annotated by Michael Wodhull, 72

Piranesi, Giovanni, 1902 exhibition of etchings of ancient Rome by, 182

Pirates, 1915 exhibition on, 187

Pirie, Robert S., *John Donne, 1572–1631: A Catalogue of the Anniversary Exhibition*, 152–153; 1963 small exhibition from the collection of, 217

Pissarro, Lucien, 1974 small exhibition of drawings and printing by, 220

*Plant Illustration Before 1850*, 145; 1941 exhibition on, 198

Plantin, Christopher, publication on, 120 (P7)

Plantin-Moretus Museum, publication on, 120 (P7)

Plantin Press, 1971 Committee on Modern Fine Printing exhibition on, 223

Plants, endangered, 1977 exhibition of book illustrations of, 214

Platt, Charles A., publication on, 160 (H84); 1925 exhibition of etchings by, 190

Platt, Dan Fellows, 1937 Club speaker on Italian drawings, 196

Plimpton, George A., 1921 Club speaker on writing books and penmanship, 189; 1930 Club speaker on the formation of the English language, 193

Plimpton Press, 113; publications printed by, 142 (P93–P94)

Poe, Edgar Allan, 1949 exhibition on, 171, 203; medallion portrait of, 164

*Poems of John Donne*, 124

Poetry, illustrated by Pablo Picasso, 1972 exhibition of, 212

Poets Laureate of England, publications on, 127 (P34), 158 (H44); 1901 exhibition on, 182

Poggio Bracciolini, Giovanni Francesco, 1981 small exhibition on, 222

Polain, Louis, papers of, in Grolier Club Archives, 88

Polar exploration, 1932 exhibition on, 170, 194

Political cartoons, of the reign of Louis-Philippe, 1949 exhibition of, 203

Pollard, Alfred W., his forward to Haebler's *Study of Incunabula*, 143

Pollard, Graham, and Ehrman, Albert, *The Distribution of Books by Catalogue to A.D. 1800*, 66

*Polyhistor*, 51

Pompadour, Madame de, catalogue of her library in manuscript, 72; photograph of title-page, 27

Pond, Walter, 1977 small exhibition from the collection of, 221

Pope, Alexander, portrait of, 110

—exhibitions: in 1911, 169, 185; in 1939, 197
—publications: 133 (P54); 159 (H69)
Portalis, Roger, 131 (P46)
*Portrait of Benjamin Franklin*, 126
Portraits, exhibitions: in 1899, dramatic, 181; in 1924 from the bequest of Beverly Chew, 190; engraved: in 1887, 177; in 1935, 195; in 1922, from the gift of Edward G. Kennedy, 190; publication on, 161 (H86)
Portraits of English authors, 1891 exhibition on, 178; publications on, 122 (P13); 156 (H14), 157 (H35)
Portraits of French artists and authors, 1892 exhibition on, 178
Portraits of women writers, engraved, publication on, 157 (H26)
Posters, exhibitions: in 1890, French, 168, 178; in 1892, 178; in 1916, 187; in 1943, of World War I, 199; publication on, 155 (H10)
Potter, Beatrix, 1959 small exhibition of sketches by, 172, 216
Pottinger, David T., Club speaker: in 1926 on Fifty Books of the Year, 191; in 1940 on D. B. Updike and the Merrymount Press, 198; his Updike talk published, 144–145 (P105)
Pottle, Frederick A., his Boswell Papers catalogue, 142 (P95); Club speaker on Boswell papers: in 1931, 171, 193; in 1951, 203
Pound, Ezra, 1976 small exhibition on, 220
Powell, Lawrence Clark, 1964 Club speaker on "The Three L's: Life, Landscape, and Literature," 209
Powell, Roger, bookbinding by, 42
Prairie Press, 1976 Committee on Modern Fine Printing exhibition on, 224
Prang, Louis, 1897 Club speaker on his lithographs of Oriental porcelains in the Walters collection, 180
Pratt Institute, library school, 102
"Prelude to Independence," 1974 exhibition on printing and the American Revolution, 212
Prescott, Marjorie Wiggin, 89
Press books, exhibitions of: in 1929, German, 193; in 1978, American, 214
Press of A. Colish, publications printed by, 146–147 (P114); 154 (P143–P144); 162–163 (G14–G20/21); 113
Prideaux, Sarah, bookbinding by, 42
Priest, Richard E., 41
Prime, William C., 1890 Club speaker on history of wood engraving, 177; 1892 Club speaker on genealogy of a book, 178
Princeton University Library, Friends of, joint publication with, 150–151 (P130)
Princeton University Press, publications printed by, 150–151 (P130); 153 (P138); 113
Printed ephemera, in Grolier Club Library, 57; in Print Collection, 81–82
Printers, English, 1914 exhibition of trade cards of, 186; French, 1914 exhibition of trade cards of, 186; exhibitions of portraits of, in 1905, in 1906, in 1907, in 1910, in 1911, 183–185; 168

"Printer's Choice," 1978 exhibition of American press books, 214
Printers' social clubs, papers of, 87–88
Printing, exhibitions on: 167, 168, 172; in 1923, English, 190; in 1929, German, 193; in 1940, on bibliography and iconography of, 198; in 1950, Chinese, 203; in 1978, French, 214; Italian, publication on, 132 (P50). *See also* Modern fine printing
Printing history, exhibitions on, 170; publications on: 120 (P5); 124 (P21); 127 (P33); 132 (P52); 140 (P84, P87); 1938 Club speaker on, 197; resources for study of, in Grolier Club Library, 54–55
—American: 1893 exhibition on, 179; publications on, 143 (P96); 156 (H19)
—Spanish: 1886 Club speaker on, 176
"Printing in France, 1850–1900," 1978 exhibition on, 214
Printing ink, 1910 informal meeting on, 185
"Printmakers Observe Their Own World," 1982 exhibition on, 216
Prints, auction catalogues of, 61
—exhibitions of: miscellaneous, in 1934, 195; in 1952, from the Society of Iconophiles, 204; in 1956, 205; in 1961, 207; in 1979, 214; in 1982, 216; 172
—by place, in 1903, Italian, 182; in 1931, modern French, 193; in 1939 contemporary American, 197; in 1944, modern French, 200; in 1945, contemporary Latin American, 201
Prints, Japanese. *See* Japanese prints
Prior, Matthew, 129 (P42)
Private library catalogues, 68–73, 95; scope of collection, 68; growth of the collection, 69; difficulty of collecting, 70; relative size of Grolier Club collection, 73; American, in manuscript, 71; English, in manuscript, 70; French, in manuscript, 72; other European countries, 72
Private press books in Grolier Club Library, 57
Private presses, English, 1938 exhibition on, 197
Private presses in Lexington, Kentucky, 1975 Committee on Modern Fine Printing exhibition on, 223
"Prized Prints," 1979 exhibition from collections of Grolier members, 214
Proofs, authors' corrections on, 1967 exhibition of, 210
Propaganda, 1943 Club speaker on, 199
*Proposals for Publishing a General History of Printing*, 54
Proust, Marcel, 1972 exhibition on, 170, 211
Prouty, Charles Tyler, 1953 Club speaker on Elizabethan books, 204
Pryce-Jones, Alan, 1966 Club speaker on exiles and expatriates, 209
Publishers, autograph letters and manuscripts of, 77; exhibitions of portraits of, in 1905, in 1906, in 1907, in 1910, in 1911, 183–185; 168
Pulitzer Prize winners, 1956 exhibition of, 206
Purdy, J. Harsen, gifts of prints, 81
Purdy, Richard L., 1940 Club speaker on Thomas Hardy, 198
Putnam, George Haven, 1915 Club speaker on American illustrated books, 186

Pyle, Howard, *Friar Roger Bacon in his Cell*, 111; *William Caxton at his Press*, 111; 119 (P3)

Pynson Printers, publication printed by, 144–145 (P105)

Quaritch, Bernard, 119 (P2); catalogues of, in Grolier Club Library, 62

"Quarter of a Millenium," 1982 exhibition marking the 250th anniversary of the Library Company of Philadelphia, 215

*Quattrocentisteria*, 138

"Queen Victoria's Lady Novelists," 1969 exhibition on, 210

Quintilian, copy owned by Jacques-Auguste de Thou, 57–58

Rabi, I. I., 1958 Club speaker on 100 books famous in science, 206

Radical movements in America, literature of, 1938 exhibition on, 171, 196

Radnitzky, K., 1897 exhibition of medals and plaques by, 180

Rahir, Edouard, stock and sale records of, in Grolier Club Archives, 88

Rajon, Paul, 1890 exhibition on, 178; 1891 exhibition on, 178

Rampant Lions Press, 1971 Committee on Modern Fine Printing exhibition on, 223

Ramsaye, Terry, 1943 Club speaker on "People, Propaganda, and Motion Pictures," 199

Randall, David A., 1953 Club speaker on English book illustrators of the 1860s, 204

Randall, Lilian M. C., 1977 Club speaker on the Walters Art Gallery, 214

Rankin, Joseph T., 1977 Club speaker on Harper Bequest, 213

Ransom, Will, 117

"Rare and Endangered," 1977 exhibition of book illustrations of endangered plants and animals, 214

Ratdolt, Erhard, printer, 49

Raubicheck, Frank, 119 (P3)

Raucourt, Antoine, 56

Ray, Gordon N., on quality of Grolier Club exhibitions, 170; 1965 small exhibition from the collection of, 217

—Club speaker: in 1963 on Thackeray, 208; in 1977 on Harper Bequest, 213

Read, Thomas Buchanan, portrait of Longfellow by, 110

Reade, Charles, *Peg Woffington*, 114, 120

*Reading a Poem*, 132–133; 1910 performance of, 185

Reagh, MacCarthy, J. R. Abbey copy of his auction catalogue, 65

*Recollections of the Gilliss Press*, 140

Reed, Joseph Verner, 1970 Club speaker on artists and architects in the theatre, 211

Reese, William S., 59; 1980 Club speaker on the Brinley centenary, 215

Reichel, Anton, *Die Clair-Obscur Schnitte*, 1927 exhibition of chiaroscuro prints from, 192

Reifstahl, Meyer, 1917 Club speaker on books and miniatures from Persia and the Levant, 187

Reilley, Mrs. Ewing P., 1979 small exhibition from the collection of, 221

Rembrandt, 1891 exhibition on, 178; 1900 exhibition on, 168, 181; publication on, 127 (P31)

Renouard, Antoine Augustin, 51; recipient of Marsand letter, 77

Restoration, The, 1960 exhibition on, 207

Revere, Paul, 1936 exhibition of engravings by, 196

Reynolds, Joshua, 1965 small exhibition on, 218

Rice, Eugene, Jr., 1979 Club speaker on "Jean Grolier, the man in his time," 214

Rice, Richard A., 1887 Club speaker on Charles Storm van 's Gravesande, 176

Richards, Charles R., 1918 Club speaker on the art of the architect and interior decorator of the 18th century, 188

Ricketts, Charles, 1982 small exhibition on, 222

Riely, John C., 1976 Club speaker on gothic novels, ghost and horror books, 213

Ringel d'Illzach, Désiré, medallion portrait of Hawthorne modeled by, 164; 1893 exhibition of medals by, 179

Rippey, Arthur G., 1975 small exhibition from the collection of, 220

Rist, John, *Depositio Cornuti Typographici*, 132

Rive, Abbé, 72

Riverside Press, publication printed by, 135 (P62)

Rivington, James, 77

Robbins, William J., 1943 Club speaker on botanical books, 200

Roberts, Dudley, 1934 Club speaker on literature by medical men, 195

Robertson, David A., Jr., 1969 Club speaker on "Queen Victoria's lady novelists," 210

Robinson, Edwin Arlington, 1939 exhibition on, 197

Robinson, Lionel and Philip, gift of English auction catalogues, 40, 60

Robison, Andrew, 1981 Club speaker on 18th-century Venetian illustrated books, 215

Rogers, Bruce, 113; works in library, 39; letter of introduction to Grolier Club, 85; publication on, 154 (P143)

—exhibitions on: in 1932, 194; in 1938, 197; in 1970, 211; in 1982 small exhibition on, 222

—publications designed by: 135 (P62); 137 (P70); 138–139 (P78); 141 (P90); 143 (P99)

Rollins, Carl Purington, 113; 1949 exhibition on, 203

—Club speaker: in 1926 on type specimens and broadsides before 1900, 191; in 1928 on Fifty Books of the Year, 192; in 1938 on Bruce Rogers, 197; in 1949 on his own work, 203

—publications designed and/or printed by, 139 (P79); 141 (P88–P89)

Rollins, Philip Ashton, 1926 Club speaker on books and broadsides of the Middle West, 191; 1938 Club speaker on great trails of the Far West, 196

Romances, 1947 exhibition of, 202

Rome, ancient, 1902 exhibition of Piranesi etchings of, 182

Rome, classical, rediscovery of, in 16th century, 1972 small exhibition on, 220

Romeyn, Charles W., and Company, designers of clubhouse at 29 East 32 St., 107

Roosevelt, George E., 1938 Club speaker on history of navigation, 197

Root, Robert K., 1949 Club speaker, 203

Rosenbach Foundation Museum and Library, 1973 exhibition from, 212

Rosenbach, A. S. W., 1928 Club speaker on children's books, 192

Rosenberg, Alexandre, 1975 small exhibition from the collection of, 220

Rosenblum, Robert H., 1965 Club speaker on illustrated books of the 1860s, 209

Rosenthal, Max, etchings by, 123 (P17)

Rosenwald, Lessing J., 1966 small exhibition from the collection of, 218; 1973 Club speaker on A. S. W. and Philip Rosenbach, 212; his collection at the Library of Congress, 104

Rot, Adam, printer, 50

Rothman, John, 1980 performance of a one-man show about Mencken, 215

Roty, Louis O., 1893 exhibition of medals by, 179

Rowfant Library, 78

Rowlandson, Thomas, Sotheby auction catalogues of, 61
—publications: 136 (P67); 160 (H76)
—exhibitions: in 1916 of book illustrations and drawings, 187; in 1963 small exhibition, 217

Roxburghe, 3rd Duke of, auction catalogue of library, 60

*Rubáiyát of Omar Khayyám*, 119

Rudge, William Edwin, 113; publications printed by, 138–139 (P78); 141 (P90); 142 (P95); 143 (P97)

Ruskin, John, 1978 small exhibition on, 221

Russell-Rutter Company, publications bound by, 148 (P122); 149 (P124); 150 (P128); 151–152 (P133)

Ruzicka, Rudolph, *New York: A Series of Wood Engravings in Colour*, 115, 135; his illustrations to Irving's *Notes and Journal of Travel in Europe*, 137; book decorations by, 144–145 (P105); publications designed by, 147 (P115); 1938 Club speaker on Bruce Rogers, 197
—exhibitions on: in 1920, 189; in 1948, 202

Ruzicka, Veronica, wrapper design by, 147 (P115)

Ryskamp, Charles A., 1974 small exhibition from the collection of, 220


Saffron, Morris H., 1963 small exhibition from the collection of, 217

Sage, Dean, 43

Saint-Mémin, Charles Balthazar Julien Fevret de, 1899 exhibition of portraits by, 181; publication on, 157 (H37)

Salloch, William, 1976 small exhibition from the collection of, 221

Salmon, John H. M., 1979 Club speaker on "Jean Grolier, the man in his time," 214

Salmon of Paris, publication printed by, 121–122 (P11)

Samuels, Jack H., 1963 small exhibition from the collection of, 217

Sappho, 1895 exhibition of engraved portraits of, 180; publication on, 157 (H26)

*Scarlet Letter, The*, 115, 131; 1909 exhibition of Boughton's watercolors for, 184

Scharff, A., 1897 exhibition of medals and plaques by, 180

Scheide, William H., 48; 1967 small exhibition from the collection of, 218

Schieffelin, George M., gift of papers from Scribner's Rare Book Shop, 88

Schiff, Mortimer L., Club speaker: in 1919 on historical bookbindings, 188; in 1921 on 100 illustrated books, 189; in 1922 on Molière, 189

Schild, Marion, joins Grolier Club Cataloguing Project, 104

Schimmel, Herbert D., 80; 1967 small exhibition from the collection of, 218

Schimmel, Stuart B., 1961 small exhibition from the collection of, 217
—Club speaker: in 1977 on Harper Bequest, 213; in 1977 on literary and historical forgeries, 214

Schless, Howard H., 1961 Club speaker on Dante in America, 208

Schlosser, Leonard B., 1969 small exhibition from the collection of, 219; 1981 Club speaker on color in books, 215

Schoenbaum, Samuel, 1977 Club speaker on literary and historical forgeries, 214

Scholarship, its relationship to book collecting, 90–91

Scholz, Janos, 1960 Club speaker on exhibition of his collection of Italian drawings, 207; 1945 musical performance by, 201

Schwartz, S., 1897 exhibition of medals and plaques by, 180

Scientific books, 1891 exhibition of, 178; small exhibitions of: in 1971, 219; in 1973, 220; publications on: 151 (P131); 155 (H12)

Scott, Robert, auction catalogues of, in Grolier Club Library, 60; autograph letter of, 75; Twysden-Phillipps copy of his 1674 catalogue, 62

Scribner, Arthur H., on Committee on Publications, 114

Scribner's Rare Book Shop, papers of, in Grolier Club Archives, 88

Sea in literature, 1953 exhibition on, 204

Seaman, Lazarus, auction catalogue of his library, 60; photograph of title-page, 26

Second editions, 1956 exhibition of, 206

"Second Thoughts," 1967 exhibition of authors' corrected proofs, 210

Seitz, Don C., Club speaker: in 1915 on pirates and highwaymen, 187; in 1923 on Japanese prints, 190; in 1927 on American humor, 191

Selch, Frederick R., 1976 Club speaker on "Europe in 1776," 213

"Selection from Our Shelves, A," 1973 exhibition from the Rosenbach Foundation Museum and Library, 212

*Selective Check Lists of Press Books,* 117

Self-portraits by living American artists, 1939 exhibition of, 197

Seltzer, Daniel, 1964 Club speaker on "Shakespeare's rivals," 209

Senefelder, Alois, 1934 exhibition on, 195; *A Complete Course of Lithography,* 55

*Series of Six Reproductions of Additional States of Whistler's Etchings,* 133–134

Seznec, Jean, 1947 Club speaker on romances of chivalry, 202

Shackleton, Robert, 1969 Club speaker on the Bodleian Library, 211

Shakespeare, William, 1916 exhibition on, 169, 187; publications on: 136 (P66); 160 (H75)

"Shakespeare's rivals," 1964 exhibition on, 209

Shattuck, Roger, 1972 Club speaker on Proust, 211

Shaw, George Bernard, 1952 exhibition on, 204

Shelley, Percy Bysshe, 1922 exhibition on, 170, 189; 1969 small exhibition on, 219; publication on, 138 (P76)

*Shelley Library, A,* 166

Shellman, William F., 1975 Club speaker on landscape architecture, 213

Sherborn, C. W., 1931 exhibition of bookplates designed by, 193

Sherburn, George, 1939 Club speaker on Pope, 197

Shipman, Carolyn, her translation of *Researches Concerning Jean Grolier,* 46, 131

*Short History of the Printing Press, A,* 57

*Short List of Microscopic Books in the Library of The Grolier Club, Mostly Presented by Samuel P. Avery,* 133

Shugio, Heromich, 1887 Club speaker on Japanese and Chinese books, 177; gift of *Strife of Good and Evil,* 111

Sign of the Chorobates, publication printed by, 141 (P89)

Silesius, Andrea Jociscus, *Oratio de ortv, vita, et obitv Ioannis Oporinus Basiliensis,* 54

Silhouettes, American, 1932 exhibition of, 194

Silve, David, 1927 Club speaker on Fifty Books of the Year, 192

Simmonds, Harvey A., Club Librarian, 46

"Since *The Waste Land,*" 1964 exhibition of modern English poetry, 209

*Six Hundred Years of Sport,* 145

Sizer, Theodore, 1927 Club speaker on Geoffroy Tory and his times, 192

Sloan, John, drawings by, 83

Slocum, John J., 1982 Club speaker on James Joyce, 215

Smith, Charlotte, *Elegiac Sonnets,* printed by Isaiah Thomas, 58

Smith, David A., his foreword to *Bibliography, its History and Development,* 154

Smith, F. Hopkinson, 1903 Club speaker on "The Quality of the Picturesque," 183

Smith, Richard, auction catalogue of his library, 60

Smith, Sidney L., 87

Smith, William Jay, 1966 Club speaker on French Parnassian and Symbolist poetry, 209

Snell, Charles, *Art of Writing,* 54

Sneyd, Walter, 40

Society of American Wood Engravers, 1886 exhibition on, 176; 1890 exhibition on, 177; 155 (H9)

Society of French Bibliophiles, life of Count Hoym written for, 126 (P28)

Society of Iconophiles, 82; archives of, 87; 1920 joint meeting to honor memory of William Loring Andrews, 188

—exhibitions of prints, portraits, and views published by: in 1898, 181; in 1919, 188; in 1952, 204; in 1967 small exhibition, 218

"Society's Chief Joys, A," 1969 exhibition of Americana from the American Antiquarian Society, 210

Solinus, *Polyhistor,* 51

Sora, Gabriel, catalogue of his library, 72

Sotheby catalogues, Grolier Club purchase of, 61

Sotheby Parke-Bernet Book Department, Gabriel Austin leaves Grolier Club for, 46

Sotheby, Samuel Leigh, 61

Sotheran, Henry, catalogues of, in Grolier Club Library, 62

South Kensington, Caxton Celebration (1877), exhibition of books at, 166

Southey, Robert, 51

Spanish books, 1932 exhibition of, 194

Sparrow, John, 1972 Club speaker on Donne, 211

Spenceley, J. Winfred, 1910 exhibition of engraved work of, 185

Spenser, Edmund, 1899 exhibition on, 169, 181; publication on, 157 (H39)

Spies and intelligence, 1960 exhibition on, 207

Spiral Press, 113; publications printed by: 147 (P117); 149 (P126); 150 (P128); 151–152 (P133); 152 (P135); 161 (H89)

"Splendid Occasions," 1964 exhibition of festival books, 209

"Splendor in Books," 1977 exhibition of items from the Walters Art Gallery, 214

Sporting books

—exhibitions: 170; in 1925, 191; in 1937, American, 196; in 1940, 198; in 1971, small exhibition, 219

—publications: 144 (P104); 145 (P106)

Stamperia del Santuccio, 1975 Committee on Modern Fine Printing exhibition on, 223

Stanbrook Abbey Press, 1974 Committee on Modern Fine Printing exhibition on, 223

*Standard Rules of the Round and Round Text-hands,* 54

Stanford University, J. Terry Bender leaves, to come to Grolier Club, 45

Stanhope, George, 54

Index   Stanley, William, 70

Stargardt auction of Barnheim library, 50

Starkey, John, autograph invoice of, 75

Starkweather, William E. V., 1916 Club speaker on Goya, 187

Starr, Nathan Comfort, 1972 small exhibition from the collection of, 220

Stationers' Company, *Orders, Rules & Ordinances*, 55

Stauffer, David McNeely, *American Engravers upon Copper and Steel*, 130

Steele, Frederic Dorr, 1939 Club speaker on American life as portrayed by American illustrators, 197

Stefansson, Vilhjalmur, 1932 Club speaker on polar exploration, 194

Stein, Aaron Marc, 1973 Club speaker on "Murder by the Book," 212

Stein, Gertrude, 1974 exhibition on, 212

Stern, Edward, & Co., publication printed by, 161 (H86)

Sterner, Albert, 1939 Club speaker on American life as portrayed by American illustrators, 197

Stevens, Edward F., 192

Stevenson, Robert Louis, *A Lodging for the Night*, 139; Beinecke Collection of, 45

—exhibitions: in 1914, 169, 186; in 1941, 198

—publications: 135 (P63); 160 (H74)

Stillman, E. Clark, 1973 small exhibition from the collection of, 220

Stilson, Walworth, 134 (P58)

Stinehour Press, 113; publication designed and printed by, 151 (P132); publications printed by: 150 (P129); 152–153 (P137); 153–154 (P141); 154 (P142); 162–163 (G22/23–33/34); publication typeset by, 151 (P131)

Stinehour, Roderick D., 113; 1983 Club speaker on Grolier Club publications, 216; his introduction to "The Grolier Club and the Spiral Press," 154 (P142); publications designed by: 150 (P129); 151 (P131)

Stockhausen, William E., 1966 small exhibition from the collection of, 218

Stockton-Hough, John, 1891 Club speaker on the library of Demetrius Canevarius, 178

Stoddard, Roger E., 1982 Club speaker on the Houghton Library, 216

Stokes, I. N. Phelps, 1915 Club speaker on iconography of Old New York, 187

Stone, Hampton. *See* Stein, Aaron Marc

Storm, Colton, 1952 Club speaker on the American Revolution, 204

Storm van 's Gravesande, Charles, 1887 exhibition of etchings by, 176

Stowaways, The (printers' dining club), 88

Strahan, William, 77

Stralem, Donald S., 1960 small exhibition from the collection of, 172, 217

Streeter, Edward C., Grolier's 1504 Aldine Homer purchased from, 43

Streeter, Frank S., 1977 Club speaker on Harper Bequest, 213; 1978 small exhibition from the collection of, 221

Streeter, Thomas W., catalogue of 1959 exhibition from his collection, 149–150 (P127); 1959 exhibition, 207

*Strife of Good and Evil*, 111

Strouse, Norman H.

—Club speaker: in 1960 on modern fine printing, 207; in 1973 on John Henry Nash, 212

—small exhibitions from the collection of: 172; in 1960, 216; in 1964, 217; in 1973, 220

Strozzi, Tito Vespasiano, *Poetae*, Frederic Warde's copy, 57

Stuart, Gilbert, 1901 exhibition of engravings after, 182

*Study of Incunabula*, 143

Sturgis, Russell, 1888 Club speaker on Turner's *Liber Studiorum*, 177

Subject collecting, exhibitions on, 170, 172

*Summary of the Work of Rudyard Kipling*, 142

Surimono, 1924 exhibition of, 190

Swann, Arthur, collection of his business papers, 79

Sweeney, John L., 1964 Club speaker on modern English poetry, 209

Swift, Jonathan, 1945 exhibition on, 201

Swynheym, Conrad, and Pannartz, Arnold, 51

Syracuse University, J. Terry Bender leaves Grolier Club for, 45

Szathmary, Louis, 1977 small exhibition from the the collection of, 221


Tanenbaum, Charles J., Club speaker: in 1974 on printing and the American Revolution, 212; in 1976 on Europe in 1776, 213

Tanselle, G. Thomas, 165

Tapley, J. F., Co., publications bound by: 150 (P129); 150–151 (P130); 151 (P131–P132)

Tasso, marble bust of, 109

"Taste of 1884, The," 1983 exhibition on collectors and collecting and the founding of the Grolier Club, 216

Tate, Allen, 1948 Club speaker on little magazines, 171, 202

Tautenhayn, J., 1897 exhibition of medals and plaques by, 180

Taylor, Archer, *Book Catalogues: Their Varieties and Uses*, 72

Taylor, Francis Henry, 1940 Club speaker on Grolier Club Library, 198

Taylor, Henry C., 1970 small exhibition from the collection of, 219

Taylor, Robert H., 1969 small exhibition from the collection of, 219; his "Authors at Work" talk published, 149 (P124)

—Club speaker: in 1953 on English book illustrators of the 1860s, 204; in 1955 on "Authors at Work," 205; in 1963 on "Other People's Mail," 208; in 1966 on dedication copies, 209; in 1969 on "Queen Victoria's lady novelists," 210; in 1971 on Max Beerbohm, 211; in 1976 on gothic novels, ghost and horror books, 213

Tennyson, Alfred, Lord, 1897 exhibition on, 169, 180; publication on, 157 (H31)

*Tentative Scheme of Classification for the Library of the Grolier Club*, 128

Terry, Seth Sprague, gift of Grolier binding by family, 43

Thackeray, William Makepeace, his play, *Reading a Poem*, published, 132–133; 1910 performance of, 185

—exhibitions: in 1910, 185; in 1912, 169, 185; in 1963, 208

—publications: 133 (P56); 160 (H71)

Theatre, 1968 exhibition on, 210; 1970 exhibition on, 211; in 19th-century New York, 1977 small exhibition on, 221

*Thesauro de scritto*, 54

"The World and *The New Yorker*," 1975 exhibition on, 213

Thinking, art of, 1928 Club speaker on, 192

Thistle Press, publication designed and printed by, 149–150 (P127)

Thomas à Kempis, translated by Dibdin for Pickering, 77

Thomas, Evan, 1967 Club speaker on authors' corrected proofs, 210

Thomas, Isaiah, 58; autograph letter of, 76

Thompson, Cephas Giovanni, portrait of Nathaniel Hawthorne by, 109

Thompson, Edmund Burke, publication printed by, 144 (P101)

Thompson, Lawrance R., on Elmer Adler, 150–151 (P130); 1955 Club speaker on retrospective of Grolier Club exhibitions, 205; and Lathem, Edward Connery, *Robert Frost and the Lawrence, Massachusetts, "High School Bulletin,"* 151

Thompson, Thomas, 78

Thoreau, Henry David, 1954 exhibition on, 205

Thorndike, Ashley H., 1916 Club speaker on William Shakespeare, 187

Thorp, Willard, "Trollope's America," 148 (P119)

—Club speaker: in 1949 on Trollope, 203; in 1957 on American literature of the South, 206

Thorpe, Thomas, catalogues of, in Grolier Club Library, 62

Thou, Jacques-Auguste de, his copy of Quintilian, 57–58; catalogue of his library, 65, 71; autograph letter by, 74–75

*Three Essays: I. Book-Buying, II. Book-Binding, III. The Office of Literature*, 139

Tietze, Richard G., wood engravings by, 122 (P12)

Tindall, William, 61

Tindall, William York, 1962 Club speaker on Irish literature, 208

Tinker, Chauncey Brewster, Club speaker: in 1933 on Pepys, 194; in 1950 on the *Oxford Book of English Verse*, 203

Tinker, Edward Larocque, Club speaker: in 1935 on Joseph and Elizabeth Robins Pennell, 195; in 1947

on contemporary American hand bookbindings, 202

Title-pages and frontispieces, engraved, 1898 exhibition of, 181; publication on, 157 (H34)

*Title-Pages as Seen by a Printer*, 127

"To Delight, Surprise, and Inform," 1976 exhibition of literary sources of opera libretti, 213

Tobacco, 1941 exhibition of books on, 170, 199

Tobin, Robert L. B., 1983 Club exhibition from the collection of, 216

Torio de la Riva y Herrero, Torquato, *Arte de escribir*, 54

Tory, Geoffroy, *Champ fleury* (1529), copy in Grolier Club Library, 53–54; *Champ Fleury* (1927), 115, 141

—exhibitions: in 1927, 192; in 1937, 196

Toulouse-Lautrec, Henri de, 1967 small exhibition on, 218

Townsend, Horace, 1918 Club speaker on mezzotints from Dixon to Cousins, 188

Toyokuni, 1922 exhibition on, 190; 139 (P82)

Trade books, 1979 exhibition of, 215

Trade cards, 1914 exhibition of, 186; 1921 exhibition of, 189; in Grolier Club Print Collection, 81

"Trade Roots," 1979 exhibition of fine trade books, 1920–1950, 215

*Transactions of the Grolier Club*, 162

*Translation of Giovanni Boccaccio's Life of Dante, A*, 126

Travel of Tudor and Stuart periods, 1936 exhibition on, 196

"Travelers in the Desert," 1967 exhibition on, 210

"Travellers in Greece and the Levant," 1970 small exhibition on, 219

Treaties, and maps reflecting their effects, 1951 exhibition of, 203

Trent, William P., 1917 Club speaker on history of English prose fiction, 187; his introduction to Irving's *Notes and Journal of Travel in Europe*, 137

Trichet du Fresne, Raphael, catalogue of his library, 71

Tritheim, Johann, *Catalogus illustrum virorum*, 52; *Compendium*, 53

Trollope, Anthony, 1949 exhibition on, 203; publication on, 148 (P119)

"Trollope's America," 148 (P119)

*Truthful Lens, The*, 115, 153–154; 1974 exhibition on the photographically illustrated book, 170, 212

Tsarkoe Selo, Russian imperial summer palace at, 51

Tuckerman, Bayard, on Committee on Publications, 114

Turner, Dawson, manuscript library catalogue of, 70

Turner, J. M. W., 1888 exhibition on his *Liber Studiorum*, 177; publication on, 155 (H4)

Turnpike era, Fox's 1940 talk on, 198

Turnure, Arthur B., on purpose of Grolier Club exhibitions, 165–166; at first meeting of Grolier Club, 176

*Two Note Books of Thomas Carlyle*, 125

Twysden, William, 62

Type designers, American, 1948 exhibition on, 171, 202

Type foundry, catalogue for auction of, 54

Type specimens, 1926 exhibition of, 191; publications on, 120 (P5); 161 (H85); in Grolier Club, 80

*Typographic Years*, 154

Typography as a fine art, 1924 exhibition on, 190

Typophiles, joint publication with, 150–151 (P130)

Typophiles Chapbooks, 1973 Committee on Modern Fine Printing exhibition of, 223

Typothetae of America. *See* United Typothetae of America

Uffenbachiana, 72

Unique books, pamphlets, and broadsides, 1944 exhibition of, 200

United Nations, *belles-lettres* from countries in, 1950 exhibition of, 203

*United States Navy 1760 to 1815*, 114

United Typothetae of America, 112; reproduction of its gold medal, 142 (P92)

Universitätsdruckerei H. Stürtz AG, publication printed by, 153 (P140)

University of Heidelberg, 66

University of Kentucky, King Library Press. *See* King Library Press

University of Nebraska at Omaha, Abattoir Editions. *See* Abattoir Editions

University of Wisconsin, printing by students of Philip M. Hamilton at, 1974 Committee on Modern Fine Printing exhibition on, 223

Upcott, William, autograph letter of, on autograph collecting, 78

Updike, Daniel Berkeley, gift to library, 58; 1938 Club speaker on Bruce Rogers, 197; his edition of Mores's *Dissertation Upon English Typographical Founders*, 140; 1940 exhibition on, 198; publication on, 144–145 (P105)
—publications printed by: 132 (P52); 133 (P53); 137 (P72); 140 (P84); 143 (P96); 145 (P106–P107)

"Upon Subtler Wings," 1966 exhibition of French Parnassian and Symbolist poetry, 209

Urdang, Laurance, 1978 Club speaker on Webster's dictionary, 214

Uzanne, Octave, *Le Livre Moderne*, personal set of, 42, 56

Uzielli, Giorgio, 1962 small exhibition from the collection of, 217

Vail, Robert W. G., 1946 Club speaker on caricatures relating to America, 201

Valois, Henry de, manuscript library catalogue of, 72

Vander Lyn, John, 1977 small exhibition on, 221

Vatican type specimen book (1628), in Grolier Club Library, 54

Vellum, books, manuscripts, and documents, 1958 exhibition of, 206

Venetian books, exhibitions of: in 1944, 200; in 1981, 18th-century illustrated, 215

*Vers de société*, books of, 1895 exhibition of, 180

Vershbow, Arthur, 1969 small exhibition from the collection of, 219
—Club speaker: in 1970 on French books, 211; in 1979 on prints from members' collections, 214

Victoria, Queen, 1970 small exhibition on, 219

"Vintage of 1884," 1983 small exhibition of books published in the year of the Grolier Club's founding, 222

*Vitae Sanctorum Patrum*, 49–50

Von Siegen, Ludwig, Grolier Club publications on, 160 (H78); 1918 exhibition of mezzotints by, 187

Vostre, Simon, 50

Voynich, Wilfrid, papers of, in Grolier Club Archives, 88

Wagstaff, David, Club speaker: in 1925 on Gosden, 191; in 1937 on early American sporting books, 196; in 1940 on sporting books, 198

Wagstaff, Samuel J., Jr., 1983 small exhibition from the collection of, 222

Wainwright, Alexander Dallas, on Elmer Adler, 150–151 (P130)

Wakeman, Stephen A., gift of Hawthorne portrait, 109

*Walden*, 1954 exhibition on, 205

Walker, Emery, publication printed by, 137 (P70)

Wall, Alexander J., 1942 Club speaker on "New York City Then and Now, 1626–1942," 199

Walpole, Horace, 1936 exhibition on, 171, 195; *The Duchess of Portland's Museum*, 143–144

Walters Art Gallery, 1977 exhibition from, 214

Walters collection, 1896 exhibition of lithographs of Oriental porcelains from, 180

Walton, Izaak, 1893 exhibition on, 168, 179; publication on, 156 (H21)

Wang, Chi-Chen, 1935 Club speaker on Chinese illustrated books, 195

War of 1812, 1912 exhibition of prints, portraits, and books relating to, 186; publication on, 160 (H72)

War Posters, 1916 exhibition of, 187; 1943 exhibition of, 199

Warde, Frederic, 1938 Club speaker on Bruce Rogers, 197; publication designed by, 144 (P103); books and papers of, in Grolier Club library, 57, 87

Warne, Roger, autograph invoice of, 75

Warner, Frank M., 1951 Club speaker on American music, 204

Warren, Arthur, *Charles Whittinghams Printers*, 125

Warren, Lloyd, 1918 Club speaker on the art of the architect and interior decorator of the 18th century, 188

Washington, George
—exhibitions: in 1899, of engraved portraits, 181; in 1904, of engraved portraits, 183; in 1931, 194
—publications: 129 (P39); 158 (H40)

*Waste Land, The*, 1964 exhibition on, 209

Waterloo, Anthonie, 1912 informal discussion on, 185

Webster, Jerome P., 1966 small exhibition from the collection of, 218

Webster, Noah, and his dictionary, 1978 exhibition on, 214

Weddell, Alexander W., 1942 Club speaker on color printing, 199

Weil, Hope, 1979 small exhibition from the collection of, 221

Weitenkampf, Frank, his sketch of the life of Saint-Mémin, 157 (H37)

—Club speaker: in 1916 on Goya, 187; in 1926 on Gavarni, 191; in 1927 on Beurdeley, 191; in 1929 on Currier and Ives, 193; in 1934 on lithography and Alois Senefelder, 195

Wendelin de Spire, printer, 51

Wescott, Glenway, 1960 Club speaker, 207

West, Andrew Fleming, 1887 Club speaker on *The Philobiblon*, 177; his translation of *The Philiobiblon*, 121 (P8)

*What I Am Pleased to Call My Education*, 116, 147

Wheatland, David P., 1973 small exhibition from the collection of, 220

Wheeler, Monroe, on Committee on Publications, 114

"When This You See Remember Me," 1974 presentation of a documentary film about Gertrude Stein, 212

Whicher, George F., 1951 Club speaker on important books in English, 1901–1950, 204

Whistler, James McNeill

—exhibitions: in 1890, 177; in 1891, 178; in 1894, 179; in 1900, 181; in 1904, 183; in 1907, 184; in 1910, 184; 173

—publications: 131 (P49), 133–134 (P57); 137 (P71); 138 (P75); 158 (H51); 159 (H60); 115

White, W. A., 1916 Club speaker on William Shakespeare, 187

White Knights Library, auction catalogue of, 61

Whitehill, Walter Muir, his introduction to Ruzicka catalogue, 147 (P115); 1948 Club speaker on Ruzicka, 202; 1962 Club speaker, 208

Whitman, Walt, 1955 exhibition on, 205; 1964 small exhibition on, 217

Whitridge, Arnold, 1971 Club speaker, 211

Whittingham, Charles, 125 (P24)

Wick, Peter A., 1978 Club speaker on French printing, 214; 1981 small exhibition from the collection of, 222

Widener, Harry Elkins, letters to Beverly Chew, 79; catalogue of his library, 71

Wiegand, Willy, 1929 Club speaker on contemporary German printing, 193; 1931 Club speaker on German illustrated books, 193

Wightman, Julia Parker, 1978 small exhibition from the collection of, 221

Wilbur, Richard, 1982 small exhibition on, 222

Wilde, Oscar, 1965 small exhibition on, 218

Wilkinson, Charles K., 1962 Club speaker on oriental books, 208

*William Blake's Illuminated Books*, 148–149

*William Caxton at his Press*, 111

William L. Clements Library, 1977 exhibition of its Harper Bequest acquisitions, 213

Williams, John, medallion portrait of Emerson cast by, 164; medallion portrait of Lowell cast by, 164

Williams College, 45, 46

Willis and Sotheran, catalogues of, in Grolier Club Library, 62

Wilmerding, Lucius, interest in collecting auction catalogues, 40; gifts of French auction catalogues, 64; gifts of private library catalogues, 69; his Grolier binding sold to Club, 43; 1936 Club speaker on Renaissance bookbindings, 196; 144 (P103); 194

Wilson, Adrian, 1973 Committee on Modern Fine Printing exhibition on, 223

Wilson, Carroll Atwood, on Committee on Publications, 114

Wilson, H. W., Foundation, financial support for Grolier Club Cataloguing Project, 105

Wilson, Robert A., 1977 small exhibition from the collection of, 221

Wilson, Stanley Kidder, his introduction to Leech catalogue, 134 (P61)

Wimsatt, William K., 1949 Club speaker on Poe, 203

Winchell, Edward Everett, his illustrations to *The Culprit Fay*, 138

Wing, Donald Goddard, 1948 Club speaker on little magazines, 202; 1960 Club speaker on the Restoration, 207

Winship, George Parker, Club speaker: in 1916 on Shakespeare, 187; in 1920 on fine printing from Didot the Edler to the Ashendene Press, 189; in 1926 on Cruikshank, 191; in 1929 on Fifty Books of the Year, 193

Winterich, John T., on Society of Iconophiles, 82

—Club speaker: in 1946 on 100 influential American books, 201; in 1954 on an exhibition of items from the collections of Grolier members, 205; in 1963 on Elmer Adler, 208

—works: *The Grolier Club, 1884–1950: An Informal History*, 147; *The Grolier Club, 1884–1967: An Informal History*, 116, 151–152; his 100 influential American books talk published, 146–147 (P114); his talk on Elmer Adler published, 150–151 (P130)

Wise, Thomas J., 79; his Ashley Library catalogues, 70; letters of, in Grolier Club Archives, 85

Witchcraft, 1962 exhibition on, 208

Wither, George, 1893 exhibition on, 179; publications on: 123 (P16); 129 (P42); 156 (H20)

Witten, Laurence C., II, 1958 Club speaker on vellum, 206

WNET-TV, its documentary film on Gertrude Stein shown at 1974 Club meeting, 212

Wodhull, Michael, 65, 72

Woffington, Peg. *See Peg Woffington*

Wolf, Edwin, 2nd, Club speaker: in 1957 on William Blake, 206; in 1971 on great American book collectors, 211; in 1982 on the Library Company of Philadelphia, 215; and Keynes, Geoffrey, *William Blake's Illuminated Books*, 148–149

Women, 1901 exhibition of engravings, etchings, and lithographs by, 182; publication on, 158 (H45); 1908 exhibition of mezzotint portraits of, 184

Women writers: American, 1948 exhibition on, 171, 202; Victorian, 1969 exhibition on, 210; engraved portraits of, from Sappho to George Eliot: 1895 exhibition of, 180; publication on, 157 (H26)

Wood engraving, 1890 exhibition on, 177; publications on: 135 (P64); 155 (H8); American: 1886 exhibition on, 176; 1888 exhibition on, 167, 177; modern: 1890 exhibition on, 177; publications on, 155 (H9); 15th–16th centuries: 1886 exhibition on, 176

*Wood-Engraving: Three Essays*, 135–136

Woodberry, George E., his introduction to *100 Books Famous in English Literature*, 128

Woodbury, Charles H., 1921 exhibition of etchings by, 189

Woodcuts, exhibitions: in 1901, German, of 15th and 16th centuries, 182; in 1912, 186; in 1914, 186; in 1915, of American books illustrated with, 186; in 1930, 15th-century, 193

Woodhouse, Samuel W., Jr., 1934 Club speaker on the China trade, 195

Woodring, Carl, 1982 small exhibition from the collection of, 222

Woodworth, Samuel, 141 (P88)

World War I, 1943 exhibition of posters of, 199

Wotton, Thomas, autograph letter of, 74

Wrangham, Francis, 57

Wrenn, John Henry, catalogue of his library, 71

Wright, Louis B., 1957 Club speaker on American literature of the South, 206

Wright, Richardson Little, Club speaker: in 1941 on "Diaries: Why People Keep Them, Why Others Collect Them," 199; in 1943 on botanical books, 200; in 1947 on iconography of American industry, 202

*Writers of Knickerbocker New York*, 134

Writing, Chinese, 1950 exhibition on, 203

Writing books, 1921 exhibition of, 189; 1933 exhibition of, 171, 194; in Grolier Club Library, 54

Wroth, Lawrence C., 1930 Club speaker on early American books and broadsides, 193; 1940 Club speaker on Updike and Merrymount Press, 198; *The Colonial Printer*, 143; his Updike talk published, 144–145 (P105)

Wyllie, John Cook, 1956 Club speaker on second editions, 206

Wyman, Loraine, 1920 performance of old English children's songs, 188

Yale University Library, 149–150 (P127)

*Yearbook of the Grolier Club*, 161

Yeats, William Butler, 1962 exhibition on, 208

Yonge, Theodore, 1975 Club speaker on Thomas Frognall Dibdin, 213

Young, Mahonri, 1920 exhibition of etchings by, 189; 1921 Club speaker on 100 illustrated books, 189

Zeltner, Johann Conrad, *C. D. Correctorvm in typographiis ervditorvm centvria . . .* , 54

Zigrosser, Carl, 1946 Club speaker on architectural prints, 201

Zilboorg, Gregory, 1956 Club speaker on Freud, 205

Zilcken, Philip, 1892 exhibition of etchings by, 178; publication on, 156 (H15)

Zitner, Charles, 1978 small exhibition from the collection of, 221

The Grolier Club, 1884–1984

was designed by Stephen Harvard, who also made
the hand-lettered title page and initial letters.
The type was set and the letterpress printed by
The Stinehour Press, Lunenburg, Vermont, on Mohawk
Superfine paper. The plates were printed by The
Meriden Gravure Company under the direction of
Stephen Stinehour. The Grolier Club centennial
seal was designed by Jerry Kelly. The book was
bound in Dutch cloth by The Stinehour Press
in an edition limited to 600 copies.